CW01081453

Northern Arcadia

❊

Hammerfest
NORTH CAPE
BARENTS SEA

Tromsø

RUSSIA

ICELAND
Reykjvík

Narvik

WHITE SEA

FINNMARK

LAPPLAND

NORDLANDET

Torneå (Tornio)

VÄSTERBOTTEN

Luleå

ÖSTERBOTTEN

Oulu

FINLAND

FÆRØ
Tórshavn

Trondheim

Umeå

Vasa (Vaasa)

Gulf of Bothnia

NORRLAND

TRØNDELAG

THE KEEL

JÄMTLAND

Viborg (Viipuri)

OLD FINLAND KARELIA

Lake Ladoga

Anjala

Fredrikshamn (Hamina)

Borgå (Porvoo)

St. Petersburg

SWEDEN

DALARNA

Gävle

Helsingfors (Helsinki)

Åbo (Turku)

Gulf of Finland

Narva

NORWAY

Bergen

Eidsvoll
Christiania (Oslo)

ØSTLANDET

VÄRMLAND

Uppsala

ÅLAND ISLANDS

DAGÖ

Revel (Tallinn)

ESTONIA

Stavanger

VESTLANDET

Moss

Karlstad

Stockholm

ÖSEL

RUSSIA

Christiansand

SØRLANDET

Arendal

Örebro

Norrköping

LIVONIA

Marstrand

Visby

Riga

NORTH SEA

Skagerrak

Skagen

Kattegat

Gothenburg (Göteborg)

Jönköping

GOTLAND

Ålborg

Kalmar

ÖLAND

BALTIC SEA

POLAND

Tilsit

Århus

Karlskrona

JUTLAND

Helsingborg

Lund

Copenhagen

Malmö

BORNHOLM

Danzig

DENMARK

SJÆLLAND

Kiel

SCHLESWIG-HOLSTEIN

SWEDISH POMERANIA

Stettin

DUTCH REPUBLIC

Berlin

HANOVER

PRUSSIA

SCANDINAVIA, 1765–1815

0   100   200   300 Miles

Northern Arcadia

FOREIGN TRAVELERS IN SCANDINAVIA, 1765–1815

H. Arnold Barton

Southern Illinois University Press

Carbondale and Edwardsville

Frontispiece: Map of Scandinavia, 1765–1815. Cartography by Bill Nelson

Library of Congress Cataloging-in-Publication Data

Barton, H. Arnold (Hildor Arnold), 1929–
Northern Arcadia : foreign travelers in Scandinavia,
1765–1815 / H. Arnold Barton.
p.   cm.
Includes bibliographical references and index.
1. Scandinavia—Description and travel.
2. Travelers—Scandinavia—History.
3. Travelers' writings. I. Title.
DL11.5.B36 1998
914.804'89—dc21   98-15892
ISBN 0-8093-2203-X (alk. paper)   CIP

Contents

CONTENTS

❖

4

The Inhabitants of the North

5

Ultima Thule

6

The Rise and Fall of a New Arcadia

Conclusion: "The Eye of the Beholder"

Notes

Select Bibliography

Index

Illustrations

Acknowledgments

As ALWAYS, I am grateful for the stimulation, ideas, and help I have received, directly or indirectly, from others. In this regard let me mention in particular Thorkild Kjærgaard, Matti Klinge, Jørgen Schou-Christensen, Sverker Sörlin, Jarl Torbacke, and Eva Tedenmyr. I also want to thank Letterstedtska Föreningen and Nordisk Kulturfond for their generous support for this project. I am greatly indebted to the staffs of the Royal Library, Stockholm, and of the Morris Library at Southern Illinois University at Carbondale, as well as to Kathryn Koldehoff for her meticulous editing of my manuscript. My Swedish-born wife, Aina, has been my constant, patient, and supportive companion during my travels—both actual and intellectual—in the North.

Finally, this study is dedicated to the memory of three friends who over the years gave me constant inspiration and new insights into the wide fields it covers: Sigvard Cederroth of Uppsala, Karl-Gösta Gilstring of Linköping, Lennart Seth of Stocksund.

H.A.B.
Tyresö, Sweden

Northern Arcadia

�֎

Introduction:
Travel and Travel Literature in
the Eighteenth Century

THE LITERATURE OF TRAVEL held a particular fascination for eighteenth-century European readers. It was a genre to which Scandinavians contributed in no small measure. One recalls, in Sweden, Carl Linnæus (von Linné) and his celebrated notebooks, such as his *Iter Lapponicum* and *Iter Dalicarlicum*, or the accounts of his disciples from far parts of the world, like those of Pehr Kalm from North America, Carl Thunberg from Japan, or Daniel Solander, who sailed with Captain James Cook in the South Seas. In the neighboring Danish kingdom—which then included the duchies of Schleswig and Holstein, Norway, the Færø (Faroe) Islands, and Iceland— Bishop Erik Pontoppidan produced his magisterial descriptions of Norway and the other Danish domains, stimulating numerous local topographical works, largely by learned Norwegian pastors. Literary Scandinavians who wrote of their travels in Europe—although rarely other parts of the North— included such figures as Ludvig Holberg, Jens Baggesen, Franz Mikael Franzén, Henrik Steffens, Adam Oehlenschläger, and Erik Gustaf Geijer.[1]

A growing number of foreigners meanwhile visited and left accounts of Scandinavia, even if relatively few compared to those who followed the well-trodden high roads of the classic Grand Tour. To many, the Northern kingdoms seemed a Hyperborean wilderness and to journey there an exotic adventure. "It may possibly excite curiosity to know," Giuseppe Acerbi prefaced his account in 1802, "why a native of Italy, a country abounding in all the beauties of nature, and the finest productions of art, would voluntarily undergo the danger and fatigue of visiting the regions of the Arctic Circle"; but, he added, "there is no people so advanced in civilization, or so highly cultivated, who may not be able to derive some advantage from being acquainted with arts and sciences of other nations, even of such as are the most barbarous."[2]

To study this eighteenth-century travel literature is to raise a number of significant questions. What conditions existed at the time in the lands the travelers visited? In what ways do these stand in contrast to conditions there today? What were the purposes of travel during that period? What motives led travelers to find their way to particular regions? Who comprised the reading public for travel accounts and what did they seek in such literature? At a deeper level, what preconceptions, prejudices, and values did confrontations with other peoples and places bring to the fore?

Down to the mid eighteenth century, travel was undertaken on the whole for essentially practical, useful purposes: for trade, diplomacy, war, geographic discovery, education, employment, or scientific investigation. Such travel might result in published works, but these were the by-products of sojourns abroad, however interesting they might be to a select readership.

Even the Grand Tour, which by the eighteenth century had become well-established practice among young members of the aristocracy—characteristically accompanied by their preceptors—and in time even of the wealthier bourgeoisie, was intended to serve practical ends. Young men of birth and breeding, destined to play prominent roles in public or commercial affairs, hereby acquired familiarity with other lands, languages, and practices, while establishing networks of direct personal contact with those who controlled the destinies of other nations, or who would do so in the future.[3]

While travel for utilitarian purposes naturally continued, new motives for travel began to emerge after the middle of the eighteenth century. The growth of the middle class in numbers, wealth, and education created a burgeoning demand for literature of new kinds. These came to include most notably lyric verse, the novel, the essay, the didactic drama—and the travel account. The cosmopolitanism of the Enlightenment aroused interest in unfamiliar parts of the world, even of Europe itself. There was a growing fascination with the strange and exotic. Descriptions of other regions and their inhabitants both questioned and confirmed the familiar assumptions and values of European life and culture. At first, travel simply to experience and observe was not always easy to understand. Nathanael Wraxall, visiting Denmark in 1774, wrote that it was "sufficient" for him to be "publickly talked of . . . because I come from England, and have no avowed motive, except curiosity and knowledge."[4]

Throughout the century, there was meanwhile a sentimental countercurrent to Enlightenment rationalism and utilitarianism, which in time came to be best personified by Jean-Jacques Rousseau. In his native Switzerland, Rousseau found a new Arcadia, where a sturdy peasantry, uncorrupted by the evils of civilization, lived simple and virtuous lives amid natural surroundings inspiring in their awesome grandeur. Poets like the Scottish James Thomson and the English Edward Young and Thomas Gray dwelt upon nature in its somberer and more majestic aspects and upon the unfathomable mysteries of human existence. Laurence Sterne introduced the sentimental traveler, for whom a journey was above all the occasion for philosophical reflection and emotional introspection.

Travel for its own sake, to provide direct and indirect experiences and sensations to the travelers and to those who read their published accounts, became increasingly fashionable. As William Combe's Dr. Syntax declares in 1812, "I'll make a tour—and then I'll WRITE IT." The year before, the Englishman Henry Holland, recently returned from Iceland, commented wryly to Maria Edgeworth that "nobody, you know, travels now a days without writing a quarto to tell the world where he has been, & what he has beheld."[5]

A combination of circumstances made the Nordic lands the goal of an increasing number of literary travelers by the end of the eighteenth century, a trend culminating in the late 1790s. Old Icelandic literature was brought to the attention of European readers by the Swiss scholar Paul Henri Mallet's *Introduction à l'histoire de Dannemarc* and *Monumens de la mythologie de la poésie des Celtes, et particulièrement des anciens Scandinaves*, published in Copenhagen in 1755 and 1756. These works were in turn adapted and translated into English under the title *Northern Antiquities* by Thomas Percy, published in London in 1770, which created a veritable vogue for the ancient North, especially in Britain. To the preromantic generation seeking new and novel sensations, beyond the bounds of the Græco-Roman canon, and fascinated by James Macpherson's mythical Celtic twilight, Nordic antiquity exercised a powerful enchantment.

Well-established political concepts likewise underlay interest in the Nordic or "Gothic" past, especially in Great Britain, as to it was attributed the origins of human freedom. This belief is widely reflected in writings on Nordic life and culture during the eighteenth century and beyond.

Growing numbers of travel accounts during the later eighteenth century created an increasing need for novelty in the genre to compete for the interest of the reading public. This novelty could include new foci of interest, such as description of the manners and mores of the inhabitants or the landscapes of the countries visited. It could also direct literary travelers to regions previously neglected in published accounts, including the Nordic lands.

"Fashion," Acerbi wrote in 1802, "which extends its influence over every thing, appears in our day, to favor travels and expeditions to the North: and the prevalence of this may, perhaps, have been increased by the political troubles in the South of Europe."[6] Revolution and war thus also played their part by the turn of the century in directing travelers toward the Nordic lands. Here there remained an oasis of peace and tranquility, a goal for pre-romantic reveries—until these lands themselves were drawn into the maelstrom of the Napoleonic Wars.

Scandinavia comprises both a typical and in certain ways a unique example of travel and its uses in the eighteenth century. What literary travelers found in the Northern kingdoms—as well as what readers derived from their accounts—was as much the product of their own cultural and personal backgrounds as of what they actually saw and experienced. Their writings provide invaluable insights into the conditions and mentalities of the age in which they lived.

Considerable attention has in recent years been given to the history of travel, perhaps especially during the eighteenth and nineteenth centuries.[7] Excellent bibliographies on travel in Sweden and Norway have been compiled.[8] Literature on foreign visitors to the Nordic lands is, however, scanty. It remains essentially limited to popular surveys briefly summarizing, in succession, the observations of selected visitors to individual countries, with little attempt at commentary or interpretation.[9] Most of the foreign travelers, moreover, visited more than one—in some cases all—of the Nordic lands, and their constant comparisons between them, as well as with other countries, provide much of the particular value and interest in their writings. No attempt has been made thus far to study these travelers, taken together, in the entire region and in the broader context of their times. That is my objective in the chapters that follow.

The writings of more than thirty foreign visitors to the Nordic lands during this period provide the foundation of this study, although others are drawn upon where they shed further light upon particular details. For Sweden alone, meanwhile, Samuel Bring's authoritative bibliography lists and describes no fewer than 210 accounts of travel undertaken between 1765 and 1815, published during the period or since, up to 1950. Of these, ninety-eight were written by (or in some cases, about) foreign visitors, in addition to one hundred Swedish works and twelve by other Scandinavians. (In contrast, Bring shows only fifteen foreign travel accounts of Sweden between 1700 and 1764.) Most of the foreign works Bring cataloged deal with other Nordic countries as well.[10]

It is more difficult to arrive at comparable figures for Norway and, at present, practically impossible for the rest of Scandinavia. However, an overall estimate of some one hundred fifty foreign travel accounts from the entire region during this period—including those that do not include Sweden at all, many of them, to be sure, very brief and summary—would seem reasonable.

One may, therefore, legitimately ask, On what basis did I select those travelers (and their accounts) given particular attention in this study? Scandinavians writing about their own or other Nordic countries fall outside of my purview. Similarly, I do not concern myself with accounts by long-term foreign residents of the Nordic lands, such as diplomats or the pastors of foreign congregations.[11] My focus is upon outsiders who viewed the North with fresh and unaccustomed eyes.

The foreign works I have selected include, as might be expected, those most widely read and influential during the period itself, as witnessed by numbers of editions, translations, and references by others. Those of certain less well known travelers have also been included for their unusual itineraries, for notable perceptiveness, and for evocative style, or, conversely, for views especially characteristic of writing on Scandinavian travel during the period, taken as a whole. For both variety and balance, a spectrum of nationalities and of social and occupational backgrounds is represented.

I cite the original English translations of works composed in other languages when available; otherwise the translations are my own. Forays into the accounts of others from the period, both foreign and Scandinavian, meanwhile, serve to reinforce and fill out the composite picture of the Nordic world presented by those who provide the foundation of this study. Quotation marks surround original captions for period illustrations. When I have prepared the captions myself, they do not.

Since childhood I have been fascinated by travelers' accounts of faraway places. This interest was powerfully stimulated by my own first, extended encounter with Europe—including Scandinavia—at the age of eighteen, in 1948–49, during which, in letters to family and friends, I myself sought to describe my own experiences and impressions.

In my research on Scandinavia during the revolutionary-Napoleonic era, as well as on the Swedes in America, I have been much concerned with questions involving the perceptions of insiders versus outsiders and have thus repeatedly made use of the observations of contemporary travelers. Increasingly I became convinced that those who visited the Nordic lands during the tumultuous era of political and intellectual conflict between the High Enlightenment and the defeat of Napoleon deserved a study in their own right.

The wind is fair—let us embark!

I

Travelers and Travel in the North, 1765–1815

ALTHOUGH THE NORTHERN KINGDOMS lay off the beaten track, occasional travelers had found their way there over the centuries and had left accounts of their sojourns. Several noteworthy visitors come to mind. There was, for instance, the Venetian merchant Pietro Querini, who was shipwrecked on the northern coast of Norway in 1431; Charles Ogier, secretary to a French diplomatic mission to Sweden in 1651; Sir Bulstrode Whitelocke, the English Commonwealth's envoy to Sweden in 1653–54; Francesco Negri, the priest from Ravenna who journeyed to the North Cape in 1664–65; the Florentine Lorenzo Magalotti, who visited Sweden in 1674; Robert Molesworth, William III's Irish-born envoy to Denmark in 1692; and Pierre-Louis Moreau de Maupertuis, leader of a celebrated French scientific expedition to Swedish Lapland in 1736.[1]

After the mid eighteenth century, there was, nonetheless, a notable increase in the numbers of foreign visitors to the North. They were from a variety of European countries, even from the New World. They represented an increasing variety of occupational and social groups, and their motives for traveling and for writing about their experiences became ever more diverse, reflecting new ideas about the very nature and significance of travel. Before attempting any generalizations about the foreign visitors to the Nordic lands during the later eighteenth and early nineteenth centuries, I present those foreign travelers upon whom this study is principally based.[2]

The German Johann Beckmann (1739–1811), went to Sweden in 1765 from St. Petersburg, where he had been a teacher of mathematics and natural history, attracted above all by the renown of Carl Linnæus (von Linné), whom he visited in Uppsala. He recorded his experiences in a travel diary, first published in 1911.[3]

In the winter of 1769–70, a young Italian, Count Vittorio Alfieri (1749–1803), spent some months in Denmark and Sweden. His trip coming between visits to despotic Prussia and Russia, Alfieri was enthusiastic over the freer atmosphere of the Scandinavian lands. Later, as one of the leading Italian poets and playwrights of his day, he recalled in his memoirs how his poetic vein had first been aroused by the severe majesty of the wintry North.[4]

William Windham (1750–1810), who would begin his long and distinguished career in the British Parliament in 1784, visited the North in 1773. His travel diary covers his adventurous journey overland from Bergen to Christiania in Norway, offering only brief glimpses from his further progress down Sweden's west coast to Helsingør and Copenhagen. He offers on the whole a sympathetic view, especially of Norwegian peasant life.[5]

Sir Nathaniel William Wraxall, Baronet (1751–1831), later best remembered as a writer of historical memoirs, visited Denmark and Sweden in 1774 on his way to Russia, following three years' service with the British East India Company in Bombay and a visit to Portugal. His published letters to his patron, the earl of Clare, provide a lively and highly personal picture of the Northern capitals during a key period of ferment and change.[6]

William Coxe (1747–1828), an English divine and fellow of King's College, Cambridge, later archdeacon of Wiltshire, became in time known for a number of historical writings and the editing of historical documents. He is perhaps best remembered for his voluminous account of his travels in eastern and northern Europe, including the Scandinavian kingdoms, which he visited in 1779. This work appeared in numerous editions and was translated into several languages. He went back for a second visit in 1784. Coxe's work abounds in factual information but contains relatively few personal anecdotes or reflections.[7]

A young English scholar, Matthew Consett, went to Sweden and Denmark in 1786, as a traveling companion to a wealthy, aristocratic amateur of the arts and sciences, journeying as far north as Torneå (Tornio) on the Bay of Bothnia. While he gave due attention to high society and culture, he also showed a marked sensitivity toward nature and folklife.[8]

Surely the most exotic and colorful of the foreign visitors to the North during our period was Francisco de Miranda (1750–1816), from Caracas in present-day Venezuela, who visited the Nordic countries in 1787, after sojourns in the United States and in various European countries, most recently the Ottoman Empire and Russia. His diaries came out in print over a century later, revealing an exuberant and venturesome traveler.[9]

A young Scot, Andrew Swinton, passed through Denmark in 1788 on his way to St. Petersburg to seek an appointment in Russian service through the influence of his illustrious kinsman, Sir Samuel Greig, commander of Catherine II's Baltic fleet, then engaged in war with Sweden. He claimed this to have been his third visit to the North. His account is of interest principally due to the speculations he offers concerning the mythical origins of the Nordic peoples.[10]

Some obscurity surrounds the published accounts of a visit to Denmark and Sweden in 1790–91 of two French émigrés, former officers and men of letters, Alphonse Fortia de Piles (1758–1826) and Pierre Marie Louis de Boisgelin de Kerdu (1758–1816). Fortia was the first to bring out his account, in Paris in 1796. Boisgelin's appeared in English fourteen years later in London. The two works are virtually identical, word for word. Due to the circumstances under which they appeared, it is impossible to know what to attribute to each of the two men. (Boisgelin claimed in his preface that his manuscript had been lost through fire.) Recognizing that the two accounts must be regarded as essentially a joint effort, I cite Boisgelin's in preference to Fortia's, as it is more complete than the English translation of the latter, and Boisgelin's English is better. Fortia and Boisgelin provide a treasure trove of detailed—including statistical—information on the Northern kingdoms, together with sensitive and sympathetic observation of the lands and their inhabitants.[11]

In 1795 Mary Wollstonecraft (1759–97), the English champion of women's rights, spent some months in Scandinavia, mainly in Norway, together with her infant daughter. In letters ostensibly written to her lover, the American Gilbert Imlay, in Paris, published the following year, she gave a romantic yet insightful account of her experiences.[12]

Christian Ludwig Lenz (1760–1833), a teacher from the pedagogical institute at Schnepfenthal in Saxony, visited Denmark and Sweden in 1796. He gave particular attention to schooling and to the conditions of the poorer classes in a manner revealing his sympathies with the ongoing Revolution in France.[13]

A fellow Saxon, the writer Carl Gottlob Küttner (1755–1805), left one of the most insightful accounts of the Scandinavian lands, following his visit there in 1798. He had an eye, it seems, for everything, and his comments, not least on economic matters, are both sympathetic and objective.[14]

That year and the following, the young Italian dilettante Giuseppe Acerbi (1773–1846) traveled widely in Sweden, Finland, and Norway, as far as the North Cape. His exuberant account combines Continental *mondanité* with romantic enthusiasm for unspoiled nature and those who lived in close communion with it.[15]

In 1798 a French émigré, Jacques-Louis de Bourgrenet de La Tocnaye (born 1767) arrived in Gothenburg from Ireland, then on the verge of revolt. Over the next two years, he ranged widely through the Scandinavian lands, priding himself on gaining, in his enforced leisure, a truer understanding of conditions and culture than did those who, after rapidly and superficially surveying the passing scene, cataloged pedantic detail from accessible sources or rhapsodized over picturesque or sentimental impressions.[16]

The Scotsman Henry Peter Brougham (1778–1868), later Lord Brougham, went to continental Scandinavia in 1799, after finding the season too far advanced to visit Iceland, as he had originally hoped. His reminiscences from this journey, published posthumously, are somewhat haphazard and impressionistic but sober and generally evenhanded.[17]

The same year, the Reverend Thomas Robert Malthus (1766–1834) visited the Nordic lands, recording his warmhearted and enthusiastic observations in a diary published long afterwards. The information he gathered there would be valuable in the preparation of the second, revised edition of his celebrated *Essay on the Principle of Population*, which came out in 1803.[18]

Among Malthus's companions at the beginning of his journey was a man of note, Edward Daniel Clarke (1769–1822), whose far-reaching travels as preceptor to John Marten Cripps, a wealthy and adventurous nineteen-year-old, and at first with his friend the Reverend William Otter—often, it would seem, at breakneck speed—took him from Scandinavia on to Russia, the Ottoman Empire, and the Levant. Clarke's celebrated account of this journey ultimately filled six stout volumes. Although he had visited the Scandinavian lands first, volumes V and VI, dealing with the region, were the last to appear (in 1819 and 1823, the latter posthumously). During the intervening two decades, he made various additions reflecting the later course of events. His published account may be supplemented with the biography of him (which includes Clarke's letters written during his travels) by his friend William Otter, later bishop of Chichester, who accompanied Clarke and Malthus as far as Vänersborg in Sweden, before continuing on with Malthus to Norway.

Clarke's *Travels* came out in numerous editions and languages. He was interested in virtually everything, discussing matters as they arose along the way. Thus many of his most interesting reflections consist of asides in the midst of his ongoing narrative. He was a scholar, even occasionally a pedant, yet at the same time an enthusiastic preromantic soul. Altogether, his account—which drew liberally upon the unpublished notes of his companions, Malthus and Otter—provides the fullest panorama of the Nordic countries during our period.[19]

John Carr (1772–1832), a well-known English travel writer, journeyed through Denmark and Sweden (including Swedish Finland) on his way to St. Petersburg in 1804. His account shows much literary polish, and he added atmosphere by liberally embellishing it with verse, others' as well as his own. While much of what he said was what had come to be stereotypical regarding the North by the turn of the century, he seems in turn to have had some influence upon the interests and observations of those who came after him. His tone is, on the whole, good-natured and positive, and toward Denmark more so than that of many other travelers of the time.[20]

The celebrated mineralogist or, as he described himself, scholar of "geognosy," Leopold von Buch (1774–1853), a member of the Royal Prussian Academy of Sciences in Berlin, traveled in 1806, via Denmark, up the Norwegian coast as far as the North Cape, thence through Sweden back to Christiania, where he remained until 1808. His account is filled with geological and topographical data while revealing high hopes, in the spirit of the cosmopolitan Enlightenment, for the future exploitation of the region's still largely untapped resources.[21]

Robert Ker Porter (1777–1842), an English artist known for his battlefield scenes, visited Sweden in 1808, following a prolonged sojourn in Russia. His account is illustrated with his own interesting engravings, but coming from a time of crisis, following Russia's invasion of Finland, it presents a generally gloomy view.[22]

Surely the most dramatic entry onto the Scandinavian scene was that of the Scotsman James Macdonald, when the merchant vessel on which he was traveling, evidently to Gothenburg, was shipwrecked on the Skagen Peninsula in November 1808. After his daring rescue by local fishermen, he was taken prisoner by the Danish authorities, since Denmark was then at war with Britain. He was conveyed to Copenhagen, where he was permitted to cross over to Britain's ally, Sweden, in January 1809. His account, which ends after his arrival in Gothenburg in February, is unusual in its treatment of North Jutland and of Denmark during the Anglo-Danish conflict.[23]

A visitor of a very different type was Aaron Burr (1756–1836), former governor of New York and vice president of the United States, who after killing Alexander Hamilton in a duel and suspect secret dealings with Spanish Louisiana, went into exile abroad. Much of the year 1809 he spent in Sweden and Denmark. His diary, interspersed with letters to his daughter, Theodosia, in South Carolina, published two years after his death, concerns mostly day-by-day occurrences and observations, with relatively little reflection, but it contains some interesting glimpses of life in Scandinavia.[24]

The Scottish chemist and mineralogist Thomas Thomson (1773–1852) visited Sweden in 1812. While he confessed that his journey from Gothenburg to Stockholm and Dalarna, then back via Helsingborg, took no more than six or seven weeks, he proved a keen observer. His principal interest was geology, of which he provided a detailed account, but his observations of Swedish life and institutions, not least the practical aspects of travel, are sober and objective. As a natural philosopher, Thomson reflects the heroic age of chemistry and geology, showing little sign of the romantic mood of the time.[25]

The newly married Lady Sarah Lyttelton, née Spencer (1787–1870), the daughter of an earl, visited Sweden between July and October 1813 with her husband on the first lap of their extended European wedding trip. Young and ebullient, Lady Sarah, in letters to her family and friends, reveals the attitudes of both her nationality and her exalted social status, alternating between enraptured enthusiasm and lighthearted irony over what she encountered.[26]

As a young student, the Englishman John Thomas James (1786–1828) spent much of 1813–14 in the Sweden now led into the Allied camp by Crown Prince Carl Johan, the former Napoleonic marshal Jean-Baptiste Bernadotte, as the Napoleonic Wars drew to a close. Like several of his fellow travelers, James was an accomplished artist and illustrated his own account of his travels.[27]

What broader characteristics may be discerned within this heterogeneous group? Although the travelers were of different nationalities, the British clearly dominated. Wealth and leisure, commercial and imperial connections had made them pioneers of tourism, so that the foreign traveler abroad would long be almost axiomatically taken for an English milord.

Compared with earlier times, these travelers represented a greater variety of social and occupational groups, as well as of motives for travel. Some, such as Alfieri, Windham, Acerbi, Brougham, James, and Lady Sarah Lyttelton, were persons of leisure with the means to satisfy their curiosity about the remoter parts of Europe, as were numerous others who never left accounts of their visits. Such notables were frequently accompanied by more scholarly tutors or companions, who traveled at their employers' expense and who wrote of their experiences, such as Consett, Malthus, and Clarke. Some traveled in connection with their professions, including Beckmann, Swinton, Lenz, Küttner, Buch, Porter, and Thomson. Others were political exiles, living a footloose and peripatetic existence, such as Miranda, Fortia, Boisgelin, La Tocnaye, and Burr, and perhaps to a degree Wollstonecraft.

Several of these visitors to the North are noteworthy because of the renown they would in time acquire in other connections. Mary Wollstonecraft already enjoyed a certain celebrity (or notoriety) for her defense of women's rights, published in English and French in 1792 and thereafter in numerous editions and translations. Malthus brought out the first edition of his treatise on population and its natural limits the same year he visited Scandinavia. Burr was, at the time of his visit, infamous for his alleged treason against the United States. Others would, however, become well-known primarily on the basis of their travels and the accounts they left of them, such as Coxe, Acerbi, Clarke, and Carr, whose works came to enjoy great popularity.

These differences in turn point to a fundamental distinction between types of travel accounts. In the first instance, there were those that were deliberately conceived and written for publication. These became ever more frequent by the later part of our period and include most notably the accounts by Coxe, Consett, Swinton, Fortia, Boisgelin, Küttner, Acerbi, La Tocnaye, Clarke, Carr, Buch, Porter, Thomson, and James. Such publications were generally well prepared and gracefully written, sought to cover a wide spectrum, if not a country as a whole, and are filled with factual information. Basically similar were letters addressed to private persons but evidently written with an eye to publication, such as Mary Wollstonecraft's and perhaps Aaron Burr's.

Alfieri's and Brougham's accounts were included in their memoirs, written long after the event, which has its interest in showing what aspects of their experience of the North seemed most significant to them in long perspective. Others, such as Beckmann, Windham; Malthus, and above all Miranda, wrote diaries, and Lady Sarah Lyttelton wrote letters apparently never intended for the public eye. These are of particular value as they concentrate on what most captivated the diarists and letter writer at the time, including piquant, colorful, and often intimate details that would not have found their way into print. Such accounts often contribute a sense of freshness, immediacy, and excitement to the broader panorama of time and place seldom found in more formal writings.

The reactions of the travelers to what they saw and experienced in the Nordic lands could be affected by a variety of circumstances. Obviously nationality—national preconceptions and prejudices—played a prominent part. The same would be true of social class and of educational and cultural background. Often the extent and locations of previous travel left their mark. Clearly those who had traveled most widely had the broadest basis for comparison.

Moreover, the routes by which the travelers went to the Nordic lands could play some role; thus Miranda, after visiting the East in 1787, could compare Stockholm with Constantinople, while Porter, arriving from St. Petersburg in 1808, was less inclined to be impressed by the Swedish capital than were visitors arriving by way of the petty courts of northern Germany. Even within Scandinavia the travelers' judgments of different localities could be affected by what they had already seen of the region. Clarke, for instance, seems to have been notably impressionable in that respect.

In large degree, the visitors' reactions derived from their relative inclination toward, respectively, the rational values of the Enlightenment or the emotional values of preromanticism. While both currents coexisted throughout the period, the romantic worldview became ever stronger, as expressed in the travel literature on the North, especially up to the turn of the century. Thus the age of the visitors at the time of their Scandinavian travels and their basic attitudes would seem to show some rough correlation. There are, nonetheless, exceptions: Vittorio Alfieri, born in 1749, was clearly a pre-romantic, whereas Leopold von Buch, born in 1774, held staunchly to the rationalism and utilitarianism of the Enlightenment.

Finally, the time of travel and the circumstances prevailing both in the Scandinavian kingdoms and elsewhere in Europe exercised a powerful influence upon the ways in which the visitors saw and experienced the North. Above all, the vagaries of revolution and war would leave their unmistakable mark.

In considering the conditions under which these visitors journeyed in the North, we must first determine what sources of information they had available to them. Little enough to begin with. A few scholars before 1760 might have been familiar with Linnæus's Latin writings on Dalarna and Swedish Lapland. Better known would have been the Norwegian bishop Erik Pontoppidan's ambitious survey of his native land, published in English translation in 1755, which for instance E. D. Clarke in 1799 noted to be of particular value.[28]

Later there appeared certain foreign compendiums of varying usefulness. One was the first part, from 1767, of the German Anton Friedrich Büsching's multivolume descriptive geography. A large work of uncertain origin but attributed to one "Joseph Marshall" came out in London in 1772 and thereafter in several translations. While allegedly based on a journey to the North in 1769, it eventually became evident that its author had never actually visited the region and that the information it contains was culled from other sources. It thus proved a particularly notorious example of the numerous bogus travel accounts of the period. Of obviously greater value were Johann Georg Canzler's work on Sweden from 1776 and John Williams's on the Northern kingdoms from the following year. While Canzler had served as the Saxon minister to Stockholm and Williams had visited the region in 1770, neither of these works can really be described as a travel account. Rather, each is essentially a handbook of basic factual information.[29]

The appearance of William Coxe's *Travels into Poland, Russia, Sweden and Denmark* in 1784 set a benchmark for travel literature on the North, which later travelers generally considered the authority against which to test their own observations. Increasingly the travelers referred in their writings to each other's works. Coxe warmly praised Canzler's "accurate account of

Sweden." Consett in 1786 modestly did not "pretend . . . to vie with such celebrated Travellers as Coxe or Wraxal [sic]." Upon arriving in Stockholm the following year, Miranda promptly bought both Canzler's and Coxe's works on Sweden, and he later mentioned reading Williams's. Swinton remarked in 1788 that during the prior fifteen years only two travelers, Wraxall and Coxe, had published accounts of Scandinavia. Küttner and Acerbi took exception to some of Coxe's pronouncements. Boisgelin in 1810 provided useful bibliographies of writings available on both the Swedish and the Danish monarchies, including those by Canzler, Consett, Küttner, Wollstonecraft, and Acerbi.[30]

The volume of travel writing on the North became so great by 1799—the peak year—that La Tocnaye foresaw that, if the European war continued, it would swell to vast proportions as ever more "sublime folios" were delivered each year to the printers. It was significantly increased with the publication in English, by the enthusiastic Scottish Scandophile John Pinkerton, of a number of earlier accounts of the region, by both Scandinavian and foreign travelers.[31]

Various sojourners, moreover, encountered each other during the course of their travels. This was particularly the case with E. D. Clarke, who at the start traveled with Malthus. He and Acerbi met first in Uleåborg (Oulu) in northern Finland. Their paths later crossed in Stockholm, where Brougham met them both. Clarke, in Trondheim, met La Tocnaye, whom Brougham likewise met in Christiania.[32]

Thus, by the turn of the century, a growing corpus of travel writings about the Nordic lands was establishing something of a canon. Increasingly foreign visitors to the region had preconceptions about it and looked for what they by now expected to find there. The genre began to assume those characteristics that would persist for generations to come.

"This is my third expedition to the north," Andrew Swinton confessed in 1788; "It is a strange whim to get in love with deserts, with ice and snow. I delight to see Nature in her Winter uniform; to be surrounded with rugged rocks and frozen oceans." "Journeys in the North," wrote Giuseppe Acerbi in 1799, "will be undertaken by those only who have a just and masculine taste for nature, under every aspect, and are actuated by a desire of enlarging their own information, and of instructing others."[33] Indeed, few women were prepared to face the rigors involved, the most notable exception being that determined nonconformist Mary Wollstonecraft.

The Northern kingdoms covered an immense expanse, from the Elbe to the North Cape, well above the Arctic Circle, from Finland's eastern frontier to Iceland's westernmost capes. While there were great local variations, to visitors from the European heartland, the region as a whole seemed vast, rugged, and remarkably underpopulated. Areas of settlement were often separated by great, empty tracts of forest, mountain, and wasteland. There were innumerable lakes and rivers, while coastlines were deeply penetrated by inlets and fjords or shattered into mazes of islands, large and small.

Both topography and climate imposed formidable obstacles to travel in the North. Scandinavian children were traditionally taught, until recently, that land separates, whereas water unites. It was the open waters that held together Denmark, with its many islands, Norway, with its long coastline and mountainous interior, and the remote Atlantic islands of Iceland and the Færøes, making possible their dynastic union since the fourteenth century. Similarly the Baltic provided the essential link between Sweden, Finland, and Swedish Pomerania. Local travel and transport was everywhere heavily dependent upon rivers, lakes, and coastlines.

Sea communications, nonetheless, were beset with perils, as Buch was reminded when sailing off of Jutland, where he claimed to have seen "thousands of masts and skeletons of vessels run like an alley or range of palisadoes the whole seventy-three miles of our course along the coast." After himself being shipwrecked on that shore in 1808, Macdonald claimed to have counted thirty-five wrecked ships within one Danish mile (3.5 English miles) along the coast heading south from Skagen. Contrary winds or periods of calm could hinder the movement of vessels. Mary Wollstonecraft's ferry was, for instance, becalmed for ten hours in attempting to cross the narrow Little Belt in Denmark, whereas Miranda had made the same crossing in twenty-five minutes. It took Clarke over a month to cross from Grisslehamn in Sweden to Åbo in Finland via the Åland Islands under the most arduous conditions at the turn of the year 1799–1800, whereas Otter wrote that it had taken only two days for Malthus and himself to make the same passage in fine weather, and to them "it seemed too short." Coastlines could be closed by ice during the long winter months, especially in the Baltic. On occasion, as in early 1809, the Sound, between Denmark and Sweden, could freeze over. Wartime blockades, together with the vagaries of wind and weather, could largely isolate different parts of the Scandinavian kingdoms from each other. This combination of circumstances delayed Leopold von Buch's return from Norway to Berlin for several weeks in 1808. Macdonald was, as mentioned, shipwrecked in a storm on the treacherous North Jutland coast the following year. Yet travel afloat could also provide its exhilarating moments, such as when Buch's ship from Kiel, two years before, rounded the chalk cliffs of the Danish island of Møn and the sea "appeared as if alive," as "far and near the vessels of the Sound floated around us. We saw at least a hundred at once."[34]

Understandably, however, most of the visitors were eager to travel by land, to see landscapes and their inhabitants. The usual conveyances for persons of their station were thus carriages, or in winter, sleighs. Several of them had acquired their own—or later rued that they had not. These were drawn by relays of horses hired in the localities through which they passed. On occasion they might have to make do with such carts or sledges as the local people were able to provide, which could be "so very bad," according to Malthus, that "we could not sit on them with tolerable ease, & were continually losing the small parts of our luggage." The even more difficult conditions of travel in the Far North—Swedish Lapland and Norwegian Finnmark—and on Iceland are discussed in chapter 5.

Such travel, however, often proved less arduous than the visitors might have expected. The roads could be surprisingly good. In Denmark, Clarke and his companions traveled from Copenhagen to Helsingør on "the finest paved road we had ever seen." But it was the roads in Sweden that drew the greatest praise from those visitors who commented on them. Matthew Consett well expressed their pleasant surprise in 1786: "Tho' we have no great reason to complain in England of our public turnpike roads, yet nothing there is comparable to these; swamps, morasses, &c. are all equally made good." "In travelling more than twelve hundred English miles," Aaron Burr wrote from Sweden in 1809, "I have never found a bridge out of order, nor an obstruction in the road that could retard your progress for a second. There is no country in which travelling is at once so cheap, expeditious, and secure." Lenz and La Tocnaye were particularly impressed with provisions for snowplowing the roads. Malthus, however, noted in 1799 that the road from Christiania to Trondheim in Norway was "almost covered with grass, & apparently little used."[35]

Teams of horses and their local teamsters were naturally a constant concern to travelers everywhere at that time, and about them experiences and opinions could vary considerably. Acerbi, who was much inclined to criticize facilities for travel, declared in exasperation, shortly after arriving in Sweden in 1799, that "such a Babylonish confusion is not, I believe[,] to be met with in any other part of the world." Küttner, who gave the matter closer attention, was of the opposite view: "In Sweden," he wrote, "there are neither post-masters nor post-horses; but the government has adopted such regulations, that I know no country in Europe where we can travel extra-post, in every direction, so well as in this."

Certain peasant farmers were assigned the responsibility of constantly keeping available teams and drivers for the convenience of travelers. While this system of *skjutshåll* provided some income, Küttner, Lenz, and Macdonald realized it could impose heavy burdens upon the peasants involved. Küttner noted, moreover, that the Swedish horses, though sturdy, were small. It was advisable to engage a *förbud*, or courier, to ride ahead to order fresh relays of horses in advance; if one did not, La Tocnaye complained, "one would go much more quickly on foot." Curiously, Thomson in 1812 hired for this purpose a "black man from North America," who was fluent in Swedish.[36]

The most arduous traveling conditions—outside of the Far North—were those encountered by Windham and La Tocnaye on the rugged mountains and deep fjords of Norway's west coast. The journey from Molde to Bergen, La Tocnaye claimed, although not more than forty miles as the crow flew, took him "eighteen long days" to cover.[37]

Though the cold could be severe in winter, that season proved in many ways the most favorable for rapid land travel, as well as for the transport of heavy goods, thanks to long periods of snow cover and the freezing of lakes, rivers, and coastal waters, permitting the use of sleighs and sledges. La Tocnaye also noted the use of skis in Sweden and felt it would be well if the inhabitants of the Alps would adopt them. Traveling over "deep snow" and "frozen lakes" from Copenhagen to Stockholm in 1770, the young Vittorio Alfieri was filled with "wonder and delight." Miranda, too, declared that persons from more southerly regions could scarcely imagine the charm of racing in a sleigh over the snow. "Winter is the festival time for all the inhabitants of these Northern latitudes," Clarke declared. "They are all abroad, in a state of the most lively activity, and easy revelry." And later: "It is, with them the season of visiting and travelling to the most distant markets." Coxe left a vivid description of a crossing by sledge over the ice from Stockholm, via the Åland Islands, to Åbo in Finland: "The vast extended plain of ice, broken in abrupt ridges, the boundless and dreary track marked only by a line of trees and boughs, and the rugged rocks starting up on every side, afforded one of the most desolate scenes imaginable." Following a harrowing winter crossing over the same route in 1800, Clarke found the annual midwinter market in Åbo thronged with people from all over Finland and even from as far afield as Russia.[38]

Communications could be in places transmitted remarkably quickly and elsewhere surprisingly slowly. La Tocnaye reported that semaphore, or optical telegraph, stations connected Drottningholm Palace with Dalarö on the coast via Stockholm's Katarina Church. He also found that, although Frösö in Swedish Jämtland and Trondheim in Norway lay only twenty-five miles apart in a direct line, all mail between them had to travel via Christiania and Stockholm![39]

An unquestionable advantage to traveling in the Scandinavian kingdoms was the remarkable security of both travelers and their possessions, at a time when theft and brigandage were all too common elsewhere. In Copenhagen, Wraxall wrote in 1775, one need fear neither robbery nor assassination, "cloaks" nor "stillettos," as in "the Southern Kingdoms of Europe." "Indeed, it is usually almost as quiet at eleven o'clock at night, as in a country village, and scarce a coach rattles through the streets." Even in the poorest and most desolate parts of Sweden he felt no apprehensions. Others, too, gratefully expressed the same assurance. Despite often extreme poverty in Sweden, Lenz observed in 1796, there were "neither beggars nor thieves."[40]

Besides transportation, the travelers' main practical concern was accommodation, and on this point opinions again varied, depending upon background and expectations. Here too the sophisticated Milanese, Acerbi, was the most critical. The whole way from Helsingborg to Stockholm, he complained, "nothing that can be considered as an inn is to be met with. . . . [A] small village in Italy is better provided with all the necessities and conveniences of life, than the most eminent provincial towns in Sweden."

In that connection, travel fare could pose problems, especially for more demanding travelers like Wraxall, who complained of his journey through southern Sweden, "Had I not taken the precaution to carry wine and provisions with me in the chaise, I must have almost starved in three or four days journey through these miserable provinces, where the peasants are strangers to every kind of aliment, except bread, and salt pork or fish." And such coarse bread of rye and oats!

Clarke complained that the inns in Stockholm were "very dear, and very bad," so that it was preferable to hire lodgings, even if this too was expensive. Elsewhere he seems to have accepted public accommodations as he found them with a British stoicism that was apparently seriously shaken only by those he encountered in southern Finland, on the way to St. Petersburg.

Although he observed that the inns in Sweden were "very much decried," Küttner owned that his own impressions of them were not unfavorable, except that they were too few and far between. The inn at Kongsvinger in Norway indeed "would do honour to any city, even in the most polished countries of Europe; and except in the large towns, I did not find its equal in all Italy." In view of what he must earlier have experienced in both South and North America, as well as in Turkey and Russia, it seems not surprising that Francisco de Miranda was most unreserved in his praise of the public accommodations he found in many parts of Scandinavia. An inn in Skåne, in southernmost Sweden, for instance, he considered "very well run and as clean as in England," while his night's lodgings at Os, near Mangor in Norway, were "better than in all the inns of Paris." Somewhat surprisingly, Lady Sarah Lyttelton was on the whole well pleased in 1813 with both the accommodations and the fare she and her husband were able to find—and amply afford—in Sweden.[41]

Meanwhile, foreign persons of birth and breeding were frequently spared the need to put up in public lodgings, thanks to the often overwhelming hospitality they encountered. When a Swedish lady in rural Västergötland invited Clarke and his companions to stay as guests in her home, he marveled, "This polite and hospitable invitation, to persons who were perfect strangers, astonished us; but we hesitated not to accept it; and we after-

wards found, that such attention to strangers, whenever they have an opportunity of shewing it, is always characteristic of the *Swedish* gentry."

Acerbi, to his relief, followed the established custom almost everywhere
in the Swedish dominions of requesting lodging in the homes of the local
clergy, who, "wearied with the dull uniformity of living in those sequestered
regions, cut off from all society, are extremely happy to receive a stranger
who is acquainted with what is passing in the world." It did not escape his
notice that such clerical households often included "extremely handsome
and amiable young ladies," who, even if they spoke only their own tongue,
were delighted at the visit of educated travelers. All the foreign visitors had
stories to tell of the frequently astonishing hospitality they had encountered
in Scandinavia, even in poor and humble homes.

While this was in most instances a great advantage to the foreign visitor, in some cases it could be a mixed blessing. The traveler might on occasion be compelled to seek shelter in a peasant hut, which in poorer regions
could prove a harrowing experience.[42]

Despite all the hardships and uncertainties of travel in the North, it may
come as something of a surprise how well the traveler of ample means could
manage to fare, even in the most desolate regions. The Lytteltons in 1813
traveled in the style befitting the English milord, in a commodious barouche,
accompanied by their English servants, male and female, and a cart carrying
"beds, trunks, canteens, [and] breadbaskets." Clarke reported in 1799 from
Lapland—perhaps not without a touch of envy—that "the march of *Acerbi*
and his companions resembled that of a small caravan: they carried with
them nine servants, besides tents, and every other convenience which might
enable them to encounter the difficulties of such a journey." The last lap of
his pilgrimage to the North Cape, by sea from Alta Fjord, Acerbi himself
described as "very pleasant and comfortable." The boat was outfitted with
cushions and mattresses, bedclothes and covers. "By way of provisions, we
had everything that was good, such as white wine, claret, brandy, fresh
salmon, roasted fowls, veal, hams, coffee, tea, with the necessary utensils.
. . . It was, indeed, nothing but a party of pleasure on the icy ocean."[43]

2

The Public Visage: Culture, State, and Polite Society

Surely no period of western history has been so cosmopolitan in its outlook and values as the Age of Enlightenment. Civilization, deriving from ancient Mediterranean origins, was regarded as one and indivisible. Its essential attributes, wherever they manifested themselves, were judged by the standards of Europe's cultural capitals, above all Paris and London. These attributes included cities, literature and the arts, science, scholarship and learning, royal courts, government and its functions, and the manners and mores of polite society. Together, they comprised a nation's "public visage," on the basis of which outsiders determined its level of civility.

The Scandinavian kingdoms lay on Europe's northern periphery, separated from its cultural centers by long and arduous travel. They were afflicted by a severe climate, only modestly endowed with the basic resources of a preindustrial economy—above all, fertile plowland—and thinly populated. Under such conditions, visitors were not inclined to hold overly sanguine expectations regarding civilization's blessings in the North. Depending upon experience and temperament, they tended to react either with dismay over how few or, conversely, with surprised delight over how many of them they found there.

Since the dawn of the historic era, cities have been regarded as the very foundation of civilization, as the word itself implies. It was largely on the basis of cities that travelers appraised the lands they visited. In most of Scandinavia, however, towns of any kind were few and far between. There were, for instance, none at all in the whole of central Finland before Gustav III chartered four municipalities in the region in 1775.[1] In Italy, within the equivalent distance from Helsingborg to Stockholm, Acerbi declared grandiosely, there would be fifty towns, "in neatness and elegance, and every comfort of life, equal if not superior even to the capital of Sweden."[2] There were indeed few municipalities in the Northern kingdoms that could properly be considered cities by contemporary European standards. Hence the particular importance of the capitals, Copenhagen and Stockholm.

The Danish capital, then a city of some eighty-five thousand inhabitants, drew its share of praise from several of the travelers. "Copenhagen is the best-built city of the north," Coxe declared, "for although [St.] Petersburgh [*sic*] excels it in superb edifices, yet it contains no wooden houses, it does not display that striking contrast of meanness and magnificence, but in general exhibits a more equable and uniform appearance." Boisgelin regarded it in 1790 as "very handsome and well built, although for a capital, not large." Parts of the city were indeed "magnificent."

Most of the visitors arrived after the great fires of 1794 and 1795, which destroyed, respectively, the royal palace of Christiansborg and much of the central city. Wollstonecraft, who arrived shortly after the latter conflagration, was horrified by the devastation and saw its victims encamped in tents. Clarke found Copenhagen in 1799 "risen with renovated splendour from her ashes; a great improvement being visible in its streets, and many magnificent houses substituted in place of antiquated mansions, that wanted repair, and had been burned." Küttner, likewise noting the reconstruction, declared it a "handsome city . . . certainly one of the finest capitals of Europe." He especially admired the new Amalienborg quarter, centering on the new royal residence. "This part of the city," he wrote, "would not make a despicable figure either in London or Paris, Rome or Turin, Vienna or Berlin." Brougham, however, considered the city's location unhealthy and its streets "uncommonly dirty."[3]

Stockholm, meanwhile, attracted far more commentary. Approaching it from the south, Wraxall, Boisgelin, and Brougham found few signs that they were approaching a capital with at that time a population of around seventy thousand; to Brougham its outskirts "appeared first like a village scattered among rocks and rising ground." But reaching the heights overlooking the city he found it to be a "large, well-built city" with a location that was strikingly romantic—more so than any other capital in Europe. Other visitors likewise marveled at the vista. Wrote John Thomas James in 1813,

Uniting every beauty of wild nature, with the charms attendant upon the scenes of more active life; echoing the clamour of the bustling populace amidst rocks, that have not ceased to ring with the woodsman's axe; rivalling at once the boasted cliffs of Edinburgh, the broad lake of Geneva, and the streets and shipping of Venice: its view presents a romantic vision, that not even the highest powers of the art of description could ever attempt to delineate.

Boisgelin, Küttner, Clarke, and Buch offered similarly picturesque and enthusiastic descriptions. Even Robert Ker Porter, arriving in 1808 from what he called the "finest city in Europe"—St. Petersburg—was overcome by the overall prospect. Miranda could compare it only with Constantinople.[4]

"If external appearance alone were to be relied on, this might be deemed the most magnificent city in the world," Clarke maintained. While the royal palace and a few other public buildings were impressive, closer acquaintance with the city revealed its shortcomings. Many of the houses, in James's view, were built in a "meagre and hungry style," lacking variety and grace. The streets were narrow, steep, and poorly paved. There were few public promenades or squares. Worse, much crowding, poverty, and dirt were in evidence. Küttner summarized the overall effect: "I never beheld from one point of view any thing so beautiful, so magnificent, and so sublime, nor yet any thing so mean, so rude, and so wild, within the circumference of a metropolis."[5]

As Norway was until 1814 part of the Danish monarchy, Christiania (now Oslo) was not yet a capital. It was, however, the local administrative and cultural center, as well as the emporium for southeastern Norway's thriving timber trade, with a population of some nine thousand. While the foreign visitors were much impressed with its prosperity and social amenities, as will be seen, they had less to say about its overall appearance. Clarke nonetheless described Christiania as "very striking, owing to the throng of shipping before the town, and the number of islands lying off, in its extensive bay. . . . There is less of a *Scandinavian* character in Christiania than in any other town of the North; the houses are built of stone; *log-houses* being confined entirely to the suburbs." Its streets were wide and straight, intersecting at right angles. Brougham, too, noted that the town was "regularly built" and that it contained some splendid private residences. Mary Wollstonecraft complained, however, that its "large, square wooden houses offend the eye, displaying gothic barbarism. . . . [S]ize, without grandeur or elegance, has an emphatic stamp of meanness, of poverty of conception, which only a commercial spirit could give."[6]

Bergen, meanwhile, was Norway's largest town. La Tocnaye, who visited it in 1799, noted there the presence of foreigners from all of Europe, arriving and departing by sea; but few left descriptions of the town. Yves-Joseph de Kerguélen-Trémarec, later renowned as an explorer of the South Indian Ocean, visited Bergen in 1767 as commander of a French naval expedition to the North Sea. Of it he wrote: "The city is very extensive. The streets are not straight, and are irregularly paved with large and small stones, but are kept very clean. The houses, although built of wood, afford a very pleasing appearance, from the diversity of colours with which they are painted. . . . The city of Bergen may contain three thousand houses, and more than twenty thousand inhabitants." La Tocnaye in 1798 contrasted its picturesque and prosperous appearance with the rugged, mountainous hinterland that largely isolated it from eastern Norway. Clarke noted the same year that the inhabitants of Christiania and Trondheim seemed little familiar with Bergen. As a prominent citizen of Christiania put it, "*Bergen* is less known to the inhabitants of this place than *London* or *Paris*: in fact, we hardly consider it as forming a part of our country; or as inhabited by *Norwegians*." Its citizens were indeed of largely foreign origin, principally German, Dutch, and Scottish.[7]

Clarke was particularly taken with Norway's third largest town, Trondheim, which then had somewhat under nine thousand inhabitants. "Considered only in point of picturesque beauty, the Bay of *Trönjem* does not yield to the Bay of Naples," he wrote. The town was of "very considerable size: its streets are wide, well paved, and filled with regular, well-built houses, generally plastered and whitewashed. There is no part of *Copenhagen* better built or neater in its aspect than the streets of *Trönjem*." Clarke found Christiania "neither so grand nor so picturesque." Buch in 1806 also made a flattering comparison: "Drontheim possesses the patriotism and public spirit of a solitary republic; and Christiania the spirit of a trading town."[8]

Many, if not most, of the travelers passed at some time through Sweden's west coast port of Gothenburg (Göteborg), about which opinions varied. Boisgelin considered the town "very handsome, though much inferior to those of the third order in France," with fourteen to fifteen thousand inhabitants. Küttner owned that, as Gothenburg was Sweden's second city, "I was certainly disappointed in my expectations," yet he gave on the whole a favorable description, noting that in its suburbs the wooden houses of the well-to-do were kept freshly painted and had a "neat and clean appearance, which quite delighted me." Acerbi found its environs "almost everywhere naked, barren, and dreary," but he gained a fairly positive impression of the town itself, which, he observed, constantly strove to emulate the capital. Brougham noted that the central town was built mainly of brick by seventeenth-century Dutch settlers "in the style of Rotterdam."

Gothenburg underwent great fluctuations of prosperity and poverty, depending upon the possibilities for maritime trade during the revolutionary and Napoleonic Wars. Brougham found its trade languishing in 1799. When Sweden was later allied with Great Britain, Aaron Burr in 1809 found the streets of the "lower town" filled with drunken English sailors, "God d——ning everything that was not exactly as in England." He also learned that no fewer than six American ship captains were then in port there. By 1813, at the time of James's visit, Sweden, following a brief period of unwilling alliance with France, was again in the Allied camp, and Gothenburg prospered greatly as Napoleon's Continental System collapsed. "On entering the place," he wrote, "we were struck with the symmetry and splendor of the buildings, and admired, at leisure, the several bustling groups that thronged its canals, bridges, and quays, where their never ceasing activity seemed to bespeak the important concerns of this great emporium of the country."[9]

Third in importance among the towns of the Swedish monarchy was Åbo (Turku), the local administrative and cultural center of Finland, with a population of about ten thousand. Wraxall in 1774 declared it the "wretched capital of a barbarous province," but Clarke was much taken with the place in 1799, especially its university and its thriving winter fair.[10]

Not until 1812, after the vagaries of war had transformed Finland into an autonomous grand duchy under the Russian tsar, would Helsingfors (Helsinki) become its capital. Up to that time, it served primarily as the garrison town for Sveaborg, a fortress located on islands offshore and—as the "Gibraltar of the North"—the key to Finland's defense. Few of our travelers got that far off the beaten track. Boisgelin in 1791 noted "as many cows as people passing through the streets." He was, however, duly impressed with Sveaborg, as was Clarke, who in 1799 briefly described Helsingfors as a "small but handsome town, containing many stone houses," which had an "appearance of comfort."[11]

The travelers also remarked on various of the smaller towns they visited in the Northern kingdoms. There was no town in Denmark except Copenhagen, according to Küttner, "that can be compared with the middle class of German towns, or even with Chemnitz in Saxony, or Zittau and Gürlitz [sic] in Lusatia." Most, too, were remarkably similar in appearance. As outside of Denmark and the duchies they were constructed mostly of wood, the natural building material of the region, they were repeatedly ravaged by fire. Bergen, for example, was devastated, according to Kerguélen-Trémarec, in 1248, 1472, 1623, 1640, 1702, and 1756, losing on the latter occasion some sixteen hundred houses. In some cases, such fires may have been something of a blessing in disguise. Traveling through Denmark in 1808, for instance, Macdonald found Nyborg on Fyn a particularly "pleasant little town," surely thanks to its having been rebuilt after a conflagration four years earlier.[12] Indeed, few secular urban buildings from earlier than 1700 still exist in smaller Nordic towns, most of which even today show an essentially eighteenth- or early-nineteenth-century character. Clarke noted the basic similarity of Swedish towns:

> Having once figured to the imagination a number of low red houses, of a single story, each covered with turf and weeds, a picture is presented to the mind which will serve to give a correct idea of all the oppidan scenery of *Sweden*. There is no other country in the world, excepting perhaps *Russia*, that exhibits, over an equal extent of territory, such unvaried uniformity; and this, not only in the appearance of its buildings, but also of its inhabitants and landscapes.[13]

Still, the visitors did comment favorably on numerous smaller Scandinavian towns. Miranda found Flensburg in Schleswig, which he compared to Philadelphia, "the most flourishing town in Denmark," excepting only Copenhagen. In Norway, Frederikshald (now Halden) and Moss caught Küttner's and Burr's fancy; Clarke was "greatly surprised" by the imposing appearance of the copper-mining town of Røräs; and Buch found Tromsø in remote Nordland a prosperous town with some merchants' houses that would do credit even to Trondheim. In Sweden, Wraxall was well pleased with Jönköping after traversing the desolate wastes to the south. Küttner liked Eskilstuna and Uppsala; Clarke, Karlstad and Filipstad; Burr, Västerås. James wrote of the wartime prosperity of Karlshamn in 1813.

Clarke, after traveling along both sides of the Bay of Bothnia, meanwhile, stated that the towns on the Finnish side, including Åbo, Vasa (Vaasa), Gamla Karleby (Kokkola), and Uleåborg (Oulu), were "magnificent" compared with those on the Swedish side, with the exception of Gävle, "although they enter into no comparison with the towns of *England*, *France*, *Italy*, *Germany*, or *Holland*." Their citizens, too, were "persons not only of local but of national importance and consideration." Nykarleby (Uusikaarleppyy) afforded, in his view, "the most pleasing and picturesque appearance of any town in *Sweden* or *Finland*."[14]

It was in the larger cities—especially the capitals—and in the university towns that cosmopolitan visitors looked for the recognized attributes of civilization as they knew it. E. D. Clarke, manifestly no friend of the Danes, declared:

> To our eyes, it seemed, indeed, that a journey from *London* to *Copenhagen* might exhibit the retrocession of a century; every thing being found, in the latter city, as it existed in the former a hundred years before. This observation extends not only to the amusements, the dress, and the manners of the people, but to the general state of every thing connected with *Danish* society; excepting, perhaps the commerce of the country, which is on a good footing. In literature, neither zeal nor industry is wanted: but compared with the rest of *Europe*, the *Danes* are always behind in the progress of science. This is the case, also, with respect to the Fine Arts.[15]

It is worth noting, however, that Clarke, like most of the literary travelers, spent relatively little time in the Danish capital. Much the best and most sympathetic picture of Copenhagen is, meanwhile, to be gained from Miranda's exuberant diary of some three months' visit during the winter of 1787–88. Thanks largely to the favor that had been shown him by Russia's Empress Catherine II, all doors, even in the highest social and government circles, were open to him. He was, moreover, in Denmark during a particularly fortunate time: the beginning of the era of reforms under the regency of Crown Prince Frederik, before the short but unhappy war with Sweden later in 1788 and the devastating fires of 1794 and 1795 in Copenhagen.[16]

In the capitals were to be found most of the region's more notable architectural monuments. Stockholm's royal palace was especially impressive.
Boisgelin considered it one of the "handsomest modern palaces in Europe";
Küttner, one of the finest he had ever seen; and Thomson, the finest. Porter
described it as "commanding, in a grand and simple taste." For one who had
"never seen any but Saint James's," Lady Sarah Lyttelton enthused, it seemed
"almost sublime."

Boisgelin found the nearby summer palace of Drottningholm "extremely
grand," and Küttner was both astonished and delighted to find there "the
elegance, the taste, the luxury, and the magnificence of Versailles" as he had
seen it in 1787 and 1788, albeit in Sweden on a smaller scale. Wraxall in 1774
admired its formal baroque gardens, "the triumph of cultivation and elegance, opposed to that of a savage wilderness"; while Clarke, twenty-five
years later, reflecting the taste of a later generation, disliked them. "We soon
saw enough," he wrote, "to convince us that nature had done every thing
for *Dröttningholm* [*sic*], and man worse than nothing." Boisgelin admired
Gustav III's opera house and the Princess's Palace on what is now Gustav
Adolf's Square in Stockholm, as well as the seventeenth-century House of
the Nobility. Küttner was much taken with the royal pavilion at Haga.[17]

The palaces of Copenhagen and its environs fared less well. Of Christiansborg Palace, Wraxall wrote in 1775: "It is of prodigious size; and if I was
inclined to find fault with it, I should say, it is too splendid and too magnificent for a king of Denmark; on the same principle, as foreigners constantly remark, that the palaces in England are far beneath the dignity and
greatness of the British empire." To Boisgelin in 1790, "The architecture of
this edifice, upon the whole, is not fine, nor even elegant; it is, however,
an imposing pile of building, which announces the habitation of a sovereign." Christiansborg burned in 1794, before most of the literary visitors arrived, although Küttner found its ruins imposing. Wraxall found a certain
appealing "air of antiquity" in the little baroque Rosenborg Palace. Fred-
eriksberg Palace on the outskirts of the capital Clarke, meanwhile, found
"meanly furnished, and in no way worthy of a moment's observation." Miranda, with his republican sympathies, inveighed against the wastefulness
and "absurdity" of the Danish king's owning fifteen palaces on Sjælland
alone, not counting ruins![18]

Outside the capitals, there were at least a few architectural monuments that elicited comment from the visitors. Coxe considered Sveaborg fortress in Finland "really stupendous and worthy of the ancient Romans." Miranda found Roskilde's cathedral, the burial place of the Danish kings, "grandiose and well proportioned." La Tocnaye admired Lund's cathedral. In Trondheim, Clarke described the cathedral as a "*Gothic* structure of extreme pristine beauty" and, with some hyperbole, considered military commander General Krogh's residence, "although built of wood . . . the most magnificent palace in all *Scandinavia*, containing a theater, and a most stately suite of apartments." Of Åbo's cathedral in Finland he wrote, "There is no building in all *Scandinavia* more worth seeing." Thomson, meanwhile, commented in 1812 on a notable lack of castles in Sweden and wondered if this were due to its security against outside attack or to its lack of a feudal system and baronial wars in past centuries.[19]

Much attention, for instance in the accounts of Beckmann, Wraxall, Miranda, Brougham, and especially Fortia and Boisgelin—whose joint work comprises a veritable Baedeker for the areas they visited—was devoted to the royal collections of paintings and sculpture, objets d'art and curiosa. On occasion, too, private collections attracted attention, such as the wealthy Christiania merchant Peder Anker's splendid array of Italian paintings, acquired at great expense during his travels and filling several rooms.[20]

While such collections consisted primarily of older European works, the eighteenth century marked a new phase in Scandinavian culture. Until that time, the practice of the arts in the North had been reserved almost entirely for foreigners. Now native Scandinavians, working in the established international styles, came to dominate creative activity in their homelands. Some even achieved international standing, such as the Swedish rococo painters Alexander Roslin and Nils Lafrensen (Lavreince), the younger, or later the neoclassical sculptors Johan Tobias Sergel from Sweden and Bertel Thorvaldsen from Denmark, all of whom spent much of their careers abroad.[21]

Küttner noted that "Stockholm contains a greater number of artists than a stranger would expect to find in such a city." Yet few of the visitors paid very much attention to them, even though Fortia and Boisgelin, with characteristic thoroughness, duly listed the better-known ones. Miranda, to be sure, greatly admired the sculpture of Sergel, whose studio he visited. Both Boisgelin and Brougham commented in particular on the Swedish landscapist Elias Martin. The former recognized that Martin possessed "genius and taste, but works so rapidly, that his productions are incorrect and unfinished. These views, however, have a very pretty effect, and he sells them for about two ducats and a half a piece." Brougham dismissed him with the comment, "Mr. Martin is an R.A. of London; his *forte* seems to be caricature painting, for his landscapes are daubs."

Such attitudes reveal the gulf that separates the classical canons of that time from present-day taste. Sergel is more admired nowadays for his rapid, burlesque, and often bawdy pen sketches, which were never intended for the public eye, than for his polished neoclassical marbles; while Martin enjoys a place alongside his better preromantic English contemporaries. Miranda was more in tune with the present preferences in his warm admiration for the pen drawings of Sergel's boon companion, the artistic Swedish admiral and aesthetician Carl August Ehrensvärd, whose sketches he claimed impressed him more "than all I have seen of antique art in Italy."[22]

In Sweden, the performing arts enjoyed the generous patronage of King Gustav III, whose passion they were, up to his death in 1792; with suitable literary collaborators, he himself composed works for the stage. Several of the visitors were highly impressed by the Stockholm opera. Miranda considered its newly constructed building as perhaps Europe's finest. Thanks largely to the French artist and architect Louis Jean Desprez (1743–1804), whom Gustav had engaged in 1784, its scenic effects were especially noteworthy. Having attended over a score of performances, Boisgelin declared that "the decorations and machinery are equal, in every respect to those of the first theatres in Europe. . . . The wardrobe of the Opera House is very rich, and there is no theatre where the actors, dancers, &c. are more handsomely dressed. The same characters which are dressed in stuff at Paris are here attired in silk." Brougham concurred entirely.

Performance, meanwhile, tended to draw a more mixed response. Brougham noted no outstanding singers, although "the *figurantes* are far superior to those in London," and he noted the large numbers of performers onstage. Boisgelin, who himself was something of a composer, commented on the orchestra of "more than forty musicians, who are tolerably good performers." Clarke's judgment in 1799 was harsh: "Little needs to be said of the style of performance at a *Swedish* opera," he complained; while the orchestra was not bad, the singers and dancers were "equally below mediocrity." It would be only fair to point out that royal patronage of the arts had languished since Gustav III's death by assassination in the opera house in 1792.

Comment on opera in the Danish monarchy is much sparser, although Miranda, after seeing a Danish comedy in Copenhagen, noted that "the actors were poor, the orchestra excellent and large, so that it would have been much better if it had given a concert throughout the whole performance."

Due to language, it is not surprising that the visitors had little to say about the nonoperatic theater. La Tocnaye regarded it as fortunate that the Swedish theater was based on the French rather than on the "monstrosities" of the English stage, although he had little use for Swedish comedy. Burr, who made some effort to learn Swedish, dutifully attended and pronounced the Stockholm theater good. Porter, around the same time considered it, "like all others on the continent . . . dismally dark and as dismally stupid." A related phenomenon was the great public spectacles occasionally held in the capitals, such as those James enthusiastically described in Stockholm.[23]

Few of the visitors had any command of Scandinavian languages, the most notable exception being the scholarly La Tocnaye, an enthusiast for Nordic antiquity who knew medieval Icelandic and who cited passages from the saga literature in the original and translation, as well as quotations in Swedish and Danish. He even claimed to have read all the plays of Holberg, which he had greatly enjoyed; indeed, he preferred Ludvig Holberg's *Niels Klims underjordiske Reise* to Jonathan Swift's *Gulliver's Travels*, which it resembled. Lacking such familiarity, the contemporary literatures of the Nordic lands were, however, literally a closed book to most foreigners, except in those rare cases where translations existed.

They had naturally little enough to say on the subject. Mary Wollstonecraft believed that the frequent use of French by the "well-bred Swedes of the capital" might be advantageous in some ways but imagined that it must prevent "the cultivation of their own language, and any considerable advance in literary pursuits." She believed the Norwegians had little taste for literature. Clarke, meanwhile, opined that Norway was more advanced in literature than was Denmark and had produced some eminent writers, especially Ludvig Holberg and Bishop Erik Pontoppidan. In Norway poetry had been cultivated since the earliest times, long before any literary contacts with other, more civilized lands. "Their poetry," he concluded rather fancifully, ". . . such as it is, must be regarded as their own: it may be compared indeed to the streams from their native mountains, rolling impetuously along their valleys, but unmixed with a single drop from any of the waters of *Helicon*." Acerbi pointed out the much larger numbers of journals and periodicals published in the Danish monarchy, thanks to its relative lack of censorship (up to the fall of 1799), as contrasted with Sweden, with its more tightly controlled press. Malthus noted "most perfect freedom of opinion" in Denmark and found Thomas Paine's writings in French and German.[24]

Various travelers gave much attention to libraries, archives, and manuscript collections.[25] But it was a repeated complaint among the more learned of them that booksellers were few and far between and books hard to obtain. In 1790 Boisgelin noted fourteen or fifteen booksellers in Copenhagen, but in 1799 Clarke claimed that "good books are seldom found in any of the booksellers' shops." Booksellers in Stockholm were unable or unwilling to provide much help to the inquiring foreigner. Clarke further stated that there were no booksellers at all in the whole of Norway, nor, he was convinced, were there any north of Åbo in Finland, where he found three or four that were worse than those in Stockholm.[26] Although they did not remark on this, it is evident that many wealthy and cultivated Scandinavians at that time arranged for book purchases abroad.

The visitors occasionally mentioned Scandinavian learned societies but left little comment on them, except Acerbi, who had the young radical's skeptical view of academies in general.

> Let the academies found orders, and grant to their favourites crosses or any other particular marks of distinction; all these may be innocent; but they should not pretend, by the magic of their election, to make philosophers of men who perhaps scarce understand the expression. Intrigue, cabal, and envy of real merit, the little vices of some academies and learned societies, have an unavoidable tendency to expose them to the attacks of wit and ridicule.

Yet he was thereupon prepared to admit that "there is notwithstanding in Sweden, and even in the academies, much genius and industry directed to useful purposes."[27]

James was far more positive when he declared in 1813: "There is no country in Europe which, in proportion to her numbers, has contributed so largely to the advancement of science as Sweden, and none where it is still more steadily and successfully pursued."

When Wraxall in 1774 had professed a "reverential awe" over the "immortal and sublime spirits" Sweden had produced, he was looking back in the baroque spirit to its Age of Greatness (1611–1718), its warrior-kings Gustav II Adolf and Karl XII, and its generals in the Thirty Years' War, such as Lennart Torstenson or Johan Banér. Most of the travelers tended, meanwhile, to look to the newer, peaceful ideal of the Enlightenment: the man of science or "natural philosopher." And if there was one area of cultural activity in which Scandinavians, most specifically Swedes, had won international acclaim during the eighteenth century, it was natural science, and particularly natural history.[28]

Carl Linnæus (1707–78)—or von Linné as he was called following his ennoblement in 1757—was the great dominating and symbolic figure of Swedish natural science, but several of his widely traveled disciples, including Pehr Kalm, Daniel Solander, and Anders Sparrman, also enjoyed international reputations, as did a number of other Swedish scientists. Their activity—centered above all at Uppsala University—was at its height by midcentury, and it unquestionably provided one of the most powerful attractions to the foreign travelers of the following decades.

Certain of the most scholarly visitors indeed journeyed to Sweden expressly to meet the great Linnæus, up to his death in 1778. The adulation he enjoyed is well expressed in a brief account in Latin verse, with English and French prose translations, describing such a pilgrimage to Uppsala in 1769 by the Englishman Frederick Calvert, Lord Baltimore, who proclaimed, with a preliminary invocation to Nordic antiquity,

> Upsal was formerly the glory of this northern Empire, she directed the long reigns of government. Now she enjoys an Academy happy in the great learning of its Doctors. . . . Nature was miserable buried in darkness, and mournful science lay prostreate in eternal night. Linneus brought her forth from obscurity, and unveiled her, illustrating with his knowledge and with labours the whole world. O Linneus! I send the most trifling and wretched works to a Lucretius! . . . May the flowers, the birds, the fish, and the beasts of Sweden remain famous by your means. O most happy sage! The threatening thunder of your judgment terrifies me. . . .

Johann Beckmann had, meanwhile, spent ten months in Sweden in 1765–66, mainly in Uppsala, in the constant company of Linnæus and his colleagues.

Against such a background, E. D. Clarke's eager anticipation in 1799 may well be understood:

> A long avenue of stately firs at length opened upon *Upsalia*. . . . Its appearance, in the approach to it, is really noble . . . calling to mind the names of *Celsius, Linnæus, Wallerius, Cronstedt, Bergmann, Hasselquist, Fabricius, Zoega*, and a long list of their disciples and successors, which had contributed to render this University illustrious; the many enterprising travellers it has sent forth to almost every region of the earth; the discoveries they have made, and the works of which they were the authors. For since the days of *Aristotle* and of *Theophrastus*, the light of *Natural History* had become dim, until it beamed, like a star from the *North*; and this was the point of its emanation.

In Sweden, "There is hardly an apothecary or physician," Clarke noted, "who has not either a collection of stuffed birds or of insects, or of other living or dead animals."[29]

Still, the later eighteenth century was becoming a time of scientific epigones. Already in 1765 the otherwise enthusiastic Johann Beckmann realized that, aside from Linnæus and a few others, "the love of natural history has already died out even in Sweden. . . . One likewise does not find as much instruction or opportunity at Uppsala as foreigners imagine."

Uppsala University proved an undoubted disappointment to visitors by the turn of the century. That it had seen better days was attested to by its declining enrollments. Wraxall noted in 1774 that its students were not "young men of family and condition as with us, but for the most part are miserably poor." Boisgelin observed that, whereas as late as 1730 they had numbered some two thousand, there were now, in 1791, only six to seven hundred. Acerbi mentioned five hundred in 1799 and James the same number in 1813. Consett, meanwhile, claimed in 1786 that they included "many foreigners and Students of different nations, even from England"; while Clarke met a young American, whose republican views aroused his ire.[30]

It is above all the Cambridge don, E. D. Clarke, who provides the fullest outsider's description of Uppsala University and its denizens at the end of the eighteenth century, and it is not on the whole complimentary. His "high expectations" were not realized, and "everything seemed to dwindle into insignificance, when reality was opposed to our ideal picture." Lectures by some of the better-known professors in botany and chemistry, which he sat in on, were attended by only handfuls of bored and "slovenly boys," some of them evidently not over the age of fourteen. Clarke deplored the lack of any "peculiarity of habit" to distinguish academics from the "lower orders." "In *Upsala*," he complained, "a student in the street is not a whit better clad than any working coachman or carpenter in *England*." Dress was symptomatic of behavior and attitudes. "Every one studies what, and when, he pleases: of course, very little real application to learning takes place among them." Clarke described the dingy taverns where they whiled away their time, their addiction to drink, and their boisterous sallies through the town to harass unpopular professors. Worse yet, the staunch English Tory caught the scent of what indeed at that time was widespread enthusiasm among the students and even some of the faculty for French Jacobinism.

"Considering the manner in which lectures are given, and sort of people which attend as students, and the total want of all Academical discipline and all incitement to emulation in *Upsala*," Clarke nonetheless concluded, "it is quite wonderful that it has produced such a number of persons eminent in every branch of science."[31]

Brougham's briefer observations from the same year are of the same character. The more liberal-minded Acerbi, who visited Uppsala the same year, however, provides something of an antidote with his considerably more positive view of the university. He particularly praised its emphasis upon the "cultivation of real science, and the pursuit of objects which are of great importance and utility" and "the very proper degree of familiarity" that appeared to exist "between those who teach and those who are taught," resulting in a free interchange of ideas.[32]

Lund University, in southern Sweden, was, it seems, generally bypassed by visiting foreigners in this period, although Miranda found some three hundred students there in 1787. Clarke, meanwhile, provided a good description of Åbo University in Finland, with an enrollment at the time of some three hundred students, which in his view was "as much superior to *Upsala*, as the latter is before the University of *Lund*." "At Upsala," he wrote, "science was made a matter of conversation; at *Åbo* it was a subject of real and industrious research." Of the professors, he wrote to William Otter, "They beat Upsal out and out." He added that he here became the "student" of Henrik Gabriel Porthan, the pioneer scholar of Finnish language and folk culture, and of the poet Frans Mikael Franzén. He also found none of the "drunkenness and riot" that pervaded the streets of Uppsala. The students were serious and orderly, thanks, in Clarke's view, to the absence there of ruinous "*French* principles." In Åbo, "the older *Swedish* manners and customs were prevalent, not having been yet liable to such mischievous innovations: a love of truth, and a sincere ardour in the pursuit of science, seemed to be the natural growth of the place, where the force of good example were added to precept."[33]

The University of Copenhagen, the sole such institution for Denmark and Norway, attracted little attention. Miranda reported its enrollment to be only some two hundred fifty students in 1788. Brougham, who visited it in 1799, later recalled, "The University is an old and shabby quadrangle. We were present at an examination of the students, who were very mean-looking, and seemed to be questioned by the master, who sat in his chair, like boys at school." Still, at the University of Kiel, in Holstein, where Miranda found some two hundred students in 1788, Buch noted in 1806 that the Danish students there had "by far the quickest capacity" for learning, as opposed to the German Holsteiners. Reflecting the views of Norwegian acquaintances, Küttner deplored the lack of a university in Norway. Coxe, visiting Christiania in 1784, found only thirty-seven scholars in its preparatory Latin school.[34]

When it came to the state and its public institutions, the attitudes of foreign visitors varied according to nationality and political orientation. Denmark, which since 1665 had in theory been Europe's most absolute monarchy, had begun to allow its subjects by the mid-1780s progressively greater personal liberties; whereas Sweden, in principle a constitutional monarchy, in which the monarch shared power with the estates of the realm, became in practice increasingly authoritarian from the same period.

The Swedish constitution of 1720, which had established a parliamentary regime in significant ways similar to Great Britain's, was widely admired in enlightened circles, although Gustav III's coup of 1772, resulting in a new constitution providing a strengthened monarchical authority, was generally welcomed in Europe as a necessary corrective. Most of the visitors, being British or admirers of British political institutions, were inclined to admire the Swedish regime, at least before Gustav III in 1788–89 largely overrode his own constitution of 1772.[35] Hence their increasing disillusionment as the system grew ever more despotic in practice during Gustav III's later years and under his successor, Gustav IV Adolf.

The French royalist émigré Boisgelin, under the shadow of violent revolution in his homeland, could warmly praise Sweden's government in 1790: "Indeed the Swedes have so much reason to be satisfied with a constitution which, in most particulars, is so superior to those of other countries, that they are very ready to tolerate the few abuses which still subsist; for they fear, if they attempted to lop the branches, they might possibly injure the trunk." However, Miranda in 1786 already deplored Gustav III's introduction of police espionage as a harmful import from Paris. Clarke, in praising Swedish eminence in the sciences, believed that "centuries may elapse before *Sweden* will produce a *Locke*, or a *Montesquieu*." Acerbi, a warm admirer of republican France, was particularly critical in 1799 of censorship and obscurantism in Gustav IV Adolf's Sweden, which he was convinced stifled true cultural creativity, as compared, paradoxically, with the relative freedom in the Danish state. Attending the Stockholm opera the same year, La Tocnaye was "almost scandalized" by the coldness of the public toward the young monarch.[36]

Vittorio Alfieri had noted as early as 1769 a freer atmosphere in Denmark than in autocratic Prussia or Russia. Yet Miranda could not refrain from occasional private tirades against Danish "despotism"; his cosmopolitanism was, for instance, offended by the Law on Indigenous Rights (*Indfødsretslov*) of 1776, which restricted state appointments to Danish subjects. In 1790 Boisgelin declared, however, that despotism was not the same as tyranny. Although Denmark had a "despotic" government, "we never think of pitying the Danes, though, according to the philosophers of the present day, the subjects of an absolute prince must necessarily become objects of compassion." Worse still was the despotism of "the many," of which "it is easy to find examples in Europe. The greater the number of tyrants, the heavier the yoke." Mary Wollstonecraft, whose initial enthusiasm for the French Revolution by then had cooled, wrote in 1795 that, although their king was an absolute monarch, "from all I can gather, the inhabitants of Denmark and Norway are the least oppressed people in Europe."[37]

The reigning princes embodied and symbolized the state. About Christian VII of Denmark (r. 1766–1808), there was little to say. By 1770 he had already become hopelessly insane and had fallen under the influence of his German physician, Johann Friedrich Struensee, who became both Denmark's virtual ruler and the lover of Queen Caroline Mathilde, a sister of

George III of England. Struensee was overthrown by a palace revolution in 1772 and executed, while the unfortunate queen was first imprisoned at Kronborg Castle in Helsingør (Elsinore), then exiled to Celle in Hannover, where she died in 1775.

Following various makeshift arrangements, Christian VII's son, Crown Prince Frederik, made himself de facto regent in 1784, at the age of sixteen. Although dedicated and conscientious, the young prince at first delegated responsibility to the able Count Andreas Peter Bernstorff and his associates, who over the next two decades implemented an ambitious program of social, economic, and legal reforms. Miranda in 1788 regarded the crown prince as "highly energetic, but ignorant" and feared that "his heart is filled with the thoroughly false idea that everything must give way before the unlimited authority of an absolute monarch as the foundation of good government." Mary Wollstonecraft wrote from Norway in 1795 that the "prince royal" was "well-disposed" but "tractable" in the hands of Count Bernstorff, the "real sovereign." Bernstorff had impressed Miranda as "well informed" but "rather dictatorial" in manner. The Swiss phrenologist and mystic Johann Caspar Lavater, who visited Copenhagen as Bernstorff's guest in 1793, was highly impressed by the count and his associates.[38] Not until after the count's death in 1797, and especially after the crown prince succeeded to the throne as King Frederik VI in 1808, did he exercise an increasingly personal authority. Austere and withdrawn, he shunned courtly ceremony, thriving best in the company of his military adjutants. Few foreign visitors seem to have had anything to say about him.

Nor, at the beginning of the period, was there much to remark about the colorless and virtually powerless King Adolf Fredrik of Sweden (r. 1751–71). In striking contrast stood his son, Gustav III (r. 1771–92) — restlessly active, intelligent, cultivated, ambitious, avid for glory at home and abroad, the author both of dramas and of vast political scenarios, and a recklessly extravagant patron of the arts. Few Scandinavian monarchs achieved such renown on the international scene, aroused greater adulation or hatred, or remained, to the present, the object of more historiographic dispute.[39]

Such a sovereign naturally drew much commentary from foreign visitors, providing a classic example of the degree to which this kind of discussion — from outsiders unfamiliar with the national languages, with little prior background, and based upon relatively brief sojourns — was bound to reflect their preexisting national and personal values, as well as the divided views of those natives with whom they consorted.

Wraxall's account from 1774 reflects the widespread popularity, indeed adulation, the young Gustav III enjoyed during the early years of his reign, following his successful "revolution" two years earlier. "His person, character, and actions, are all subjects so agreeable and flattering," he declared, "that there is little need to request a Swede to converse upon them." The king frequently paid unexpected visits to "persons of very inferior rank, where he behaves with an ease and politeness which must infallibly render him beloved." Diligent in controlling his subordinates, he was accessible to the "meanest subject." His soldiers adored him and, with "his disdain of fatigue, and undoubted courage," he was, in Wraxall's view, a worthy successor to his heroic, warlike predecessors.[40] Not surprisingly, Boisgelin, too, warmly praised Gustav III and venerated his memory. He contrasted Sweden's bloodless revolution from above of 1772—guided by the single will of the king himself—with the wild, anarchical revolution from below in his native France, both of which had led to the replacement of an old regime by a new. "What happened in Sweden is a proof that the dreadful excesses that have stained our history might have been prevented: though the philosophers and logicians of the present day insist upon the impossibility of bringing about a revolution without bloodshed, and sacrificing many victims to the cause." As for Gustav's second coup, following a bitter struggle with his nobility on the eve of the French Revolution in the winter of 1789, Boisgelin held that the king, by dealing firmly with them had indeed saved them from the fury of the mob, unlike in France. La Tocnaye—who had seen the Swedish king in 1783, when the latter had reviewed his regiment in France—ruefully compared his courage and resolution with the fatal weakness of Louis XVI. It was Gustav, he wrote, who had first recognized the cruel spirit of the French Revolution and had striven selflessly to rally monarchical Europe against it. This was precisely the version of the recent past that Gustav and his supporters sought to propagate.

Reflecting the nostalgia of Swedish artists and literati for their late king, Carr declared in 1804 that "what Frederick the Great was to Berlin, Gustavus the Third was to Stockholm: almost every object which embellishes this beautiful city arose from his patronage, frequently from his own designs."[41]

Those who visited Sweden after Gustav III's assassination through an aristocratic plot in March 1792 were inclined to reflect the attitudes of the late king's bitter opponents. Brougham, for instance, wrote that "the conduct of the late king gave rise to the profligacy of the Court," which had in turn encouraged a general moral dissoluteness in society. "He introduced and encouraged effeminate habits, and pursued a system of favoritism that led to his own destruction." He did, however, mention a detail that adds substance to Boisgelin's (and Gustav's own) view. The French consul in Gothenburg told him that the king, anticipating in 1788 a coming upheaval in France, had said, "I must hasten to finish my revolution before this begins, and before it becomes dangerous to call together the states [i.e., estates]."[42]

Clarke spoke of Gustav's ruination of the state finances and of his "polished manners and enlightened mind," which were out of place in his poor Northern realm. While he admired the splendid neoclassical church in the far northern town of Skellefteå, he could not but comment, "A *Grecian* temple upon the borders of *Lapland* may be compared to *Gustavus the Third* in *Scandinavia*, to whose magnificence and taste it must, after all, be ascribed; for, like the monarch, it has nothing in common with the country in which it has arisen."[43]

Most outspoken in his antipathy toward the late king was Giuseppe Acerbi. "His love of absolute power was sincere"; he wrote, "his zeal for literature and science affected, unnatural, and guarded." In large part this attitude was doubtless due to Gustav III's enmity toward the Revolution in France and his attempts at the end of his life to organize a monarchical crusade to crush it. To Acerbi and those with whom he associated in Sweden, Gustav III was a vain and dissolute tyrant, determined to destroy abroad the liberty he had extinguished at home.[44]

Sweden's later rulers received, in comparison, a good deal less attention from foreign visitors. Acerbi, to be sure, was given to believe by his aristocratic Swedish acquaintances that Duke Carl of Södermanland, Gustav's brother, who served as regent for the young successor, Gustav IV Adolf, from 1792 to 1796, was a friend of liberty who had served Sweden well by abandoning the late king's antirevolutionary fantasies and restoring relations with the new France. He was, however, somewhat taken aback by the duke's weakness for esoteric Freemasonic mysticism.[45]

Gustav IV Adolf (r. 1792–1809) proved remarkably unlike Gustav III and similar to his Danish cousin, Frederik VI. Clarke wrote that many stories circulated in Stockholm about him: "The general tenor of all of them was to represent the King as a haughty, imperious, but benevolent man, destitute of sound judgment and literary talents; without any love of the Fine Arts, but desirous of enforcing strict obedience to the laws, both by precept and example; and the Queen [Fredrika of Baden] as a giddy, cheerful romp, more disposed toward laughter than serious reflection." He was taciturn, solitary, and uncomfortable with the representative aspects of royalty. While La Tocnaye admired his dignity—as well as his firmness toward republican France—Küttner reported that "he has never been seen to laugh." Acerbi commented pessimistically upon the revival of royal despotism and clerical obscurantism, particularly in the form of press censorship, following the end of Duke Carl's regency.[46]

At a time when it was common for foreigners of birth and breeding to gain entrée to courts and royalty, several of the travelers met, or at least saw, the Scandinavian monarchs. Malthus witnessed a military review in Copenhagen attended by the Danish royal family in 1799. Poor, mad Christian VII was "treated quite as an idiot. The officers of the court have all orders not to give him an answer. Some . . . observed him talking very fast & making faces at an officer who was one of the sentinels at the tent, who preserved the utmost gravity of countenance & did not answer him a single word."

Gustav III quietly sought out Miranda in 1787, believing him to be privy to the secrets of his Baltic rival, Catherine II of Russia, from whose court he had just come, meeting him, as though by chance, in various places, including the sculptor Sergel's studio. Fortia and Boisgelin were received by Gustav, who not surprisingly talked with them not only "of the French revolution, but of that which took place in Sweden in 1772, and the factions which disturbed his country." Clarke saw Gustav IV Adolf at a gala at the Stockholm opera, surrounded—to his discomfiture, one may imagine—by his entourage in full feather. Porter, who saw the king and queen at a ball in 1808, was, meanwhile, impressed by their dignity and bearing, as well as the evident loyalty of their subjects.[47]

That loyalty would prove illusory, for as a result largely of Sweden's disastrous war with Russia beginning that year, Gustav IV Adolf was deposed by a revolution in March 1809. Aaron Burr observed him in captivity from a distance at Gripsholm Castle and saw his family, held at Haga Palace, before they went into permanent exile at the end of the year.

In May 1809, the Swedish estates elected his uncle, Duke Carl, as King Karl XIII. Burr met the new king, noting that he appeared older than his sixty-one years and had an "air usé"; to James, who met the king in 1813, he "appeared in an extremely feeble state."

As Karl XIII had no heir, the estates in 1810 elected as his successor none other than the French field marshal, Jean-Baptiste Bernadotte, who, as Crown Prince Carl Johan (from 1818 King Karl XIV Johan), became the actual ruler of Sweden on his adoptive father's behalf and led Sweden into the anti-Napoleonic coalition by 1812. J. T. James met him in Prussia in 1813, where he commanded the Allied northern army against his erstwhile master. "His countenance (for every trait of so noted a character bears an interest)," James wrote of one of Scandinavia's most remarkable rulers and founder of the present Swedish dynasty, "was one of extreme penetration, joined to a prepossessing appearance of great affability; his manner was equally pleasant and courteous." The new crown prince, Thomson declared in 1812, had the opportunity to make himself "a figure not inferior to that of Gustavus Adolphus," as the Germans "want only a leader of ability to free their country." This would assure the outcome of the struggle with Napoleon, making the crown prince "one of the most glorious characters in history."[48]

If foreign visitors were only able to grasp the internal politics of the Northern kingdoms in an indistinct and derivative fashion, they had clearer ideas regarding their external relations, based on nationality and political ideology. The fate of the unfortunate Caroline Mathilde, consort of the mad king Christian VII, was bound to arouse sympathies, especially among the British travelers. Wraxall was greatly moved upon visiting her chambers at Kronborg Castle in 1774 and gave a lengthy account of her and Struensee's fate. Due to the strained relations with Britain to which the episode had given rise, Wraxall was suspected in Denmark of being a British spy. What he did not mention was that he himself became deeply involved in a Danish plot to return Caroline Mathilde to Copenhagen as regent. He noted, meanwhile, that he was plied with "a thousand questions, in every company, about the inhabitants of Boston, and relative to the East India affairs. They are unanimous in opinion, that the colonies will be soon absolutely free."[49]

The numerous travelers around the turn of the century were much concerned about attitudes toward the respective sides in the war between revolutionary France and its monarchical enemies. Acerbi, as seen, warmly approved Sweden's rapprochement with France under Duke Carl's regency. British visitors, including Wollstonecraft, Malthus, Clarke, and Brougham, were much concerned at the time by disquieting manifestations of Anglophobic Jacobinism in the North. So determined "to excuse every thing, disgracing the struggle for freedom, by admitting the tyrant's plea of necessity" were some of the inhabitants of Moss in Norway, Mary Wollstonecraft wrote, "that I could hardly persuade them that Robespierre was a monster." La Tocnaye described the fury of the Vikings as a "truly *Jacobin* passion." He was apprehensive of the harmful influence, among the merchants and common people, of the "republican corsairs" who frequently put into neutral Norwegian ports, while he admired the staunch royalism of the peasantry in Swedish Dalarna. A British diplomat in Copenhagen described the Danish literati to Brougham as "a set of the greatest Jacobins on the face of the earth." Clarke's indignation over student radicalism at Uppsala and relief over its absence in Åbo has been noted.

Still, Clarke wrote that he and his companions had found in Sweden "more to admire than to disapprove, and very little to censure," and that "the generality of *Englishmen* visiting the country will probably coincide in this opinion."

Clarke was, meanwhile, particularly moved—perhaps especially in retrospect when he prepared his account for publication a decade or more later—by the partiality of the Norwegians he met toward Great Britain:

> Of all the nations to whom the *British* character is known, the *Norwegians* are the most sincerely attached to the inhabitants of our island. . . . Every *Englishman* was considered by the *Norwegians* as a brother; they partook even of our prejudices; and participated in all our triumphs. . . . Their houses were furnished with *English* engravings, and *English* newspapers were lying upon their tables. . . . [T]here was nothing which an *Englishman*, as a sincere lover of his country, might more earnestly have wished for, than to see *Norway* allied to *Britain*.[50]

After the beginning of the Swedish-Russian War of 1808–9, a new concern emerges: that Russia, as France's ally under the Treaty of Tilsit, threatened to engulf all of Scandinavia. Speaking in June 1809 of an upcoming opera performance in Stockholm, Aaron Burr commented wryly, "It is not impossible, nor altogether improbable, that we may have a Russian audience," in view of their recent landings to the north. "It is the universal opinion," he added, "that if they come, there will be general plundering and other worse enormities." Fortunately, they did not arrive. In a footnote, added to his manuscript at this time, Clarke feared Sweden's imminent extinction at the hands of the Russian colossus. Yet once the conflict ended, James was well impressed in 1813 with Tsar Alexander I's liberality toward his new autonomous grand duchy of Finland. "The more wealthy and thinking classes," he wrote, "cannot but feel the advantages of their present situation." They no longer needed to fear war, and they enjoyed freer trade, "while, as far as it can be made compatible with the Russian system, they are granted the exercise of their ancient liberties, customs, and privileges."[51]

La Tocnaye in 1799 noted among the Norwegians a growing sense of self-awareness and pride vis-à-vis the Danish regime. Those traveling or, like Clarke, completing their accounts during or after the last phase of the Napoleonic Wars tended to be warmly sympathetic toward the fate of Norway, which suffered severely as a result of Denmark's alliance with Napoleon from 1807 and was thereafter forced by the Allies into an unwelcome dynastic union with Sweden in 1814, a measure highly unpopular, especially in British public opinion. Clarke wrote of the Norwegians that, while they put their hopes in a close relationship with Britain, "they entertain a certain degree of contempt toward the *Swedes*, and hold the *Danes* in utter aversion. Whenever *Sweden* became the subject of conversation, at this time, it was the prevailing opinion that its Government was going to ruin; because every thing belonging to it was said to be in an unsettled state." James, too, was disturbed by the unstable and often violent course of Sweden's recent history and foresaw in 1814 that its present sovereign "was not likely to enter quietly into possession" of Norway.[52]

Management of the affairs of state, meanwhile, elicited the comments of foreign visitors. Of the Danish monarchy, Brougham wrote in 1799, "The administration of this Government, execrable as is its theory, is in practice mild and gentle." Mary Wollstonecraft claimed in 1795 to perceive the "cloven foot of despotism" in the "grand bailiffs" in Christiania, mostly noblemen from Denmark. However, Buch in 1806 was gratified, when witnessing the payment of taxes by the peasants in Sogness, to see the "kindness, humanity, and patience with which the boors were treated by the royal functionaries, and which they seemed to repay with the most hearty and cordial confidence." This good relationship would augur well, he felt, if the "brave Norwegians" should someday be called upon to defend their land. The difference in their perceptions is interesting, for fearing Swedish designs against Norway, the Danish government made concerted efforts during these years to improve its relations with the Norwegian peasantry.[53]

While Brougham complained in 1799 that Stockholm was badly policed and that there was much theft, especially among the soldiery, the prevailing view was that an admirable level of law and order prevailed in the Nordic lands. "The laws are clear, wise, and precise," Boisgelin wrote of Sweden in 1790. "The criminal law is lenient; which ought to be the case in countries where great crimes are very seldom committed," he added. Wollstonecraft indeed believed them so mild in both Sweden and Norway that "they rather favour than restrain knavery." Still, Aaron Burr marveled in 1809: "Only to think of a people, the most honest and peaceable in the world, and not a lawyer! No such animal, according to English ideas of a lawyer, in Sweden!"[54]

For those who fell afoul of the law, punishment could on occasion be drastic, as were the much-publicized executions of Struensee in 1772 and of Gustav III's assassin, Jakob Johan Anckarström, in 1792. Near Kalix in Lapland, Clarke purported to have seen twelve upright posts displaying the skulls or carcasses of apprehended mail robbers—it was unclear over how long a period their executions had taken place—but Clarke hastened to add that spectacles of this kind were extremely rare in the Swedish kingdom. Coxe published in 1781 a separate, laudatory study of prisons and hospitals in the Northern kingdoms, dedicated to John Howard, the English prison reformer. "So mild are the penal laws of Sweden," he wrote, "that more than 120 strokes of the rod are never inflicted; and the criminal is never sentenced to bread and water for more than 28 days." He noted, too, that Gustav III had abolished judicial torture. Boisgelin noted in 1790 that prisons in Stockholm were "very clean" and "certainly less disgusting than elsewhere." He was likewise well impressed with the so-called Spin-House (*Spinnhuset*) for woman inmates, many of them convicted for infanticide, as well as the Danviken insane asylum.[55]

Coxe had considered the treatment of criminals in Denmark rather harsher than in Sweden. Miranda, who visited Copenhagen's prisons as assiduously as he did all other public institutions, was so horrified by the conditions he found in them that he used his influence in high places to inspire the appointment of a royal commission, which thereafter carried out penal reforms.[56]

Charitable institutions could also arouse favorable comment, such as those that frequently appear in Miranda's diary. Boisgelin praised the "Great Hospital for Orphans" and the home for the widows of Stockholm burghers, the latter probably unequaled in any other country and "certainly deserving of imitation." In Trondheim, Clarke found the inmates of the poorhouse better dressed than those in England.[57]

Opinions regarding the military forces could also vary. Andrew Swinton felt in 1789 that the Danes were seriously overburdened with needless military expenditures, giving rise to discontentment that could be dangerous at a time when "revolutions are kindling over Europe." Matthew Consett, who witnessed an artillery review near Gothenburg in 1786, considered that "it would be too humiliating to draw a comparison between what we saw, and the English artillery. The soldiers, in general, look old and inactive." Yet Swinton, in St. Petersburg from the fall of 1788, testified how seriously the Russians took their war with Sweden, which had broken out in June. Porter in 1808 considered the Swedish horse guards poorly mounted and "not very martially attired." Although there were abuses, Boisgelin judged the Swedish troops in 1790 — during Gustav III's Russian War — to be "spirited and well-principled; the officers are brave, and the soldiers very like the French soldiers," not least in their use of cold steel; while Acerbi in 1799 wrote enthusiastically that "Swedish arms in the cause of liberty have always been invincible."[58]

Occasionally, though seldom, visitors touched on religious conditions. While the state church throughout Scandinavia was Lutheran, Miranda found a Catholic congregation in Copenhagen with, according to its Austrian priest, seven thousand communicants—which sounds inflated. Boisgelin noted in 1790 that, in Sweden, "liberty of conscience is every where allowed, and no mode of worship is prohibited." The Catholics had a church with some two thousand parishioners in Stockholm, he claimed, with some six thousand others throughout the kingdom, including "many families" in Finland. Such tolerance nonetheless remained limited, for Gustav III had in 1782 allowed religious freedom to foreign residents but not to Swedish members of the state church. That native dissenters at this time were still treated leniently seems evident from Boisgelin's description of a small sect, the *Skedvikare* who, after seceding from the Swedish state church in 1783 and being officially banished from the kingdom, had been quietly permitted to settle on the island of Värmdö, near Stockholm. Acerbi was concerned in 1799 with the advance in Sweden of "superstition" and clerical obscurantism; while Clarke, at the same time, noted what seemed to be a great deal of "indifferentism" in Norway.[59]

Those with whom foreign travelers of birth and breeding naturally came into closest contact were persons of their own station. Their accounts devote much attention to manners and mores among the upper classes.

The top rank was both small and exclusive; Boisgelin claimed in 1790, "what usually comes under the denomination of society does not amount to more than a hundred and fifty [in Stockholm]; whilst at Copenhagen there are above two hundred and fifty, and at Berlin two hundred and twenty or thirty."[60]

At the pinnacle stood the royal courts. There was little to say about that of Copenhagen during the reigns of the mad Christian VII and of his retiring son, Frederik VI. Visitors to the court of Stockholm were, meanwhile, struck by the elaborateness of ceremony introduced principally by Gustav III. At a time when "many sovereigns of Europe are endeavouring to retrench the ceremonies attendant on royalty," Coxe observed in 1779, "Gustavus III has introduced a degree of pomp and etiquette similar to that used at Versailles, and hitherto unknown in this country." Acerbi attributed the "great formality and restraint" of Swedish polite society above all to the royal court, "the most formal I believe in Europe; nay, I had nearly said the world: but there is undoubtedly still more of rigid etiquette at the court of Pekin [in China]." He nonetheless believed there was no country "where the king and princes mix more familiarly with the people than in Sweden." Clarke saw Gustav IV Adolf at the opera, surrounded by his ostentatiously garbed courtiers, which in his view produced "altogether the most grotesque effect, by combining somewhat of the manly chivalrous aspect of the warriors of antient days with the wretched effeminacy and scenic taste of the modern Court. It was enough to rouse the ghost of *Gustavus Vasa*."[61]

In discussing the Swedish court, Boisgelin derided the prevailing weakness for orders and decorations of all kinds. He would have preferred "an oaken wreath, bearing the following inscription, *the deserved gift of his country*." "It is easy to perceive," he added wistfully in a later footnote, that this comment "was written in the early stages of the French Revolution."[62]

The landowning nobility and gentry of the countryside occupied a key position in what were still strongly rural societies, and the visitors were for the most part impressed with those they encountered. During a period of vigorous agrarian reform in Denmark, Christian Ludwig Lenz warmly praised the Danish nobility, which "on the whole surely belongs to the most enlightened in Europe" in its concern for its peasant tenantry, although presumably he was not speaking of the lesser landowners, many of whom were hard-pressed and opposed to the reforms. Norway had virtually no native nobility, but Mary Wollstonecraft wrote of the principal exception, the count of Wedel-Jarlsberg, that she had "seldom heard of any nobleman so innocuous." "The real *Swedish* gentleman" Clarke considered "an honor to his country and to mankind." "In no country, since I quitted England," Coxe declared, "have I observed so many seats scattered over the face of the country as I perceived in Sweden; where the gentlemen of moderate fortunes, as with us, are accustomed to reside upon their estates in rural plenty."[63] In their contacts with clergymen and other persons of quality in rural areas, the travelers likewise had all reason to be well pleased.

The element of polite society that attracted the greatest comment was the wealthier merchant class, not only in the larger cities but even in smaller towns. Writing from far northern Uleåborg in Finland, where he spent the late winter of 1799, Acerbi found life there, among a local patriciate that as much as possible followed the fashions of Stockholm high society, more pleasant than in a "great metropolis."[64]

No characteristic of the upper classes drew more frequent and favorable comment than the hospitality they afforded the foreign traveler, not least at rural manors and parsonages. Examples are too numerous to document in detail. Wraxall, for instance, set off on a tour of Uppland in 1774 with "wine and provisions sufficient for a much longer journey," which "Swedish hospitality hardly suffered us to diminish," since he simply moved from one manor house to the next. In Christiania, Clarke spoke of "that native heartiness of a *Norwegian*, which knows no bounds to its hospitality, but as in *Sweden*, will carry its kind attention to strangers even to excess." Indeed, in Umeå, he wrote that "the *Swedish* hospitality was again displayed in all its force," which could actually be so "overwhelming" as to become "exceedingly troublesome." One was compelled "to eat until he finds it impossible to swallow another morsel. . . . [W]hen a guest is choked with such kindness, and unable to bear another mouthful, the importunity continues to a degree that is painful." (Later visitors to Scandinavian lands may well sympathize!) James Macdonald was greatly touched in 1808 by the hospitality of the leading citizens of Aalborg, who, even though he was a prisoner in wartime Denmark, invited him to their balls and entertainments.[65]

The visitors were also frequently received as guests by clubs and societies, which could surprise them with their amenities. Boisgelin praised "The Society" (*Sällskapet*) in Stockholm, frequented by the foreign diplomats. It would seem to have been the same club that Brougham described as "one of the first institutions of its kind in Europe, if not the first." Porter called it "the most rational and elegant assembly with which I ever associated." Burr spoke warmly of the Merchants' Society in the same city. Clarke was similarly well impressed with a club in Trondheim.[66]

Indeed, the Northern kingdoms could at times reveal a degree of elegance and social pretension that seem all out of proportion to their remoteness and limited resources. Boisgelin described the Swedish nobility as, on the whole, "far from rich," yet he satirized the "ridiculous vanity" of those in the far southern province of Skåne, who "never visit without great ceremony, and always take a large retinue of servants and horses . . . and, after making their tour, return home and pass the rest of the year entirely alone." Acerbi much preferred the ease and luxury he encountered in the country houses of the more prosperous Stockholm merchants, "the richest class of society," where the ceremoniousness of their town residences was laid aside. In Torneå (Tornio), at the head of the Bay of Bothnia, Clarke, just returned from the wilds of Lapland, marveled at the "luxuries of polished society." In Trondheim he wrote that "the houses of the lowest merchants are furnished with a degree of neatness and elegance very striking to a traveller in this *Hyperborean* corner of Europe: in this respect, *Trönÿem* does not yield to *Copenhagen*." La Tocnaye was much impressed by the comforts and amenities in Bergen. "The spirit of French fashion, but a little disciplined, reigns in Sweden," Carr wrote, "and gives a lightness and elegance to dress: the table, and the furniture, and even their manners, partake considerably of its gaiety."[67]

Certain magnates particularly captured the imagination and none more frequently than the fabulously wealthy merchant family of Anker in Norway. In his home in Christiania, Berndt Anker, the proprietor of 150 privileged sawmills, showed Clarke a splendid library, where public lectures were held, and "a complete apparatus for philosophical and mechanical purposes." He ordered everything he needed from England, where he even sent his laundry each year. He had thirty servants and his brother, sixty. The latter, doubtless Peder Anker, who proudly bore a coat of arms and the title of Danish court chamberlain by virtue of his alleged Swedish noble descent, received Clarke at his country residence outside the city with "as much magnificence as any foreign Prince, but with all the hearty welcome and hospitality of this country, added to the splendor of a King." La Tocnaye declared that his furniture and decor surpassed much that might be found in Italy. Küttner, meanwhile, assured his readers that the Anker brothers were "by no means the only opulent persons in this province," and Clarke was invited by a Christiania merchant named Collett to a feast so magnificent that "it would hardly be possible for our own Sovereign to afford a more sumptuous entertainment." La Tocnaye held that Christiania's luxury and sociability could compare with that of the "greatest capitals"—but only in four or five wealthy homes. He thus cautioned that Norwegian life should not be judged by that in Christiania, "which has little in common with the rest of the country."[68]

The level of personal culture among the wealthier classes could, however, leave much to be desired. "I cannot say as much in praise of the Swedish refinement or elegance," Wraxall observed in 1774, "as of their benevolence and civility." According to Boisgelin in 1790, "Learning has been very little cultivated for some years past in Sweden; reading is not the taste; and the generality of people are not desirous of improvement; the nobles, especially, when taken in a mass, are reputed ignorant." Even among the clergy, few were "particularly distinguished by their superior knowledge." Acerbi observed in 1799,

> The want of music in polite circles, or any thing approaching to that science, is not, I am sorry to say, compensated by the attractions and charms of conversation. You feel the want of many things in Sweden, which in some other countries constitute a fund of social pleasure and entertainment. There is, for instance, nothing to be met with that resembles those friendly dinners, where a small number of select friends meet, not for the purpose of indulging in epicurean extravagance, but from the sole motive of enjoying one another's company. The Swedish dinner parties are expensive arrangements of shew and formality.

Clarke was particularly dismayed by a lack of literary culture. Of Finnish Österbotten (Pohjanmaa) he wrote:

> Literature is at so low an ebb, that it may be doubted whether any traces of it can be said to exist north of *Åbo*. Books of any kind are seldom seen: there are no booksellers; nor is it possible to meet with a single copy of the works of the few celebrated authors *Sweden* has boasted, in any of the private houses. We sought in vain for the *Flora Svecica*, and the *Flora Lapponica*, of *Linnaeus*; we might as well have asked for the *Koran*, and perhaps we should have found it sooner. In the little shops, old *Latin* authors sometimes appear, as waste paper; and the apothecaries, now and then, possess a copy of the *Flora Svecica*, as a kind of shop-book, which they find so useful, that they are never induced to sell it.[69]

In Denmark Mary Wollstonecraft complained that "the men of business are domestic tyrants, coldly immersed in their own affairs, and so ignorant of the state of other countries, that they dogmatically assert that Denmark is the happiest country in the world; the prince royal the best of all possible princes; and count Bernstorff the wisest of ministers."[70]

Yet there were indeed exceptions to this rather dreary picture. In Uleåborg in northern Finland, Acerbi and his Swedish traveling companion, A. F. Skjöldebrand, found two enthusiastic musical amateurs with whom to play "quartettos," to the delight of an unaccustomed local public; this induced them to prolong their stay from five days to "a couple of months" in the dead of late winter. Here he found, among others, a local apothecary who was "well provided with books, had an electrical apparatus, and amused himself by making experiments in different departments of natural philosophy," as well as "a baron Silfverkielm [*sic*], a most famous magnetiser, and one of the greatest proficients among the disciples of Mesmer." The baron likewise entertained Clarke during his visit there. The frequent enthusiasm for cultivated company among isolated rural clergymen has already been noted.

Clarke spoke of a "thirst for literature" among younger members of Trondheim's patriciate and the widespread desire in Norway for a university of its own. Even in the tiny trading settlement of Rebvog, above the Arctic Circle in Norwegian Finnmark, Buch professed himself in 1806 not surprised to find polished and cultivated men. "Still, however, we cannot help feeling an unusual degree of pleasure when we find a few miles from the North Cape Ariosto and Dante, Moliere, Racine, Milton, and the flower of the Danish poets. The influence of great men is thus extended over the most remote spaces, and their spirit comprehends and finally diffuses itself over the whole globe."[71]

There was, as might be expected, much description of dinner parties, balls, soirees, and other social occasions, which all too often struck visitors from other climes as cold, formal, and dreary. In Copenhagen Miranda was on occasion exasperated by "these German formalities." "If a bow is not deep enough," he complained, "they would be prepared to pick a quarrel with their own fathers!" A visit to Koop Manor in Holstein caused an outburst in his diary: "Oh, my dear Americans, how many joyful and pleasant days have you not given me with your unpretentiousness and modesty!" La Tocnaye described the weakness for officious-sounding titles among the Swedish upper classes—especially the women—and noted with amusement that they were often uncertain as to how to treat him, since he claimed none. Brougham quoted a British diplomat to the effect that the "style of society" in Copenhagen was "insufferable." In summer the merchants departed for their country residences, while even in winter "the parties are said to be dull: the Court is uncommonly so." Lady Sarah Lyttelton, accustomed to London's social whirl, was soon bored in 1813 by what Stockholm had to offer.

Miranda and Acerbi complained of a lack of good conversation. "The greatest enemy to the spirit of society in Sweden, both in town and country," Acerbi declared, "and that which renders their parties the most heavy and insipid in Europe, is cards and other games of hazard. Ladies and gentlemen, old and young, neither think nor dream of any thing but cards." Though the Swedes were punctilious about etiquette, Brougham thought them rude toward strangers, an opinion directly opposed to that of virtually all his fellow visitors, which could perhaps be explained by strained diplomatic relations with Britain in 1799 or, more likely, by Nordic shyness and reserve.

In this latter respect, James in 1813 philosophized over the Swedish character:

> This nation has its singularities: and if, as philosophers tell us, the chill of a northern climate tinges the minds and manners of the inhabitants with an unimpassioned species of reserve, it is certain that there exists something of a reciprocity between the moral and physical constitution of Sweden. Rigidly ceremonious, they make their stiff and measured courtesies the essentials rather than the forms of life, and seem, in a stranger's eye, a people cold in their nature as the very snows they dwell upon.[72]

Yet some of the visitors have left vignettes of informal occasions of great charm, perhaps above all Miranda in his truly Boswellian diary. His Stockholm reflects both the winsome charm and the earthy gusto of Sweden's great balladeer of the Gustavian age, Carl Michael Bellman, and the often ribald sketches of Sergel and Ehrensvärd. His depictions of social life, in the broadest sense, in Christiania, Gothenburg, and especially Copenhagen are filled with color and immediacy. Burr's letters to his daughter, too, convey living glimpses of a relaxed and pleasant existence in enjoyable company.[73]

The women were, of course, the adornment of society, and they did not fail to draw due praise for their beauty from admiring visitors from other lands, not least the warm-blooded Miranda in his diary. Acerbi, meanwhile, largely summarized their views on the subject:

> The ladies of Sweden are, generally speaking, very handsome. Their countenances bear the characteristic of northern physiognomy, which is an expression of the most perfect tranquility and composure of mind, indicating nothing of that passion and fire, which, to every discerning observer, is visible in the features of French and Italian ladies. As there is but little gallantry or attention shown them by the men, and as they pass a great part of their

time either alone or amongst themselves, their conversation, though they are well educated, possesses but a small share either of variety or interest; and of that happy art of supporting conversation with vivacity, which so eminently distinguishes our Italian ladies, they are wholly destitute. The principal object that employs their time and attention is dress; and their anxiety is rather the effect of an ambition to outshine their rivals in elegance and splendor, than the result of an eagerness to please the men and make conquests. They are, however, not free from the imputation of coquetry, because they are certainly fond of admiration and praise; they would like to see every man at their feet, and would wish to be called the belles of the North; but their predominant passion is a desire of public notice and distinction. There is not an individual for whom they feel, in their heart, such strong and violent sentiments of friendship, tenderness, and love, as are found in those who live in warmer climates.

Porter said much the same when he wrote in 1808, "A more lovely assemblage of these demi-goddesses could not have been produced, than those I saw last night in the ball-room; however, they wanted that air which we call fashion, that ease of deportment, that, I cannot tell what, of *ton*, which the French, Russian and English fair of the same rank, so eminently possesses."

Lady Sarah Lyttelton, with her sharp feminine eye, was meanwhile rather more critical of both the appearance and dress of the Swedish ladies, while the Scot, Swinton, regarded their Danish sisters "not remarkable for their beauty." "It must be from the Saxon females," he added, "that the most considerable part of our fair countrywomen inherit their charms. The higher classes of the English, and the lower ranks of the Scottish women, are, no doubt, of Danish extraction, if we may judge from a parity of ugliness." His compatriot Macdonald was, however, prepared to recognize in 1808 that "the Aalborg ladies," while "neither so elegant nor so handsome as the English," nor so worldly as those in Copenhagen, were "good-humoured and obliging, and pay great attention to their family affairs." In Sweden, although he considered women deficient in education, he considered them more accomplished in this respect than the men, as they were in "every thing connected with the accommodations and embellishments of polished life."[74]

Whether from vanity alone, as Acerbi alleged, or from warmer passion beneath their impassive exteriors, some of the travelers were not slow to recognize that Scandinavian ladies were indeed not impervious to dalliance.

Kerguélen-Trémarec noted in Bergen in 1767 that the Norwegian women were "handsome, but not well informed," industrious and not addicted to luxury. Their men, meanwhile, were more inclined to be votaries of Bacchus and Ceres than of Venus. "They are fond of spirits, and smoak [*sic*] a great deal." Being thus neglected encouraged the ladies "in turn to revenge themselves without ceremony, by the help of more amiable and gallant strangers."

Brougham, no doubt well provided by his acquaintances with *petites histoires*, claimed that Stockholm society was "extremely dissolute," following the example of the court of Gustav III, who had sought to make his capital "a second Paris." Fashionable ladies carried on their amours in "the most scandalous and public manner." And as Acerbi noted, many prominent men kept mistresses. Although Consett was much taken with the Swedish ladies, he was dismayed to observe how the "Mask of Matrimony" was frequently used as a "covering for Levity and Dissipation, a skreen for the improper Indulgence of licentious Inclinations." Allegations, stemming largely from Gustav III's aristocratic enemies, likewise circulated to the effect that the court had encouraged "effeminate habits," in Brougham's words. Indeed, as early as 1787, Miranda had written in his diary that there were numerous pederasts and tribades at the Swedish court.[75]

Life for most ladies of quality was surely far more prosaic. Clarke praised their domesticity. Noting how they were neglected by their menfolk, La Tocnaye considered that "in truth it must be a hard lot to be a woman in Bergen. In Turkey women are not free, but they are nonetheless treated with appreciation." The "lovely ladies" of Paris and London would cry out in indignation, but La Tocnaye, who took an ironical view of Mary Wollstonecraft's "Jeremiads" in behalf of women's rights, felt "a little tour in this country would not do them great harm." "It has been said, that the women of *Norway* are domestic slaves, and their husbands domestic tyrants," Clarke wrote. "Some truth, we are ready to allow, may be found in the former part of this sweeping assertion; although there be none whatsoever in the latter. But the slavery of the *Norwegian* wife is voluntary; she delights in her labour, because it is 'the labour of love'; and if this be 'domestic slavery,' it is well repaid by domestic happiness." Danish women—and by implication those elsewhere in Scandinavia—Mary Wollstonecraft sadly observed in 1795, were "simply notable housewives; without accomplishments, or any of the charms that adorn more advanced social life." Swedish ladies grew fat in their inactivity, while she found their Norwegian sisters a "mixture of indolence and vivacity."

At a Copenhagen dinner party involving "two hours of hard stuffing," Carr observed that "the appetite of the fair ones present, was far, I might say very far from being puny or fastidious, but in the homely phrase, what they did eat did them good. . . . [T]hey much resemble the higher class of Wouvermann's figures, and very largely partake of that gay good humour, which is so generally the companion of a plump and portly figure."[76]

While visiting a Swedish family, Mary Wollstonecraft noted that "my host told me bluntly that I was a woman of observation, for I asked him *men's questions.*" In Norway, Clarke observed that "literary female characters are unknown." He no doubt felt he could speak for the North as a whole. So, indeed, it must have seemed to visitors from Britain and France in particular. Yet the day was already dawning when women played a growing role in Scandinavian cultural life. None of the visitors are likely to have had any familiarity with the able Danish novelist and dramatist Charlotta Dorothea Biehl (1731–88) or with the Swedish poets Hedvig Charlotta Nordenflycht (1718–63) or Anna Maria Lenngren (1754–1817), nor would they have known of such influential literary hostesses as Friederike Brun or Kamma Rahbek in Copenhagen or soon after, Malla Montgomery-Silfverstolpe in Uppsala.[77]

3

Landscapes and the Material Base

IN THE UTILITARIAN SPIRIT OF THE ENLIGHTENMENT, Nature was valued for the resources it offered and the ways in which these resources were exploited for human ends. This view, as expressed by foreign visitors to the Scandinavian lands in our period, is the focus of what follows, leaving their romantic reactions to Nature in the North to a later chapter.

It is against this background of Enlightenment values that the travelers' impressions of the landscapes they encountered must here be considered. This in turn requires that one determine which parts of the North they actually visited and described. The travelers to Iceland form a group apart, to be considered later with the visitors to "Ultima Thule."

The beaten track consisted generally of the triangle connecting Copenhagen, Christiania, and Stockholm. Many of the travelers entered the region via the duchies of Holstein and Schleswig, thence through East Jutland to the Great Belt, Fyn, and Sjælland (Zealand), to Copenhagen, or they departed over the same road. From there one well-traveled route led across the Sound from Helsingør to Helsingborg in Sweden's southernmost province of Skåne, up the Swedish west coast via Gothenburg, through Halland and Bohuslän, to Østfold in southeastern Norway and on to Christiania. Another led from Helsingborg, through Småland, Östergötland, and Södermanland to Stockholm. The route between Christiania and Stockholm passed through Østfold and the Swedish provinces of Värmland, Närke, and Södermanland or Västmanland. A less frequent exit or entry to the Scandinavian lands lay between Stockholm and St. Petersburg, via the Åland Islands, Åbo (Turku), and the south coast of Finland. Many of the visitors also made excursions outside the principal cities to places of special interest, such as the falls and canal at Trollhättan, the mines at Dannemora, Falun, Sala, or Kongsberg, or the university town of Uppsala. Within this network, the travelers tended to comment most extensively on the richer and more productive areas they saw, in particular Holstein and Schleswig, Østfold, and the central Swedish provinces, around Lakes Vänern, Vättern, and Mälaren.

Certain visitors, meanwhile, traveled more extensively. William Windham made his way overland from Bergen to Christiania in 1773. Matthew Consett journeyed in 1786 up the Swedish Bothnian coast as far as Torneå (Tornio). Malthus in 1799 continued from Christiania to Trondheim. Miranda, Küttner, and James visited Blekinge in southeastern Sweden, particularly its naval port of Karlskrona. Most ambitious were, however, Clarke, Acerbi, and La Tocnaye in 1798–1800 and Buch in 1806–8. Clarke traveled through the duchies, Denmark, and southern Sweden to Stockholm, thence up the Swedish Bothnian coast and into Lapland, as far north as Enontekis (Enontekiö). He then made his way down the Finnish Bothnian coast to Iskmo, near Vasa (Vaasa), crossed over to Umeå on the Swedish side and on to Trondheim via Hälsingland and Härjedalen. From there he continued to Christiania and returned to Stockholm before journeying through southern Finland to St. Petersburg.

Acerbi, at the same time, went to Sweden via the duchies and Denmark. After visiting Stockholm, he crossed to Åbo and journeyed up the Finnish coast to Uleåborg (Oulu), where he spent the late winter of 1799, before trekking through Swedish Lapland and Norwegian Finnmark to the North Cape. He returned through Lapland and down the Swedish Bothnian coast to Stockholm before departing for England via Norway, which his account does not describe.[1]

La Tocnaye journeyed in leisurely fashion through Ångermanland and as far north as Åsele in the southern interior of Lapland, thence via Jämtland to Trondheim and Molde, from which he—alone among the travelers—worked his way laboriously down the rugged west coast of Norway to Bergen. He then crossed Norway's central massif to Christiania before returning to Sweden, briefly visiting Copenhagen, then—again alone among his colleagues—traveling up Sweden's southeastern coast, via Kalmar and Västervik, back to Stockholm before departing Sweden in 1800.

Buch in 1806 traveled through the duchies, Denmark, and the Swedish west coast to Christiania, thereafter to Trondheim and up the northern Norwegian coast to the North Cape. He then crossed Finnmark and Lapland to Torneå and continued down the Swedish Bothnian coast to Stockholm before returning to Christiania. In 1808 he ran the British blockade from Christiansand to Løkken in western Jutland on his way back to Berlin.

Altogether the foreign visitors covered a great deal of ground in the Northern kingdoms. Yet almost as significant are the "white spots" that remain on the map after tracing their journeys. Except for Buch, who gives few details, only Macdonald—thanks to his shipwreck at Skagen—provides any description of Jutland north of Kolding Fjord. Most of the smaller Danish islands, including Møn, Lolland, Falster, Langeland, and Bornholm, remained unvisited. The same is true of most of southeastern Sweden—eastern Småland, together with the islands of Öland and Gotland—and most of the northern interior of the country. None ventured into the inner regions of Finland. Outside of Oslo and Trondheim Fjords, few saw anything of coastal Norway, except Kerguélen-Trémarec, who visited Bergen by sea, Windham, who did not describe the region, La Tocnaye, and, most notably, Buch, as mentioned. This seems particularly surprising in view of the vast popularity of Norway's western fjord country with nineteenth- and twentieth-century foreign tourists.

Before dealing separately with the different aspects of Nordic economic life, an overview of the comparative state of wealth and development in different regions of the North, as perceived by the visitors, is called for. Most of the travelers wrote of differences and contrasts they encountered along the way. Thomas Malthus's meticulous observations, virtually mile by mile, in Norway deserve particular mention, but most of the others likewise provide considerable detail.

The duchies of Schleswig and Holstein impressed all who passed through them in either direction as a particularly well-favored region, with their bustling towns and prosperous, well-tilled countryside. "I scarcely know a country, excepting England," wrote Küttner, "in which travelling is so agreeable." He, Boisgelin, and Wollstonecraft were agreed that this was the king of Denmark's finest domain.[2]

In contrast, southeastern Jutland, in the Danish kingdom proper, produced a poor impression, although Küttner admitted that Schleswig had already prejudiced him against what followed. The land seemed poorly cultivated. Mary Wollstonecraft spoke in 1795 of "large unenclosed tracts, not graced by trees." According to Macdonald, much of North Jutland was wilder still. Proceeding down the Skagen Peninsula in 1808, he saw "not a tree, or even a bush, or a blade of grass," although he was impressed by the government's efforts to stabilize the drifting sands of the area. Around Aalborg, he found the country "too bare and destitute of hedges." The town itself he described as "old and ill built for the capital of a considerable province." Crossing "dreary and desert heaths" on his way to Flensburg the same year, Buch reflected that "in Lapland it certainly does not look worse than this, and in many places a great deal better."[3]

Nor did the Danish islands seem much of an improvement, although Andrew Swinton in 1788 recognized their fertility to be "wonderful," despite poor cultivation. Of Fyn in 1790, Boisgelin wrote, "This country passes for being very good, but we thought it miserable: yet it supplies (together with the islands of Laaland and Falster) the capital; and these three islands are the best cultivated in the kingdom. The houses are thatched, built with wood and clay; the soil appears good, and the country flat."

Küttner made much the same observations. He found Sjælland more sparsely populated yet and its soil both thinner and more poorly utilized, even in places close to the capital. "I can at any rate assert," he wrote, "that in the interior of Sweden I have seen extensive districts, which were far more fertile and better cultivated." The towns on both islands, except for Copenhagen and Helsingør, hardly bore comparison with those in the duchies. Slagelse, for instance, "makes a miserable appearance," according to Küttner, "like all the other towns in Zealand [Sjælland] that I have seen." Macdonald considered Roskilde a "melancholy place," a "poor decaying town" in the shadow of its massive cathedral, evidently "long on the decline; for the houses are almost antediluvian in form and size, the streets narrow and ill laid out, and the population scanty."

There were, however, some bright spots. Places on northern Sjælland already in 1774 reminded Wraxall of Wiltshire, while Küttner owned that the area between Copenhagen, Frederiksborg, and Fredensborg was fertile, properly cultivated, and well populated, especially the estate of the enlightened Counts Bernstorff.[4]

The remarkable prosperity of the more developed areas of the other part of the kingdom, Norway, thus seemed all the more striking to the foreign visitors. Østfold, with its thriving sawmill and seaport towns, like Frederikshald, Sarpsborg, and Moss, together with Christiania, showed great opulence, thanks to shipping and the timber trade. Despite much rugged terrain, there were areas of rational and productive agriculture on both sides of Oslo Fjord. Between Tønsberg and Moss, for instance, Mary Wollstonecraft observed that "a greater number of comfortable farms met my eye, during this ride, than I have ever seen, in the same space, even in the most cultivated parts of England."[5]

To the north, along Randsfjord, around Lake Mjøsen in Hedemark, and in Gudbrandsdal, there was much good husbandry and rural prosperity. Beyond the snowy Dovre Fjell, fertile Trøndelag, around Trondheim and its fjord, rivaled the Christiania region in well-being and affluence. Even in places along the remote coasts of Nordland and Finnmark Buch encountered surprising pockets of prosperity.[6]

Yet Norway offered considerable contrasts, and there were areas of great poverty and backwardness, as noted on occasion by, for instance, both Malthus and Buch. The latter was in particular impressed by the impoverishment he found among the fisherfolk of the North. Visiting Bergen in 1798, La Tocnaye was struck by the wretchedness of its mountainous hinterland.[7] Had more of the travelers found their way up the deep fjords and high valleys of Norway's southern massif they would surely have discovered similarly sobering contrasts.

The neighboring Swedish monarchy, including Finland, likewise showed great regional diversity. The west coast, in particular Halland, offered an especially forlorn prospect. Küttner declared, "The country between Helsingburg and Gothenburg is, I am informed, one of the worst tracts in the south of Sweden. I found it indeed barren, sandy, extremely thin of inhabitants, and badly cultivated: I however remarked many good pieces of land, but not in a state of cultivation." Malthus found it "as desolate & noir a picture as could well be seen." Greater prosperity was seen around Gothenburg, but Bohuslän, to the north, while more picturesque, showed much poverty, especially when contrasted to the affluence across Svinesund in Norway.[8]

Southernmost and southeastern Sweden received relatively few foreign visitors, other than those who sought to pass through as quickly as possible on their way between Helsingborg and Stockholm. Their writings give little account of the area. Coming from the north in 1787, Miranda was struck by the poverty he found in Skåne—inherently Sweden's most fertile province, now regarded as the nation's breadbasket. Boisgelin, proceeding in the same direction in 1790, found villages more numerous there than in neighboring Blekinge, but "the greatest part of them have a very poor and miserable appearance." Küttner considered Christianstad a "wretched, disagreeable place," lacking buildings of the quality he was used to elsewhere in Sweden, although Ystad did not seem "quite so bad as it had been represented." La Tocnaye, meanwhile, recognized that the best parts of Skåne, particularly around Malmö and Lund, "concede nothing in fertility to any other country." Carr in 1804 and James in 1813 however, were very favorably impressed with the province.[9]

Blekinge, to the northeast, struck Küttner as picturesque, with its forests of oak, alder, and beech; but the large upland province of Småland to the north seemed empty and desolate indeed. "The tract of country between Linköping and Carlskrona," Küttner wrote, "a tract of about 260 miles, is wild, mountainous, full of naked rocks, and so covered with woods that only a very small portion is in cultivation."[10] It seems not surprising that it would be from this area, a couple of generations later, that the earliest and greatest emigration to America would take place.

The region around Lakes Vänern and Vättern contained much good plowland and were more populous. Acerbi, upon leaving the west coast, noted an improvement in the countryside between Trollhättan and Stockholm, although a good deal of poor husbandry and poverty were evident in western Västergötland. After emerging from Småland in 1774, Wraxall was "charmed" to find himself "once more in a civilized and inhabited country" in Östergötland, which offered "a cheerful appearance." Consett, too, was particularly taken with "a most delightful country" between Norrköping and Linköping, with "prospects around us which brought to our remembrance Old England. We were treated with many noble views not inferior to those of Richmond or Windsor." La Tocnaye and Thomson considered Östergötland Sweden's most fertile province.[11]

Travelers between Christiania and Stockholm passed through Värmland, north of Lake Vänern and adjoining Norway. Clarke found it poor and miserable: "The soil itself is of a nature to bid defiance to cultivation. . . . It seemed to be the very region of poverty and despair, denuded and smitten by the hand of Heaven." It soon improved as he proceeded eastward, and he admitted his initial reaction to its more desolate western part had been conditioned by the contrast with prosperous southeastern Norway from whence he had come. Küttner found Värmland rather more appealing and noted the neatness and apparent prosperity of Karlstad and Kristinehamn.[12]

To the east, around Lake Mälaren in the vicinity of Stockholm, lay what might be termed Sweden's "Home Counties" of Närke, Södermanland, Västmanland, and Uppland, which attracted much favorable comment. Küttner proclaimed these provinces "the richest, most fertile, and best cultivated of any in Sweden." Consett was especially enchanted with Södermanland, around Nyköping, Coxe and Burr with the environs of Uppsala in Uppland. Immediately to the north of this region lay Dalarna, which Consett, Clarke, and Küttner likewise found attractive, apart from the declining copper-mining town of Falun and its environmentally blighted surroundings. Küttner, who proceeded no further north, considered that the area around Avesta surpassed any in Sweden "in richness, magnificence, and fertility" and that its cultivation was equal to any in the country. Clarke likened it to Cambridgeshire.[13]

Clarke, however, was above all struck by the prosperity and good husbandry he found in Norrland, the thinly populated northern two-thirds of Sweden proper. Indeed, the further north he proceeded, the more impressed he became. He was well pleased with Gästrikland and delighted with Hälsingland. He was also especially taken with Ångermanland and parts of Medelpad and noted much solid well-being among the peasantry of Västerbotten and Norrbotten, at the head of the Gulf of Bothnia. La Tocnaye maintained that if the southern Swedes could overcome their prejudices against the north they would find its cultivation would make it "preferable to all the other provinces." There were also, of course, pockets of poverty, as Consett, for instance, did not fail to notice around Bureå.[14]

Continuing into Österbotten (Pohjanmaa), on the Finnish side of the gulf, Clarke found between Uleåborg and Vasa what he considered the most populous, fertile, and best-cultivated area in the entire Swedish kingdom, excepting only parts of Hälsingland. The country south of Brahestad (Raahe) was "as beautiful as the County of Surrey. A wide prospect of rich cultivated country extended on every side: in the midst of it appeared large farms, and husbandmen everywhere busy, with their families, getting in the harvest." Altogether, he considered the eastern side of the Gulf of Bothnia better favored in both town and countryside than the western. Later, on his way from Åbo to the Russian border, Clarke was no less impressed with the evident prosperity of the southern Finnish province of Nyland (Uusimaa). Wraxall, too, had found the region well-favored a quarter century earlier. For all who passed that way, the contrast with Russian Finland—the area beyond the Kymmene River relinquished by Sweden in 1721 and 1743—was startling.[15]

While Schleswig and Holstein, lying on the main thoroughfare into the Nordic world, drew much commentary from foreign travelers, only Küttner among our group had anything to say about Sweden's German territory. "Swedish Pomerania," he wrote, "is, on the whole, superior to what the traveller might expect; the soil is not very bad, and far less sandy than other provinces in the same latitude. The villages make a very good appearance, and possibly the impression might be more favorable because I have been for some time accustomed to those of Sweden."[16]

Agriculture was everywhere in the North, in greater degree even than in most of western and central Europe, the mainstay of the economy and the principal occupation of the inhabitants. It therefore naturally attracted the interest of foreign visitors. A number of them observed farming practices with obviously practiced eyes, offering informed and specific comments above and beyond their general impressions of local well-being or impoverishment. They found cause here both for praise and for blame, characteristically measured against the standards of English husbandry.

On the positive side, in Denmark Miranda noted a more intense cultivation on Fyn than on Sjælland, although Brougham observed near Copenhagen that "the ground seemed rich and soft, and we saw some fields of grass, heavily manured, which in England would not be touched." Clarke noted that cattle and sheep seemed plentiful on Fyn, which produced a surplus of grain for shipment to Norway. Malthus was assured in 1799 that the state of agriculture in Denmark had made rapid progress in recent years, during which land values had frequently doubled and the conditions of farm laborers had improved. Macdonald was pleased to note in 1808 that land reallocation and the moving of farmsteads out of villages onto the newly consolidated peasant landholdings were well under way in Jutland and on Fyn. "The advantages of giving every man his separate farm are so great and obvious, that, in spite of old prejudices, the new arrangement is cheerfully accepted."[17]

Norway, as usual, aroused greater admiration, despite much harder conditions for agriculture. Both Malthus and Clarke were particularly impressed with the Trondheim area in Trøndelag. Malthus declared, "I think I hardly ever saw heavier crops of barley & oats." The potato was quickly gaining ground; Buch in 1806 found it even cultivated as far north as Finnmark. Count Gottfried Schmettau in Trondheim showed Malthus, "with much self-satisfaction & a little ostentation," his model farm, where he kept a dairy herd, raised potatoes, peas, and artificial grasses, and planned to plant sugar beets. Malthus was, meanwhile, amused to see a lamb grazing on the turf roof of a house that had already been mown, "so that it might be fairly said that in Norway they mow the tops of their houses & turn their cattle in for the aftergrass."

Agriculture in Trøndelag, Clarke wrote, was said to have greatly improved over the past decade, so that whereas formerly it had been necessary to import grain in exchange for fish, the area now produced almost enough barley and oats to meet its own needs. La Tocnaye even found fine wheat growing in the area. He noted, too, an intensive cultivation of garden vegetables.

Clarke likewise found the area around Lake Mjøsen in Hedemark to be virtually self-sufficient in grain. This was, however, unusual for most of Norway, which doubtless prompted such an observation. Küttner recognized the importance of raising livestock, owing to the limited tillable land as compared with an abundance of pasturage, while Windham described a typical mountain *sæter*, where the girls of a farm tended their cows during the summer. Malthus was struck by the contrast between the affluence of the farms in "Osterdale" (Østerdal) and their small cultivated patches of rather meager soil, finding the explanation in the profitability of their timberlands with easy access to flotage.[18] Altogether, not only in Norway but in Sweden and Finland as well, successful farming depended on much more than field culture.

Sweden also gave evidence of much good husbandry. Like Malthus in Norway, La Tocnaye in Sweden observed that, although the growing season was short at such northerly latitudes, it was intense, as was the work it entailed. He noted that "nature accomplishes in three months in the north what takes six months in the south." Burr found the fertile plain around Uppsala "covered with crops as heavy as in England." And James, especially, was in places very well impressed in 1813. Near Norrköping he observed, "The agriculture, in the country through which we passed, seemed in a very creditable state; and the land bore evident marks of an increased value as we approached the metropolis [Stockholm]: the fields were in some places enclosed. . . . Besides this, surface drains were cut, their grounds well kept and clean; and the rye was already appearing above the ridges." Near Stockholm he inspected a well-managed, leased estate, "which then yielded more than double the amount of its produce in the year 1805; though fewer labourers were stated to be employed in its cultivation. The agriculture was carried on in the English system, and much money had been laid out in its improvement; yet in no one year was a sum expended greater than its annual income."

In Skåne James was impressed—unlike earlier foreign travelers—by even more thriving cultivation and livestock raising, "whose general appearance was so much better than what we had before met with, that we looked upon it as the face of a new country." This observation doubtless reflected the considerable improvements in agriculture that had taken place there over the preceding two decades. He correctly foresaw that within ten to fifteen years Sweden would become entirely self-sufficient in grain production.[19]

Of particular interest are Clarke's observations from 1799 in Finnish Österbotten, which, as mentioned, he considered, on the whole, the best cultivated part of the Swedish monarchy. "The farmers," he wrote, "are remarkable for their neatness in agriculture: the land, after ploughing and harrowing, looks like a well-cultivated garden: it is laid out in borders, into which the seed is always drilled; it is moreover kept perfectly free from weeds, all sorts of rubbish being carefully removed." Here he found crops of oats, potatoes, hops, rye, and even "the finest plantation of *tobacco* we had ever seen." South of Brahestad, he even noted the first field of wheat he had seen throughout the Swedish domains, although La Tocnaye found it growing in Ångermanland, across the Bay of Bothnia, and even in Jämtland.[20]

There was, however, criticism as well. Denmark, Küttner declared, was "susceptible of high cultivation," but the level of agriculture was not high there. Fyn, reputedly the most productive region, was, in his view, "a country which has a very inadequate population; the inhabitants of which possess more land than they want, or are able to cultivate; so that they employ themselves entirely in raising corn, while they neglect the rest of their farms, which they abandon to their cattle, without bestowing any pains on their improvement."

Describing the "delightful" countryside around Flensburg in Schleswig in 1779, Coxe said, "[I] almost fancied that I was passing through English lanes and English enclosures." Malthus and Wollstonecraft were, however, impressed by a lack of enclosures—evidently in the literal sense of hedges or fences—both in southeastern Jutland and on Fyn and Sjælland, even though land reallocations had in fact been taking place since at least mid-century and especially after 1781. Only a few years later, in 1806, Buch observed that enclosures had notably changed the countryside around Hjørring in North Jutland. Malthus, meanwhile, found that cattle and horses were generally "small & poor" on Sjælland.

Among the visitors, Macdonald offered the fullest critique of Danish agriculture as he observed it in the late fall of 1808 between Skagen and Helsingør. He saw few enclosures around Aalborg in North Jutland, where there still remained uncultivated tracts. He claimed, too, that there were few "green crops" in the area, where grain raising alternated with fallow used only for rough pasturage. Ditching and draining were much neglected. Fyn, he claimed, resembled "the worst part of Wiltshire." Here he particularly criticized the overcropping of rye, which badly depleted the soil. Still, Sjælland he found "poorer and worse cultivated" than either Fyn or the better parts of Jutland. Danish agricultural implements were far below English and especially Scottish standards, but it was hard to make way against peasant conservatism in such matters.[21]

Swedish agriculture, in Brougham's view, was generally "backward." Although he noted considerable improvement after crossing Småland to Jönköping and points north on the way to Stockholm, he considered the land poorly plowed: "the furrows are still too wide, and not always raised enough." As for Clarke, while he found the fields in Västergötland free of weeds, he was surprised to see the "awkwardness with which the *Swedish* husbandmen handle the plough, who are in other respects good farmers." In the same province, close to Lake Vänern, he also believed that fishing led to the neglect of farming. Macdonald considered agriculture along Sweden's west coast, between Helsingborg and Gothenburg, to be in the "rudest and most imperfect state imaginable," except on a few farms where "the Scotch farming system has been recently introduced."

Consett in 1786 assayed a more general evaluation:

If the knowledge of Agriculture could be learned, or by any means attained by the Swedish Peasants; and the large and almost unlimited tracts of ground be unencumbered of wood, which I have no doubt might be affected by time and industry, what a blessed change might be wrought in the face of this country! The quality of the soil appears in general no way inferior to ours in England; there is no reason therefore to suppose but that the common method of English husbandry would equally promote and produce the like vegetation in Sweden.

The most detailed analysis of Swedish agriculture was provided by Thomson in 1812, based upon the admirably detailed statistical tables compiled by the Swedish government for 1801. He too regarded it on the whole relatively undeveloped. The ratio of the population engaged in agricultural as opposed to other pursuits was nearly seven to one, as compared with a ratio of seven to eight and one-half in Great Britain, which had a population density nine times as great, while rural inhabitants outnumbered urban nine to one. Still, despite its size, Sweden proper—as opposed to Finland—did not produce enough grain to meet its own needs. Although of good quality, potatoes were not yet widely grown. More land could be cultivated than in fact was, but a major obstacle was the inadequate numbers of livestock. Grazing animals in the forest wasted valuable manure in summer, while lack of fodder limited their productivity in winter. "A very moderate degree of skill would enable [the Swedes] to increase their produce 30 fold," Thomson declared, "and thus render them an exporting instead of an importing nation." He offered the following specific advice: "Let the turnip husbandry be introduced to a considerable extent. Let part of the waste land be laid down in sown grasses to furnish a supply of hay. Let the number of cattle and sheep be at least tripled. Let a sufficient quantity of manure thus be collected. Finally, let the size of the farms be much increased; and let wheat in all places be substituted for rye."[22]

After agriculture, extractive industries provided the main basis for wealth in the Nordic lands. Iron mining and smelting produced at the time Sweden's most valuable exports, especially to Great Britain, and attracted much interest among foreign visitors. While he was little impressed with the state of agriculture in the province of Uppland, Wraxall in 1774 waxed enthusiastic over its "inexhaustible" mines. These, he claimed, provided the local peasants with their greatest employment, having in mind, no doubt, the production and haulage of the vast quantities of charcoal needed by the ironworks. Of the latter, he claimed to have visited five or six, "and certainly no Cyclops was ever more dexterous in working their materials." "It is certainly a fortunate circumstance," he continued with considerable hyperbole, "that Sweden abounds with these employments for her peasants, as from the ungrateful soil and inclement latitude, they must otherwise perish of misery and famine."

Wraxall, Coxe, Küttner, and Thomson left accounts of the country's greatest iron mine at Dannemora, reputed to produce the finest ore in Europe. Boisgelin wrote that the entire province of Närke "abounds in forges and mines." Thomson pointed out that, to obtain adequate supplies of charcoal from surrounding forests, the Swedish ironworks were generally small and widely dispersed. Various of the travelers found them as far afield as Lapland. The techniques of ironworking nonetheless did not escape criticism. Clarke held by 1799—from the perspective of the rapidly advancing Industrial Revolution at home—that the Swedes now lagged far behind the British in metallurgy. The iron forges in Avesta "are such as were used in England some centuries ago; when a single hammer, moved by an overshot-wheel, constituted the only machinery used in our iron-works." La Tocnaye nonetheless maintained that the Finspång ironworks' cast cannon were superior to those from the celebrated Caron foundry in Scotland.[23]

Norway mined and worked iron in smaller quantities for the Danish internal market. Both Norway and Sweden also mined copper and silver. Several of the travelers visited in particular the great mine at Falun, long Europe's greatest source of copper, and the Norwegian copper mines at Rørås, as well as the silver mines at Kongsberg in Norway and Sala in Sweden. In all of these they noted that production was by then declining, and they described a great deal of poverty in their communities. Thomson in 1812, meanwhile, took note of some modest coal mining in Skåne.[24]

In 1806 Buch, in Norwegian Østfold, painted a vivid picture of thriving enterprise:

> We soon arrived at Moss, where a considerable river runs foaming over rocks in the middle of the town, dashing down from one wheel to another, till at last, at the edge of the Bay of Christiania, it drives the bellows of a great iron-work, which are set in motion by these wheels at the water-falls; and stunned with the noise of the saws, the falling water, and the large iron hammers, we proceeded through the works to a high fir-wood on the other side of the town. Deals [sawn timber] and iron! We had seen collected in one place what maintains and enriches the whole of the south of Norway.

He here introduces forest products, the other great extractive industry in the North. Although Sweden, including Finland, possessed greater forest reserves, southeastern Norway, with its rapid rivers providing both flotage and waterpower to drive sawmills close to the coast, as well as its generally ice-free ports, predominated in the export of sawn timber before the age of steam. In 1773 Windham wrote of great "floats of timber," forty to fifty yards long and half as wide, on Randsfjord. Great fortunes were made from this source, as witnessed by Berndt Anker's 150 privileged sawmills and the magnificence of his household. Swinton noted in 1788, however, that much timber was damaged in flotage, while La Tocnaye held in 1799 that the forests were by then overexploited in many parts of Norway.

Clarke prefaced his account of Sweden as follows: "It may be proper to state, in the way of anticipation [for the reader], that if he cast his eyes upon the map of *Sweden*, and imagine the *Gulph of Bothnia* to be surrounded by one contiguous unbroken forest, as antient as the world, consisting principally of *pine*-trees, with a few mingling *birch* and *juniper trees*, he will have a general, and tolerably correct notion of the real appearance of the country." The Swedish region around the Gulf of Bothnia was of vital importance in international trade for the production of naval stores—masts, spars, pitch, "Stockholm" tar, and hemp—and Clarke noted in Österbotten much activity of this kind.[25]

Fishing was far more important to the economy of Norway—and of the Danish monarchy as a whole—than its modest iron production, especially for cod off the Lofoten Islands beyond the Arctic Circle, by fishermen from the long coast of Nordland who sold their catch in Bergen. While this provided a valuable export product, Buch, when he visited the area, was particularly critical of both its practice and its effects. He held that the northern Norwegian fishermen were very inefficient, especially compared with the more enterprising Russians from the Murman Coast who were encroaching into their waters. Their almost exclusive preoccupation with fishing, meanwhile, caused them to neglect their small farms, despite the availability of good land, a major cause of their impoverishment.[26]

Manufacturing and luxury crafts remained tender plants throughout the North, despite the governments' mercantilist policies throughout most of the eighteenth century, and foreign visitors had little good to say about them. Coxe and Miranda were, to be sure, much impressed with the Dan-

ish gunpowder mill and cannon works at Frederiksværk in northern Sjælland and with the good housing for its workers. The best Boisgelin could
say, however, was that "the manufactures in Denmark are carried on with
a tolerable degree of activity; but they bear no sort of comparison with those
of England, France, &c. which we have already said to be the case in all
northern countries with respect to arts and sciences."

Johan Georg Canzler provided a listing of Swedish manufactories of different types for the year 1764, when they were at their peak for the century.
Judging from this, he wrote, Sweden would appear "the best-provided
country in regard to manufactures and the nation one of the most industrial
in Europe." He cautioned, however, that this would be misleading, since
many of the enterprises existed in name only. Boisgelin also gave a detailed
account of Sweden's manufactures, particularly silk weaving in Stockholm,
as of 1790, but he declared these to be "hitherto in a very imperfect state."
The quality of skilled craftsmanship in Stockholm he considered "generally
good, though inferior to articles of the same kind in France." Clarke was
blunter in his judgment: "We could find nothing good that had been man-
ufactured in this country, excepting *iron, tar*, and *gloves*," he wrote. "It is difficult to reconcile this want of manufactures with the inventive genius
shewn by the *Swedes*." Küttner felt that Eskilstuna, the center of Sweden's
production of cutlery, gave "a tolerably correct idea of the state of Swedish
manufactures. . . . [T]he establishment is altogether insignificant; and I really believe that the annual produce of Walker's manufactory at Rotheram
[in England], amounts to twice as much as the collective produce of all the
artisans of Eskilstuna." He considered Swedish products "in general coarse,
clumsy, and far from cheap," which encouraged widespread smuggling of
foreign goods. The Swedes would, he believed, continue to export their
iron to England and to receive their hardware from there in return.[27]

The integration of agriculture, extractive industries, and manufactures
into an expanding market economy depended in high degree upon the state
of communications. The high quality of the Swedish and some of the Danish roads has already been noted and, more important yet, the possibilities
of transportation on water, both liquid and frozen. A development that attracted special attention was thus the construction of canals.

In Sweden, numerous foreign travelers visited the steeply ascending canal
at Trollhättan, with its many locks, bypassing the spectacular waterfalls and

connecting Gothenburg on the Göta River with Lake Vänern and its productive environs. Nothing in the country attracted greater admiration and wonder. "There is hardly a bolder and more noteworthy undertaking," Miranda declared in 1787. The canal, according to Acerbi, was "characteristical of the Swedish nation; for it represents them as they are, prone to the conception of great enterprises, and distinguished by mechanical invention." For James, it was "a conception far beyond the reach of ordinary minds," which, in his view, "as the speculation indeed of a company of individuals unaided by the government . . . is an example of enterprise perhaps nowhere to be met with out of the limits of Great Britain. . . . [I]n the present condition of Sweden, this facility of circulation can alone afford means of diffusing or equalising the general wealth and resources of the nation."

James was also much impressed by the Södertälje Canal, which connected Lake Mälaren with the Baltic, and the Strömsholm Canal, which provided transportation from the ironworks of Västmanland to Lake Mälaren. In the Danish monarchy, Miranda regarded the Schleswig-Holstein Canal in 1788 as "a splendid work, which does honor to the nation," through which 629 vessels had passed the year before, causing him to reflect upon the benefits of a canal through the Isthmus of Panama![28]

With their long coastlines and access to the seaways of the world, the Scandinavian kingdoms naturally maintained sizable merchant fleets. This was especially true of the Danish realm, with its ships constructed with timber and manned principally by seamen from Norway, "the brightest jewel in the Danish crown," as Swinton described it. Its exports in bulk demanded extensive shipping, which provided a "great nursery for seamen." Norway's fisheries and merchant vessels, he claimed—with some exaggeration—employed half of its population.[29]

Various of the visitors likewise concerned themselves with commerce in the Nordic lands, especially international trade. Visiting Copenhagen in 1774, Wraxall declared that, although it was "one of the finest ports in the world," it "could boast of little commerce." By 1790 Boisgelin, however, held that, while the Danes had "always been extremely attentive to commerce," only recently had it been "brought to the degree of perfection it is now arrived at, when the Danish flag may be seen in the four corners of the globe." He noted, among other things, that in favorable years the Danes shipped two thousand to twenty-five hundred slaves from Africa to their own West

Indian islands and to French Saint Domingue. What had come between Wraxall's and Boisgelin's visits had been the American War of Independence, which inaugurated what in Denmark would long be remembered as the Flourishing Era of Commerce (*den Florissante Handelsperiode*), based upon neutral maritime trade during the great European wars.

Thus the overseas commerce of the Scandinavian kingdoms, thriving though it might be at such times, was not always to the liking of foreign visitors, especially the British. Malthus in 1799 was indignant that "the Danish neutral flag has been much prostituted" during the wars of the French Revolution, being flown, with the connivance of the Danish authorities, by allies of France, such as the Dutch. In Norway, Wollstonecraft found it distasteful that the almost indecent prosperity of such small southern seaports as Risør, on the west side of Oslo Fjord, where she stayed for some time, had "no employment" other than contraband trade, through which "the coarsest feelings of honesty are quickly blunted."[30]

Much the same things could be—but less frequently were—said of Swedish trade. Boisgelin noted in 1790 that it was "not very considerable" but stated in a footnote added later that "the neutrality of the Swedish flag during the late wars, has changed this circumstance; and trade is now carried on with great success." The vagaries of war and maritime policies of Britain and France could, however, cause rapid swings of fortune in the North. Brougham, for instance, found trade in Gothenburg temporarily languishing in 1799. The eventual involvement of the Scandinavian kingdoms in the Napoleonic Wars—Sweden in 1805, Denmark in 1807—ruined their lucrative neutral commerce. But as an ally of Britain in 1805–10 and again after 1813, Sweden provided a valuable emporium for British trade, both contraband and legal, with central and eastern Europe, in defiance of Napoleon's Continental Blockade. This was, of course, a very different matter as far as British visitors were concerned, as witnessed by James's remarks on the subject.[31]

In addition to such general observations, some of the travelers offered specific details on the commerce of particular regions. Clarke, for instance, noted that the trade of the Finnish Gulf ports was directed principally to Spain, whereas Finland's Bothnian towns (which dealt primarily in naval stores) traded mainly with England. Southern Finland, he held, produced a surplus of grain for export—presumably to other parts of the Swedish monarchy. He also observed that most of Trondheim's trade was with Ireland. La Tocnaye observed that most of Gothenburg's and almost all of Christiania's export went to England, while Christiansund, on Norway's west coast, exported to Spain or to St. Martin-du-Ré in France. Buch described northernmost Norway's beneficial trade with enterprising merchants from Arkhangelsk in Russia. There was in addition to overseas trade a fair amount of presumably illicit trade across Nordic frontiers, particularly by Swedes in Norway, as La Tocnaye on occasion noted.[32]

A major problem in the Nordic kingdoms was a chronic shortage of money and monetary instability, which did not escape the travelers' notice. Küttner considered Copenhagen in 1798 very expensive. "If the Danes, in general, be poor" he commented, "the government is in the same situation. It is evidently in the greatest want of money, as every thing connected with it attests," including Crown Prince Frederik, who was an "example of great frugality." Lenz, noting the same thing, meanwhile found Swedish prices surprising cheap by German standards, reflecting the high value of foreign currency. La Tocnaye in 1799 spoke of serious inflation in Sweden, due to the excessive issuance of paper money; Thomson in 1812 found nothing else in circulation. At the end of our period, in 1813, James held that Sweden's shortage of money, while encouraging its export trade, "affords us a sure criterion of the actual poverty of the nation. Every article of life is cheap, and the private fortunes of individuals are at a low estimation, in comparison with their average amount in the rest of Europe."[33]

In sum, the consensus among the foreign visitors of the period, despite their differences, was that the Nordic lands were economically backward, relative to the more progressive European heartland, even though there were signs of progress. The travelers realized that the North faced difficult obstacles to economic advance, as a number of them commented.

Küttner, always an acute observer in such matters, perhaps largely summarized the reactions of his colleagues when, speaking of the Danish monarchy, he wrote that its population was "inconsiderable" in relation to its size. In view of the long peace it had enjoyed, it was remarkable that its economy lagged so far behind the "southern states of Europe," even though most of the latter were smaller, had been worse governed, and had been harassed by "almost constant wars." "The best portion of the Danish dominions is Sleswick and Holstein," he observed, "and these do not belong to Denmark proper." The kingdom itself, including Norway, had a population in 1785 of only some 2.3 million souls, as compared with his native Saxony, far smaller in size, with around two million inhabitants. Macdonald noted in 1808 that Fyn, reputedly the "granary and agricultural model of the Danish states," had a population of only some fifteen thousand, "which is nearly that of the second rate counties in England and Ireland."

Several others likewise regarded small populations as a serious problem, especially from the viewpoint of the "populationist" ideas of the mercantilism still so largely prevalent at the time. Boisgelin observed in 1790 that, despite its great area, Sweden (with Finland) had no more than some three million inhabitants.[34]

Various reasons for this sparsity of population were suggested. In much of Scandinavia, the terrain and especially the high northerly latitudes made agriculture difficult if not impossible. The potentially negative effects of climate upon the nature of the inhabitants aroused speculation. When, at a Stockholm dinner party, Matthew Consett expressed regret that "so large a tract of improvable ground, as I had lately passed over, should be suffered to continue in so rude and uncultivated a state, which by the hand of the industrious ploughman might become rich and fertile," a "Swedish gentleman" admitted this to be true but claimed that "indolence and inactivity are the constitutional failings of my countrymen, and may probably be ascribed to the severity of the climate in which we live." This was characterized by violent contrasts. "Each season," Consett continued, "from its intenseness deprives the body of its proper and necessary exertion. This produces inability and habitual indolence."[35]

Others also remarked on the inhabitants' lack of industriousness while seeking other causes for it. Boisgelin wrote of the "imperfect state" of Swedish manufactures, as due to

> the workmen being negligent, idle, and void of emulation. They seldom commence their work before Tuesday, and some, not till Wednesday: if by chance they appear in the business earlier, it is merely to sleep off the effects of their Sunday's drink. Notwithstanding such conduct, they are very exorbitant in their demands, and the more they gain, the more they expend on liquor; nothing indeed but empty pockets can induce them to return to their different occupations.

"The slowness of Swedish workmen is very disagreeable to a man in a hurry," Thomson declared in 1812. "It seems to me to be every where alike, and to be quite incompatible with the nation ever becoming eminent for its manufactures; as they will always be undersold by their more industrious neighbours." The Swedes, he opined, were "rather given to indolence than otherwise." A Dane who had lived some time in England and had a manufactory for stockings near Aalborg complained to Macdonald in 1808 of "the dearness of labour and the general sluggishness and apathy of his workmen."

Like Boisgelin, Lenz emphasized the ruinous effects of drink upon both population and working capacity, imagining that six to ten times as many people could inhabit Sweden were it not for this evil. Coxe held that Sweden could provide itself with sufficient grain were it not for the distillation of alcohol.[36]

The poor quality of their products, not least in relation to their prices, seemed to show in many areas a lack of up-to-date technical expertise, which in turn suggested a lack of entrepreneurial spirit. Following elaborate calculations as to the amount of arable land in the Swedish monarchy and the more limited amount actually under cultivation each year, Boisgelin found it surprising that it should still have to import any grain at all. La Tocnaye was convinced that linen weaving in northern Sweden could equal Ireland's if only the local merchants would take the initiative in providing the necessary supply of bleach. Küttner was "firmly persuaded" that Sweden's backwardness in manufactures was above all due to "a want of sufficient skill, and a proper division of labor; a want of industry and invention; and lastly, a want of capital," although the country was well endowed with natural resources, especially "rivers that save the expense of steam-engines, to which the English are so frequently obliged to have recourse, on account of the want of falling water."

Thomson was sharply critical of the Swedes' lack of competitive spirit. Instead of seeking to increase manufacturing and sales, they were "anxious only to secure the highest price possible, even though that price should limit or even diminish the extent of the sale. Where such a spirit exists we may be certain that manufactures are not in a flourishing state." On the other hand, both Coxe and La Tocnaye took them to task for a lack of financial realism. In the words of the former, "It seems as if the Swedes, in all their undertakings, formed plans much too great and expensive for their finances and power; and consequently that they seldom can finish what they begin." The

Scotsman Macdonald, meanwhile, found a number of his compatriots or their descendants who were thriving in both Denmark and Sweden, prompting an English traveling companion to remark on their "peculiar felicity in making fortunes, and rising to places of eminence and power" throughout the world, "even in poor Sweden."[37]

In part, backwardness seemed attributable to deep-rooted customs that impeded more rational ways of doing things. The *odel* right, which restricted the free sale or mortgaging of property, was highly prized in Norway for preserving the collective patrimony of the family. Malthus held that it was rightly considered to impede the country's cultivation and population and was glad it had recently been somewhat curtailed. Mary Wollstonecraft felt more divided on the issue: the "most rational men" with whom she had discussed it were convinced it was "more injurious than beneficial"; still, "if it contribute to keep the farms in the farmers' own hands, I should be sorry to hear that it were abolished."

Buch was convinced that the ingrained habit of the Nordland fishermen of sailing all the way to Bergen to sell their catches, despite the government's attempt to provide a local outlet at Tromsø, established in 1794, was needlessly time-consuming and perpetuated the Bergen merchants' oppressive, virtually monopolistic, exploitation of the northern fisheries.[38] Naturally Buch did not take into account that the northern fishermen traditionally regarded their visit to Bergen as the high point of their year!

Finally, laws and government policies came in for their share of criticism. Lack of capital was an inhibiting factor, and shortage of currency has been noted above. Weak central authority and political discord had, according to Canzler, impeded the development of manufacturing in Sweden (at least before Gustav III's coup in 1772). Lenz, on the contrary, reflecting the physiocratic emphasis on laissez-faire, was particularly outspoken in 1796 about what he considered the harmful effects of an overregulated economy in Sweden, "the deplorable limitations, suppression, and prohibitions against freedom of trade, occupations, and transportation, against free import and export, and . . . the plague of monopolies and privileges [which] still today keeps the land languishing in inactivity and in a complete lack of material well-being." La Tocnaye inveighed against the weakness of the Swedish government in giving way to the special interests of corporations or gilds, "a power," Thomson later concurred, "when it exists which proves injurious to every place."

In Denmark proper, the peasants' lack of personal freedom under the *stavnsbånd*, or Adscription Law of 1733, which effectively bound them to the manors (discussed further in chapter 4) was seen as a serious discouragement to their incentive and thus to the improvement of agriculture and of the economy as a whole.[39]

Still, to end on a positive note, by no means all were convinced that high latitudes and cold temperatures induced lethargy and drunkenness. Lord Baltimore expressed the venerable belief, perhaps best articulated by Montesquieu, that a cold climate produced a hardy and virile race, when he wrote that, while Sweden was not a fruitful land, "nature has given the Sweds [*sic*], who are void of luxury, strength of mind, and body." Acerbi agreed. A traveler from the South, he wrote, would imagine that "men, animals, and plants" in the North were in winter

> all consigned to a profound sleep . . . but one who has resided among these people will find, that they are neither less awake, less active, nor worse fed than the inhabitants of the South. . . . It is necessary to have even more activity and industry in the northern districts than in the southerly ones, inasmuch as the means of maintenance are more limited, while the wants of the natives are more pressing. How many things are men in want of in the North, that are scarcely known in the South?

Acerbi was highly sanguine in 1800 regarding Sweden's progress and future prospects:

> The state of Sweden, and particularly that of the capital, has left this general impression in my mind, that a greater progress has been made in the sciences and arts, both liberal and mechanical, by the Swedes, than by any other nation struggling with equal disadvantages of soil and climate, and laboring under the discouragement of internal convulsions and external aggressions from proud, powerful, and overbearing neighbors. Their commerce, all things considered, and their manufactures are in a flourishing state. The spirit of the people, under various changes unfavorable to liberty, remains unbroken.

And James, following Sweden's worst ordeals in the Napoleonic Wars, declared in 1813, "It must be confessed indeed, that at the present day, a new era of exertion and improvement seems to dawn among the Swedes; and every effort is made to surmount those natural impediments, which have hitherto retarded their progress towards a higher state of national prosperity."[40] The same would be no less true of the other Nordic lands.

Giuseppe Acerbi. (From Joseph [Giuseppe] Acerbi, *Travels through Sweden, Finland, and Lapland to the North Cape in the Years 1798 and 1799*, 2 vols., London, 1802. Engraving by P. W. Tomkin after a portrait by P. Violet.)

Edward Daniel Clarke, LL.D. (From William Otter, *The Life and Remains of the Rev. Edward Daniel Clarke, LL.D.*, London, 1824.)

"Vehicle for travelling with Post-Horses in *Sweden*." (From Edward Daniel Clarke, *Travels in Various Countries of Europe, Asia, and Africa*, 6 vols., London, 1810–23, V.)

"Representation of a *Sledge*, the common Vehicle for Travelling in *Northern Countries of Europe*, over the ice or snow: it is usually lined with furs and drawn by one horse." (From Clarke, *Travels*, VI.)

"Mode of forcing a Passage through the Ice, when the Sea is not sufficiently frozen to sustain the Weight of the Human Body; as practised by the Author among the *Åland Isles*:—the Thermometer of *Fahrenheit* being at that time 49° below freezing." (From Clarke, *Travels,* VI.)

View of Copenhagen, showing Nytorv and Gammel Torv, circa 1806. Attributed
to M. R. Heland. (Courtesy of Statens Museum for Kunst, Copenhagen)

View of Stockholm. (From John Carr, *A Northern Summer; or, Travels round the Baltic through Denmark, Sweden, Russia, Prussia, and Part of Germany in the Year 1804*, London, 1805. Engraving by T. Medland from a drawing by the author.)

"Christiania; taken with a *Camera Obscura*, by an Officer of the *Danish* Army."
(From Clarke, *Travels*, VI.)

"*Norrmalm Square*, in Stockholm; with a View of the Royal Palace, the Opera House where *Gustavus the Third* was assassinated, &c. &c." (From Clarke, *Travels*, V. Engraving by Letitia Byrne from a painting by Elias Martin.) The opera house is to the left, the palace in the center background.

"A Winter Scene in Stockholm." (From Acerbi, *Travels*, I.) Note the *sparkstötning*, or kick-sled, in the foreground, of a type still used in Scandinavia today.

Court reception for the birthday of Crown Prince Frederik (later King Frederik VI) of Denmark at Christiansborg Palace, Copenhagen, 1781. (Courtesy De Danske Kongers Kronologiske Samling på Rosenborg, Copenhagen)

"A Swedish Village Church." (From Carr, *Northern Summer*. Engraving by T. Medland from a drawing by the author.)

Harvest Scene in Denmark, circa 1788. Anonymous pen drawing. (Courtesy of the Reventlow Museum, Pederstrup, Denmark)

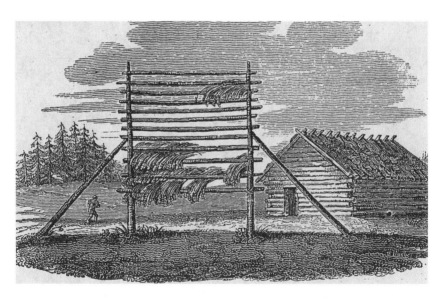

"House of a *Swedish* Peasant, with the Rack for drying the unripened Corn." (From Clarke, *Travels*, V.) This type of rack is still occasionally seen in Sweden.

A Swedish iron mine. Aquatint. (From Robert Ker Porter, *Travelling Sketches in Russia and Sweden during the Years 1805, 1806, 1807, 1808*, 2 vols., London, 1809, II.)

The falls at Hønefoss in Norway, with water-driven sawmills. Sketch by an anonymous artist, early nineteenth century. (Courtesy of the Royal Library, Stockholm)

"Representation of the Process for making Tar in the Forests of *Sweden*."
(From Clarke, *Travels*, V. Engraving from a sketch by the author.)

Copenhagen Roads. (From Boisgelin, *Travels through Denmark and Sweden*,
2 vols., London, 1810, I.)

"Aged Peasants of *Norway*." (From Clarke, *Travels*, VI.)

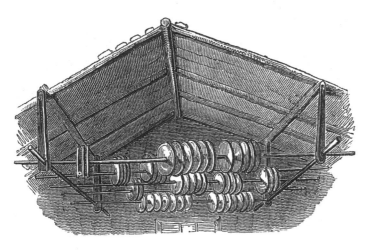

"Manner of preserving *Bread*, throughout the year, in *Swedish* Families."
(From Clarke, *Travels*, V.)

"Extraordinary Mode of Singing by Finlanders." (From Acerbi, *Travels*, I.)
The instrument is the *kantele*.

"Girl of *Westrobothnia*, blowing the *Lure*, a trumpet six feet in length, as a call for the Cattle in the Forests." (From Clarke, *Travels*, V. Engraving by R. Pollard.)

"A Finlandish Bath." (From Acerbi, *Travels*, V.)

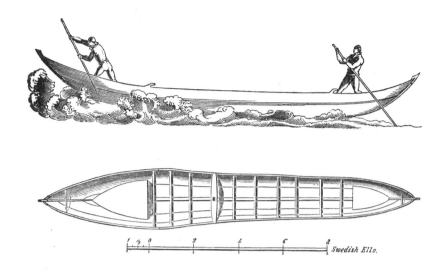

"Mode of forcing the *Cataracts* and *Rapids* of the Rivers in *Lapland*; shewing also a Plan of the Boats constructed for that purpose." (From Clarke, *Travels*, V.)

"*Nomade* or *Wild Laplander*, in his Winter Clothing." (From Clarke, *Travels*, V. Engraving by R. Pollard from sketch by the author.)

"*Nomade* or *Wild Laplander*, in his Summer Clothing." (From Clarke, *Travels*, V. Engraving by R. Pollard from sketch by the author.)

"*Laplanders*, having prepared their Winter Tents." (From Clarke, *Travels*, V. Engraving by R. Pollard from a drawing by E. Martin.) Note the reindeer in the background.

"Portrait of a Wild *Lapland* Woman and Child." (From Clarke, *Travels*, V. Engraving by R. Pollard from a drawing by E. Martin.)

"View of *Enontekis*, at the Source of the *Muonio*." (From Clarke, *Travels*, V. Engraving by L. Byrne from a sketch by the author.)

"The Faroe bird-trap and Boat house." Pen sketch. (From John F. West, ed., *The Journals of the Stanley Expedition to the Faroe Islands and Iceland in 1789*, 3 vols., Tórshavn, 1970–76, I. Courtesy of Fródska-parfelag, Tórshavn, Færø Islands.)

"View of Reikiavik." (From George S. Mackenzie, *Travels in the Island of Iceland during the Summer of the Year 1810*, 2d ed., Edinburgh, 1812. Engraving by R. Scott from a sketch by the author.)

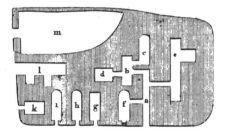

Icelandic turf houses, with typical floor plan. (From Mackenzie, *Travels*. Engraving by E. Mitchell from a sketch by R. Bright.) "*a*. The entrance passage, 40 feet long, and 4 feet wide. *b*. The kitchen. *c*. Fuel-room. *d*. Bunn, or store-room. *e*. Bed-room, 40 feet long by 8 feet wide, with recess 10 feet by 8. *f*. A wainscotted room, with bedsteads. This is an appendage only to some of the principal dwellings, and is usually crowded with saddles, harness, and implements of various kinds. It has frequently a small window in the end. *g*. Dairy. *h*. Out-house. *i*. Smithy."

"The Church of Saurbar." (From Mackenzie, *Travels*. Engraving by E. Mitchell from a sketch by R. Bright.)

"View of a Lake between *Rikleå* and *Gumboda*." (From Clarke, *Travels*, V. Engraving by L. Byrne from a sketch by the author.)

"Cataract, and Bridge, constructed of the Trunks of Pines; Shewing also the mode of conveying Water to the sawing Mills; near the Pass of *Kringlen* in *Norway*." (From Clarke, *Travels*, V. Engraving by L. Byrne from a sketch by the author.)

Vossevangsdalen in western Norway. (Engraving by M. G. Anckarsvärd. From C. J. Fahlcrantz, August and Michael Gustaf Anckarsvärd, *Samling af Svenska och Norrska utsigter*, Stockholm [1830].)

"The *Halling* and the *Polsk*, antient *Greek* Dances, as existing in *Norway*."
(From Clarke, *Travels*, VI. Engraving by W. Hughes.)

4

The Inhabitants of the North

Eighteenth-century travelers and their readers tended to hold strong and categorical ideas regarding the characteristics of various "nations." Their fascination with this subject, moreover, grew by the turn of the century with the rising preromantic mood and emphasis upon the "picturesque." In keeping with ideas best elaborated by Jean-Jacques Rousseau and Johann Gottfried von Herder, the common folk were increasingly regarded as the truest representatives of their nations. "The great people, in all countries," Andrew Swinton wrote in 1788, "have now nearly the same customs: in speaking, therefore, of the manners of foreign nations, I draw my observations from among the middling and lower classes, among whom alone is to be found a national character." Among the latter, according to John Thomas James in 1813, "we see the 'mirror held up to nature.'"[1]

Regarding material well-being, there were great variations both between and within the Nordic lands. To a degree, these paralleled the relative productivity of the different regions described in chapter 3. There were, however, significant discrepancies, for abundance of natural resources—above all, good arable land—or lack thereof could be counterbalanced by other, no less significant factors. These included above all the local ratio of population to available resources, the prevalence of peasant freeholding as opposed to manorial tenancy, and the relative juridical freedom or servitude of the peasantry. Indeed, conditions among the common folk could often prove best in seemingly unpromising environments. "The prosperity that reigns in these remote habitations," La Tocnaye wrote of thinly populated Jämtland in Sweden's northern interior, "is surely surprising and appears at first unbelievable; but reflection soon makes one realize that it is their very remoteness that assures the inhabitants' well-being."[2]

The people of the duchies of Schleswig and Holstein enjoyed, in the unanimous opinion of those foreigners who visited them, both an abundance of fertile farmland and a remarkably high level of general prosperity. Küttner largely spoke for them all when he wrote in 1798, "I scarcely know a country, excepting England, in which travelling is more agreeable." The country was fertile and well cultivated.

> In the towns every thing exceeded my expectation. The inhabitants are more conveniently lodged, and better clothed; they are more cleanly; in a word, they appear to possess greater affluence than persons of the same class in most of the small towns of Germany. I almost fancied myself in Holland. . . . Nor was this the case only in the towns; I likewise saw a great number of good houses in the country. The inhabitants appear not only to be acquainted with the conveniences and comforts of life, but likewise with a species of luxury, generally found among people who live near the sea, and who, by navigation and their proximity to seaports, procure things which the lower classes in more inland provinces scarcely know even by name. Even the smallest cottages have an appearance of cleanliness and affluence highly agreeable to the feelings of the philanthropist.

Near Aabenraa (Apenrade) in northern Schleswig, Küttner noted, for instance, that "the habitations of the country-people had, almost without exception, an appearance of neatness and cleanliness. They are very small and low, but are, in a high degree, what particularly pleases an Englishman, and what he calls a *snug neat cottage*. . . . in a word, the *tout-ensemble* gives an idea of warmth, comfort, and convenience." He was, furthermore, impressed by a relative absence of extremes of wealth and poverty in Schleswig: "as, on the one hand, every individual appears to possess a competence, so, on the other, no traces are to be found of opulence, grandeur, and splendor." It seemed worthy of note that he nowhere met anyone "but what had shoes and stockings."[3]

The inhabitants seemed healthy and happy. Miranda in 1788 noted the Schleswigers' similarity to the English, whose ancestors came from the area, and the many "pretty and healthy children." Mary Wollstonecraft spoke of an air of "chearful industry [*sic*]" in Holstein, whose inhabitants she found "very civil, with a certain honest hilarity and independent spirit in their manner." Carr was especially taken in 1804 by the "young milkmaids" in Schleswig, "whose cheeks glowed with the bloom of health, balancing their pails with great dexterity, and knitting and singing as they went."[4]

Such favorable impressions may seem paradoxical considering that serf-dom (*Leibeigenschaft*) still existed in parts of the duchies—particularly in southeastern Holstein—until 1805. Upon reaching Copenhagen in 1798, Thomas Malthus became aware that he had not passed through those areas where "slavery" still existed, and it seems evident that few, if any, of the other foreign visitors did so. Yet even in these districts, the voluntary eman-cipation of the peasantry by their manorial lords was already well under way by the 1790s, while serfs frequently worked tenancies larger than the hold-ings of local freeholders. Meanwhile, throughout the greater part of the duchies, freeholding was widespread in comparison to neighboring areas in both Germany and Denmark.[5]

Denmark and the Danes fared less well with respect to living conditions, as well as the state of their economy, as seen in the preceding chapter. Kütt-ner was unfavorably impressed from the start by southeastern Jutland, around Kolding. "The houses," he wrote, "in general have only a ground-floor, and the diminutive Duch [*sic*] style, which commences in Holstein and continues throughout Sleswick [Schleswig], dwindles away, in Funen [Fyn] and Seeland [Sjælland], into absolute meanness, without possessing that cleanliness and neatness which in the former countries produce such a pleasing affect."

Northernmost Jutland presented a melancholy picture to Macdonald, who observed on the bleak Skagen Peninsula only a "few scattered cottages," which "corresponded with the universal wretchedness of the scene," ill con-structed from the wood of shipwrecked vessels and "unfit to shelter their in-habitants from the heat of summer or the frost of winter." Here, too, he found "no other bread than a coarse mixture of rye, barley, and fish-bones, pounded and mixed together." But conditions improved notably around Aalborg. Despite the general backwardness of their farming methods, Mac-donald noted there "a general appearance of ease and comfort among the peasants; and unequivocal proof of which is the fatness of their children and sleekness of their horses."

Malthus found peasant dwellings on Fyn "exactly like English cottages formed of mud or brick, whitewashed with thatched roofs, & much smaller & less neat than those of Holstein or Sleswic," while those on Sjælland were "very poorly built, chiefly of mud, & some tumbling down, and the peas-ants had much more an air of poverty than any we had hitherto remarked." Küttner claimed that Korsør reminded him of "the most miserable villages in Ireland" or huts he had seen in the Neapolitan hinterland "and which scarcely seemed to be designed for human habitation." To him, even the villages between Copenhagen and Helsingør "wear the appearance of poverty and misery," although others did not agree. Windham, passing the same way in 1773, held that "all the houses were as handsomely built and made as neat an appearance, as any of the same degree in England; perhaps from their being generally white-washed, they looked even neater."[6]

There were indeed some brighter spots. On Fyn Miranda found not only the women better looking but the people better dressed and housed than on Sjælland, which "reveals the spirit of the inhabitants." In northern Sjælland, Küttner was impressed with peasant conditions between Copenhagen, Frederiksborg, and Fredensborg. The descendants of seventeenth-century East Frisian settlers on the small island of Amager, adjoining Copenhagen to the south, whose dwellings and dress still revealed their origins, drew praise from Coxe, La Tocnaye, and Carr. In 1795 Wollstonecraft observed that in Denmark "the distribution of landed property into small farms, produces a degree of equality which I have seldom seen elsewhere." Malthus, too, became aware of the constant improvement in agrarian conditions, especially since 1784.[7]

According to Malthus, "The Danish features & countenances are entirely English; but upon the whole not so handsome or so well made. At Copenhagen we observed very few of the same stout make that we had remarked in Funen [Fyn]." He found the Sjælland peasants generally dull and lethargic, while Swinton had complained in 1787 that "the Danes are not the most cleanly in their persons and houses." By 1804, Carr, meanwhile, found the Dane a "good natured, laborious character," doubtless reflecting the ongoing improvement of conditions in the countryside.[8]

Norway and its inhabitants attracted much greater attention and more favorable commentary from foreign visitors. Norwegians appeared in general better-off than Danes, Swedes, or Finns. Coxe considered the Norwegian peasants in 1779 more prosperous than any he had seen except in parts of Switzerland. After crossing the "mountainous parts of *Sweden*" (i.e., Härjedalen), Clarke was struck in the Norwegian Trøndelag by a "great improvement in the condition of the natives; better clothes, better bread, and even many of the luxuries of life." "From all we could hear or see," he wrote, "the lower orders appeared to live as well as in *England*." Malthus's travel diary in particular offers a wealth of detailed information on Norwegian peasant life.

Norway indeed offered Scandinavia's most striking discrepancy between available plowland and the well-being of the population. Clarke observed that male peasants in Norway had not formerly been permitted to marry until they had served in the militia, which in his view—very likely inspired by his friend Malthus—was "the cause why the lower classes of people in *Norway* were in a much better state than could be expected from the barrenness of the country." This law, he learned, was now rescinded and signs were not lacking that Norway's population was placing a growing burden upon its limited food-producing capacity. "The Norwegian women are celebrated for their fecundity," Swinton wrote in 1788, "and every inhabitable part of Norway swarms with people." Clarke noted that infant mortality was low.[9]

Coxe found peasant dwellings in Norwegian Østfold in 1779 "larger and more commodious than those we had just quitted in Sweden" (i.e., in Bohuslän). The timbered farm buildings struck Mary Wollstonecraft as highly picturesque, and Malthus noted that the Norwegians "praise much the warmth & dryness of their wooden houses." Food seemed plentiful, at least when times were good. There was an abundance of milk and, according to Küttner, "very fine white bread," such as he had not seen in Sweden, although Malthus complained of the heavily salted butter. In Østerdal, Malthus wrote, "We are told that in the farmers' houses they generally eat 6 times a day. . . . The Norwegians in general have appeared to us as if they were well fed."[10]

Wollstonecraft and Clarke were struck by the great cleanliness they found in, respectively, Vestfold and Trøndelag. Clarke declared, moreover, that the "permanent health and longevity of the *Norwegians* have long rendered proverbial the salubrity of the country and its climate." Hygienic conditions could, on occasion, still leave something to be desired. Of a peasant household at Agre, Malthus observed, "In the kitchen we saw a child about 5 weeks old swaddled & bound up almost like a mummy. The mother told us that she kept them in that state for nearly a year, & we were much surprised therefore to hear that she had had 12 children, 9 of whom were alive."[11]

The travelers could encounter surprising opulence among the Norwegian peasants. Though their roofs were commonly covered with sod, Clarke observed, "The *Norwegians*, are fond of finery: they like to have their tables and the windows of their apartments painted with showy colours: even the ceilings and beams of the room are thus ornamented, and set off with blue and red colours." William Windham left a memorable picture of the wealthy peasant proprietor of a rural inn on Randsfjord in his travel diary from 1773. The man was

> reckoned one of the most opulent boors in the province, & was what my guide calls, a pretty fellow: the whole appearance of his house and family was of a different order from anything I have seen in Norway. [I]t was built by itself on the point of a hill, with offices and yards about it, much in the stile of a large English farm; and I imagine there are few farms of five hundred [pounds] a year that produce such an habitation. [D]uring my stay there several persons came in, of the dress and appearance of farmers, or small squires; with their hair tied, & good coats on, and one I think with an edging of silver on his hat . . . every thing was of a piece with this. [T]he mistress of the house came out to meet me with a very stately deportment.

Further down Randsfjord, the wealth of the land and its farmers became more apparent still, "with houses and villages in plenty. [T]he dress too & condition of the people improves in proportion: for some time the men have had buckles in their shoes, and many of them wore large hats; and the women have covered their heads with a large wrapper of linen; but the appearance among the men of long hair hanging loose over the shoulders is not entirely past yet."[12]

In Norway greater contrasts in wealth and poverty were evident than in the neighboring Nordic lands. Clarke was disturbed, upon arriving there, by "importunate mendicants, and revolting objects, such as one sees in *Ireland*, making the most painful and disgusting exhibition to extort charity," the like of which he had never found in Sweden. Beggars were, moreover, most numerous precisely in the most fertile and populous areas: Trøndelag, Hedemark around Lake Mjøsen, Christiania and its environs. Malthus and La Tocnaye found swarms of beggars and other unfortunates in Kongsberg, Norway's "Potosí," as the latter described it. Malthus also wrote of a poor household near Dovre Fjell where "one of the old women was making oaten cakes on an iron such as they use in Cumberland, & they were to be sure the coarsest that one could conceive to be eatable. They seemed to consist more of chaff, than of oatmeal. I brought a bit away for a specimen." The poverty and misery of the peasant dwellings in a poor parish in southern Trøndelag reminded Buch of Polish villages, and he described the making of bark bread in times of famine.[13]

Norway, with its isolated fjords and mountain valleys, was a land of great local variation. "The district around Bergen," La Tocnaye wrote, "must undeniably be the most sterile and most mountainous in this kingdom, and the inhabitants, called *Horders*, are surely the poorest and least civilized race in the entire country. In truth, these fish-eaters have none of the traits that distinguish the true Norwegians." He noted that their neighbors in the Voss region immediately inland, living in their fertile valley, wanted nothing to do with them. The people east of File Fjell on the central massif he considered far superior to those of the Bergen area, "as kindly and good-hearted as the latter are quarrelsome and greedy." Some of the peasants in the eastern valleys were so prosperous and well behaved, La Tocnaye declared, that they would hardly be called peasants in other countries. Those in Gudbrandsdal Malthus found to be the tallest and most robust in Norway.[14]

Of the Swedish peasantry, Giuseppe Acerbi wrote in 1799:

> Both they and their children are well fed. Their houses and manner of clothing sufficiently protect them from the severity of the cold; their firesides are always well provided with wood, and their apartments warm and comfortable. The traits of innocence, simplicity, and contentment, which, on entering any one of their cabins, you may perceive in their countenances, form a picture that must greatly move the sensitivity of a stranger, and interest the feelings of his heart.[15]

There were nonetheless great differences in living conditions among the various parts of the Swedish realm. As seen in the previous chapter, Sweden's west coast, between Helsingborg and the Norwegian border—the area often first encountered by foreign travelers—was the most impoverished and least developed part of the country. In Halland, Küttner wrote:

> I observed scarcely any thing, all the way, but single detached cottages; or if I saw what is denominated a village, it consisted only of a few huts, with scarcely any of those accomplishments which in other countries belong to the habitation of a farmer. Here are neither stables, barns, nor gardens, to give the farm-house an appearance of comfort and respectability, to which

the Swedish cultivator is an utter stranger. The only building is a small wooden cottage, which commonly comprises the stable and barn under the same roof; and frequently not a single tree is to be seen near it. Vegetables are equally scarce.

South of Kungsbacka, Clarke declared the peasant cottages as rude or wretched as "the huts upon the moors of *Scotland*," although they thereafter improved in the environs of Gothenburg. Macdonald considered them worse than in most parts of Denmark. Küttner observed that good land was not lacking in the area, and Clarke attributed its poverty to the oppression of their tenants by manorial landowners, who could appropriate their small holdings at will.[16]

In Bohuslän, north of Gothenburg, conditions seemed, if anything, even worse. Mary Wollstonecraft, for instance, wrote that "the scattered huts that stand shivering on the naked rocks, braving the pitiless elements, are formed of logs of wood, rudely hewn; and so little pains are taken with the craggy foundation, that nothing like a pathway points out the door." Brougham even described the inhabitants as "quite different from the other Swedes we had seen; very ugly and dressed indifferently . . . apparently all having to do with the sea, as fishermen or sailors."[17]

Similarly grim conditions extended into some of the more densely populated parts of neighboring Västergötland. Near Trollhättan, according to Clarke, "We observed the interior of many of the cottages of the poor; but in this part of *Sweden* we never had the satisfaction to observe any thing like comfort or cleanliness. In this respect they are certainly inferior to the Danes. A close and filthy room, crowded with pale, swarthy, wretched-looking children, sprawling upon a dirty floor, in the midst of the most powerful stench, were the usual objects that presented themselves to our notice." Near Lidköping, he found, "Some of the *Swedish* cottages are so small, that it is quite marvellous how they can be made to contain a family." He likewise was impressed by the poverty of western Värmland, which bordered on the prosperous Norwegian Østfold and whose inhabitants were reduced to eating bark bread in times of want.[18]

Much poverty was noted, too, in the large, thinly populated southeastern province of Småland, which the travelers were inclined to traverse as quickly as possible on their way between Helsingborg and Stockholm. Here Lenz remarked on the scarcity and smallness of villages, or at least what might be described as such in Germany, while most of the peasants lived like "hermits" in wretched huts. His view was, as we shall see, in large part in-spired by a Jacobin antipathy to Europe's old regime as a whole. Brougham, about the same time, meanwhile, had a more sanguine view and provided more concrete detail. Though this area was the "wildest and most infre-quented" in the south of Sweden, he considered the inhabitants' houses to be "all good and clean—magnificent, compared with those of the English peasantry, and much better than the Danish. They are built of logs, with white plastered chimneys and windows. They are generally painted red, and either thatched or covered with timbered planks; and to preserve them from wet, they are raised on four small pillars of stone, sometimes of wood; sometimes, in the better sort, a dwarf wall is built a few feet up." Numerous lovingly preserved Swedish *stugor*, or cottages, make this picture a familiar one even today. Coxe considered the peasants of this seemingly inhospitable region "cheerful and contented."[19]

While Carr, too, noted Småland's relative poverty, he was impressed by the evident good health of its inhabitants. After describing the miserable peasant households near Trollhättan cited above, Clarke nonetheless con-sidered it "marvellous that, in spite of all these obstacles, the *Swedish* peas-ants attain to a healthy maturity, and appear characterized by sturdiness of form and the most athletic stature. Many of them seem to belong to a race of giants, with nerves of iron. But something similar may be observed among the *Irish*."

The obstacles to healthful living Clarke spoke of also included some mentioned by other visitors. James complained that the practice of closing chimney flues in winter to preserve warmth led to an accumulation of the "vapour of the carbonic acid," which annually caused many deaths from suf-focation. Mary Wollstonecraft, who traveled along Sweden's west coast with her own infant daughter, decried the "mistaken tenderness" of overdressing children, even in summer. This, together with a "sort of natural antipathy to cold water," accounted for the "squalid appearance of the poor babes, not to speak of the noxious smell which flannel and rugs retain." Macdonald noted the practice of swaddling infants for, he claimed, the first eighteen months. Malthus, too, remarked that children in that part of Sweden "gen-erally speaking did not look healthy."[20]

Hygienic conditions improved as the travelers moved inland from the west coast. Small as Clarke found the cottages around Lidköping, he added, "On entering one of these cottages, the interior denotes a much more cleanly people than the inhabitants of the more southern provinces: the furniture is not only scoured, but polished until it shines; and more of the genuine *Swedish* character and manners are conspicuous." Küttner observed that cottages around nearby Kinnekulle were better built than what he had seen heretofore and many were surrounded by small orchards.[21]

Before proceeding northward, Sweden's southernmost province, Skåne, although it received little commentary, calls for special attention. Miranda was impressed by its poverty in 1787 and the "lethargy of the people," whom he judged to be a worse lot than elsewhere in Sweden. James found the province thriving in 1814 and its people a "larger and handsomer race" than the other Swedes he had encountered. This striking difference can only be attributed to the rapid progress of land reallocation and improved agriculture in Skåne, beginning already in the mid-1780s.[22]

Conditions were on the whole good in central Sweden, around Lakes Vänern, Vättern, and Mälaren. Küttner declared its inhabitants to be "better clothed, and better lodged, in every respect more comfortable, than those on the other side of the kingdom." Thomson described in unusual detail the home of a well-to-do peasant in Södermanland in 1804:

> He appeared to be in good circumstances: he was not only a wheel-spoke maker, but likewise a farmer, and had a great number of houses round his dwelling-house, appropriated to the purpose of his farm. His house contained two rooms on the ground floor, a kitchen and parlour, into which I was shown. It was a very neat room, square, with a wooden roof whitewashed: it might have been 16 feet long, nearly as wide, and about seven feet high. The walls above the cornice were covered with paper, painted red, below it with paper painted white. There were three windows, one in the centre of each outside wall, and in the centre of the fourth wall was the stove. The furniture of this room consisted of sixteen fir chairs painted blue, three tables, one at each window, a small bed, a looking-glass, and a wooden press near the door. The floor, as usual in all the houses of the peasantry, was wood without any carpet, and seemed to be new laid. I mention these things to show that the man was in tolerable circumstances. All the family were clean and neatly dressed.

The peasants in the neighboring province of Uppland impressed the travelers with their general well-being. Clarke spoke of the numerous mines and ironworks of the region, with their neat workers' housing. Boisgelin described the Österby ironworks: "All kinds of workmen necessary in a colony are assembled in this place. The village consists of seventy houses, forming four streets, built in the Dutch style. Every house has a little garden, and contains two families; the whole amounting to seven hundred persons, five hundred of whom are workmen."

He likewise noted that many of its ironworkers were the descendants of Walloon settlers from Brabant in the seventeenth century, who preserved their "antient customs," marrying only among themselves and "holding the peasants in the most sovereign contempt." In 1790 they had, moreover, attempted to "imitate the inhabitants of Liege; but this petty rebellion was attended by no serious consequences." There were also numerous Walloon descendants at the nearby Forsmark ironworks.[23]

The southern parts of Dalarna were well cultivated and populous, although many of the proud inhabitants of the poorer northern parishes regularly migrated during the summer months to better-favored regions in search of additional employment and income. Among its poorest and most isolated inhabitants were the descendants of seventeenth-century Finnish settlers north of Orsa.[24]

"The best conditioned, as well as the most wealthy and intelligent race of peasantry, are found in the provinces lying north of Stockholm," wrote James, whose own travels did not extend very far north of the capital, "where in many districts there exists no class of great landholders, but every individual is himself the proprietor and cultivator of a small plot of land."[25]

Clarke was more specific. In general, he wrote, what he described as the "national character of the *Swedes* . . . their honesty, cleanliness, industry, and the many other virtues which will be found to belong to them," pertained above all to those dwelling north of the fifty-ninth degree of latitude, that is, north of the capital. "Scarcely had we proceeded a few *Swedish* miles from *Stockholm*," he wrote of Uppland, "before we were struck by the appearance of industry, with its attendants, cleanliness and cheerfulness."

His enthusiasm grew rapidly the further he traveled. He was much impressed with the prosperity he found in Gästrikland, with its stately churches built by the local peasants, "among whom a great degree of emulation has been politically excited; the inhabitants of the different parishes endeavouring to outvie their neighbours." In Hälsingland he was moved to write, "Judging from what we had already noticed, we considered the *North of Sweden* as being by much the finest part of the country; not only with respect to the scenery it exhibits, but to the industrious habits, the moral disposition, the cleanliness, and the opulence, of the inhabitants." The "universal characteristic" of the poor north of Stockholm, he wrote, was cleanliness; their cottages were generally "much cleaner than those of the poor in *England*." Clarke was particularly impressed by the people of Ångermanland, whom he considered "among the finest subjects of the King of *Sweden*. The men are remarkable for their healthy appearance, their strength, and gigantic stature; and the women are often handsome. . . . In their habits, they are cheerful, honest, and industrious. . . . In their dress, they are remarkably cleanly; more so than any peasants we had seen before in this country." The farmers of the region were "all yeomen, who cultivate their own estates, and will suffer no powerful lord, nor monopolizing autocrat, to reside among them. They are all in league together, to prevent any encroachment upon their little republic; refusing to sell any portion of their land, however exorbitant the sum may be which is offered for it." Nevertheless, the people of Hälsingland impressed him no less for being, in his view, "a livelier race of men than the inhabitants of the more northern provinces."[26]

"Upon the whole," Clarke declared, the Swedes "compose a hardy, active people, hitherto undebilitated by any refinement or luxury." He also commented, "From the *Arctic Circle* to the entrance into the *Baltic Sea*, the *Swedes* are, with little variation, the same. A remarkable uniformity may be considered as distinguishing not only the aspect of the country, but also the minds and persons of the inhabitants. A traveller . . . finds the natives of the most distant provinces appearing as though they were all members of the same family." This hardly agrees with his own descriptions of Swedish regional traits—but then, strict consistency was not always Clarke's strongest suit. Thomson likewise stressed the physical similarity of the Swedes, who "have all light flaxen hair, and a ruddy countenance."

Upon reaching the Norwegian border on his way to Trondheim, Clarke took a fond farewell of the Swedes: "A feeling of regret was excited at the moment; and we looked back with hearts yearning towards *Sweden*. In the pleasing recollections then suggested, we called to mind the simple and innocent lives of the arctic farmers, fishermen, and hunters; jovial *Finland*—hospitable *Westro-Bothnia*—hearty *Ångermanland*—merry *Helsingland*—sturdy *Herjeådalen*—all, all were gone!"[27]

The picture of peasant conditions in Finland presented by the foreign travel literature of this period is sparse and fragmentary at best because few of the travelers visited this part of the Swedish domain, and most of those who did passed through it as rapidly as possible on the way to or from St. Petersburg. Their recorded observations deal with the largely Swedish-speaking coastal districts, since none of them ventured into the interior, except in Lapland.

Clarke was, it may be recalled from the previous chapter, greatly impressed with the prosperity he encountered in Finnish Norrbotten and especially along the coast of Österbotten (Pohjanmaa), which he considered the best-cultivated part of the Swedish kingdom. Acerbi, meanwhile, journeying up the Bothnian coast from Åbo (Turku) encountered generally more modest circumstances. In Finnish-speaking "Yervenkyle" (Järvenkylä), he observed, "The houses of the peasants are well built, and the stranger finds every where lodging and beds." Of its inhabitants he wrote, "In comparison to those who travel among them they are poor, but in relation to themselves they are rich, since they are supplied with every thing that constitutes, in their opinion a good living." Some, moreover, had acquired some valuable objects when times were good. "You must not be surprised in Finland, if in a small wooden house, where you can get nothing but herring and milk, they should bring you water in a silver vessel of the value of fifty or sixty rix-dollars." They dressed warmly and their houses were always well heated, "indeed too much so for one who comes out of the external air, and is not accustomed to that temperature."[28]

In southern Finland, the situation was more mixed. Acerbi found on the Åland Islands that the peasants lived in modest comfort. Their dwellings were "very neat and convenient, kept in good repair, and well lighted," and the "Ålanders are upon the whole an ingenious, lively, and courteous people; and on the sea display a great degree of skill and resolution." Clarke considered them a "stout and hardy race, better clothed, and in appearance wealthier than the *Swedes* on the western side of the water." Yet poverty was evident in places, and beggars, rare in Sweden, were "very common" on Åland.[29]

Conditions in the village of Varssala, near Åbo on the mainland, were far worse. "There is nothing in the houses superior to what is found in the worst dwellings of the *Laplanders*," Clarke exclaimed. The habits of the natives were disgustingly dirty. "More barbarous than the *Laplanders*," he wrote, "[the Finns] hold in sovereign contempt all the comforts and luxuries of more refined nations. . . . The true *Finns* live in houses without chimneys, which are always filled with smoke, and, from various other causes, are black and filthy beyond description." While he noted the fertility of the land in southern Finland—an area of extensive manorial landholding—he was appalled by the conditions among the peasantry. "It seems," he wrote, "as if the natives of the dreary district between *Åbo* and [St.] *Petersburg* had exerted their utmost ingenuity, and with fatal success, to banish from their dwellings every thing that bore any relationship to comfort and cleanliness." Near Lovisa (Loviisa) "the manners of the people began to change; and we found nothing here to remark, but dirt and drunkenness."

Carr, a few years later, found peasant dwellings in southern Finland to be rudely built of logs and to present a "most savage and slovenly appearance, although some proved well furnished and comfortable inside." The country around Borgå (Porvoo) was, he wrote, "undulating and fertile, but the cottages in that part of Swedish Finland are very miserable, and the peasantry wretchedly clothed. . . . [T]heir appearance was that of extreme penury."[30]

Yet Clarke was fascinated by the Finns. He was impressed by their toughness in traveling during the dead of winter to the annual Åbo winter fair, which provided welcome insights regarding the "tribes inhabiting countries almost inaccessible to literary travellers." "Who would have thought, in *England*," he commented, "of a labouring peasant, or the occupier of a small farm, making a journey of nearly 700 miles to a fair, for the articles of their home consumption? Except in this annual journey to *Åbo*, the true *Finns* have little intercourse with the inhabitants of the maritime district." There he met a peasant he remembered from the Kemi fair in the Far North the winter before.[31]

If conditions were grim in Swedish Finland, they seemed far worse still across the Kymmene River in Russian Finland, the areas ceded to Russia in 1721 and 1743. Clarke looked back with regret at the company of Tavastehus militia at the border, his "last view of the benevolent and mild inhabitants of *Sweden*. They were a sturdy and athletic troop." He found Russian Finland "a country more inhospitable than the deserts of *Tahtary*." "We were, upon the whole, much struck with the evident inferiority, both in looks and apparent condition, of the *Russian Finlanders*, in comparison with the *Swedish*."

James in 1814 learned that much of Russian Finland was "as fertile in corn as any part of the Polar empire." Still,

> The villages we saw were of the meanest appearance and character, for whatever in this country is not made for display and shew, is poor indeed; and by our recollection of the different state of things we had left behind, Sweden was now as much raised as she had before sunk on comparison. Instead of the neat-built red ochred cottages, the road-side was disfigured by large dismal huts with walls made of the round trunks of trees barely stripped of their bark, and resembling, externally, a casual pile of timber, rather than a human dwelling.

Near Viborg (Viipuri), Carr halted at "a village of old crazy hovels, composed of trunks of trees, rudely thrown across each other, and perched upon granite rocks; every one of these forlorn abodes was out of the perpendicular, whilst, from a little hole which feebly admitted the light, the smoke issued. The inhabitants were nearly naked, and looked like a race of animals formed in the anger of heaven." Arrival in the resplendent Russian capital, which, according to Clarke, "the united magnificence of all the cities of *Europe* could scarcely equal," thereby became all the more dramatic.[32]

While the literary travelers of the 1760s and 1770s tended to concentrate upon what I have described as the "public visage" of the lands they visited — government, public institutions, higher culture, and upper-class social life — those of succeeding decades and their readers showed a growing interest in folk customs and culture. Hence their particular fascination with traditional festive occasions.

Clarke, near Lidköping, and La Tocnaye, near Gävle, witnessed the Swedish Midsummer, a celebration featuring a decorated maypole like those Brougham saw on many farms that fall, still standing with their withered flowers. In 1809 Burr was kept awake all night by Midsummer merriment outside his Stockholm lodgings. "At three the streets were full of young people," he wrote, "people, indeed of all ages and sexes, bearing little green boughs, flowers, little May-poles very prettily ornamented. They all had some good-natured wit at me. I retorted: neither comprehending a word, and we all laughed." Near Delsbo in Hälsingland, Clarke and his companions were virtually kidnapped by a festive group to share in their celebration.[33]

Peasant weddings offered lavish displays of traditional folk culture, such as one Clarke experienced in Halland, in Sweden, decorated with "garlands suspended upon upright poles, adorned like our may-poles." La Tocnaye provided an especially detailed account of the group wedding in 1799 of nine peasant couples at Drottningholm, hosted and attended by King Gustav IV Adolf himself as lord of the manor. The ceremonies interested La Tocnaye greatly and would, he wrote, have done so more "if the brides had been a bit less fat and younger."[34]

Neither peasant christenings nor funerals, also occasions for old customs and conspicuous display, attracted the same attention from the visitors. But fairs and markets—like the fair at Copenhagen that Küttner attended in 1798 or the winter markets that Clarke witnessed in Åbo in 1800 and that Buch experienced in Christiania in 1806—offered colorful displays. Buch's description provides a particularly vivid gallery of Norwegian local types:

> For several days before the annual fair, which is held on the thirteenth of January, the town is filled with country people from all quarters; and figures make their appearance, such as before were not seen in the streets. The strong and robust inhabitant of *Gudbrandsdalen*, cap on his head, walks side by the side of the comparatively elegant boor of *Walders* [Valdres], who, in features and dress, is as unlike him as if he came from beyond the sea. The rich proprietors from *Hedemarken* pass along as if they were an inferior order of townspeople; and their coats of home-made cloth are cut in an antiquated fashion, as is usual in country places. From *Oesterdalen*, on the Swedish boundaries, appears a higher class of men; but we easily see, from their carriage, that it is borrowed from their neighbours. On the other hand we see the rough and almost stupid native of *Hallingdalen*, in a true national uniform, and the sturdy men of *Oevre Tellemarken* still more rough and stupid. They alone yet continue to wear the broad northern girdle around the waist. . . . Every step and movement of these men is characteristic and definite. They have only one object in view, and nothing which surrounds them can deaden the eagerness with which they pursue that object.[35]

Buch's attention to distinctive local folk dress is characteristic of the visitors around the turn of the century. La Tocnaye especially provides lengthy and detailed descriptions. Their reactions were, however, mixed, perhaps reflecting crosscurrents between the Enlightenment and full-blown romanticism. Brougham dismissed peasant dress on Sjælland as "grotesque." Macdonald gave a fuller account of the dress of the "lower-class females" in the Aalborg area of North Jutland, which he found "as unbecoming as can well be imagined, and seems to have been invented for rendering their charms as harmless and unattractive as possible." Their upper bodies were tightly wrapped in "innumerable volumes of cloth and linen," while from the waist down they were of "such tremendous bulk, that at a distance they look like moving hogsheads." "How infants are nourished and nursed," he added, "I cannot conceive." Macdonald also condemned the use of wooden clogs in Denmark, which gave the natives a "drawling, hobbling, duck-like walk." "How great is the loss of time, strength, activity, and labour which attends the use of them," he wrote, and largely attributed to this the "general sluggishness perceptible in all the operations of this people." To him, local peasant dress and clogs were further examples of the tyranny of tradition over utility.

Of the peasant brides at Drottningholm, in their wedding crowns provided by the church, La Tocnaye found "the one more ridiculously turned-out than the next," which he felt surely must have made their bridegrooms regret not having remained bachelors. Clarke showed a more sympathetic interest, although he held that "in *Sweden*, go east, west, north, or south, there can hardly be said to be any change of costume. A change of colour, indeed, sometimes distinguishes the inhabitants of one province from those of another; but the dress, is in other respects, the same everywhere," which he thereupon described in general terms. Speaking of northern Finland, he wrote that "the pure costume of the *Finland* peasants is very elegant." Interestingly, he noted in Finnish Österbotten that, unlike elsewhere in the Swedish realm, Gustav III's "Swedish dress" was here "universally worn by the peasants."[36]

Scandinavian peasant music in its authentic, premodern form has a strange and distinctly exotic sound to modern ears. One may well imagine the impressions it must have produced upon cultivated eighteenth-century gentlemen accustomed to the classical idiom. La Tocnaye was bemused to describe the music at the Drottningholm wedding he attended. The procession to the church was preceded by "baroque instruments, half guitar, half violin, which have only three strings and, I believe [play] scarcely more than two notes." This was obviously the Swedish "keyed harp," or *nyckelharpa*, which having almost disappeared during this century has enjoyed, together with folk music in general, a remarkable renaissance in recent decades. At the celebration afterwards, La Tocnaye continued, "Four play-ers of the *Harpa* [*sic*], the instrument damned by Apollo," produced a ca-cophony, which nonetheless "did not diminish the appetite of these good people."[37]

Acerbi, who was an enthusiastic amateur musician himself, was much taken with Finnish folk music. He described the traditional *runa*, played in a five-note scale on the *harpu* or *kantele*. When Clarke met him in Uleåborg (Oulu), Acerbi performed for him on the harpsichord "one of his own compositions in the *Finnish* style." Clarke was more skeptical, although his friend William Otter later revealed that Clarke lacked "what may prop-erly be called an ear for music." Clarke described the five-stringed "lyre" a Finnish woman played for him, but "all her tunes were but variations of the same *humdrum*; which consisted of so few notes, that we could hardly give it the name of an air."

A different kind of musical experience was described by Clarke in Swedish Västerbotten, where he met a group of "wood-nymphs" in "scarlet vests with short petticoats; their legs and feet being naked, and their hair float-ing in the wind," who carried "a kind of trumpet, six feet in length, which in this country is named a *lure*: it is used, in the forests, to call the cattle, and to drive away bears and wolves." Its sound was "full and clear, [and] is heard for miles." Clarke bought one for his growing collection of memorabilia.[38]

Peasant dance likewise generally appeared perplexing to the foreigners. La Tocnaye described the dancing at the Drottningholm wedding as "scarcely more than constantly turning to the sound of the accursed *harpa*." Clarke offered a fuller account from Västmanland: "At Källback we saw a *Swedish* dance: it consisted of several couple[s], placed as in our common *country-dance*, swinging each other round as fast as possible, and marking time by stamping their feet, but never quitting the spot on which the whirl began. Like all national dances, this was grossly licentious. Such dances were some-times represented by old *Breughel*, in his pictures." Acerbi described peasant dancing near Uleåborg in northern Finland:

> Their dancing consisted in the most part of rustic jumping, without the smallest grace, mixed with certain capers; in executing which the women made their petticoats fly in the air. There was no variety in their steps, nor passion in their attitudes, nor expression in any of their countenances. They

danced with the same earnest diligence that would have influenced them in the performance of any thing by which they were to have gained their bread. . . . Their party of pleasure apparently inspired so little mirth, that one could not help believing that the people danced from a sense of duty.

While the true Finns possessed an aptitude for poetry and music, Clarke wrote, they had not "any more ability or inclination for dancing than the *bears* which inhabit their forests," thus resembling the Arabs but differing from the "whole race of *Goths*." There is less on folk music and dance in Denmark and Norway, although Swinton remarked on the fondness of the Danes and Norwegians for both. La Tocnaye, meanwhile, described a vigorous Norwegian folk dance he witnessed at the Trondheim fair: "It was truly very strange. The man throws himself, in keeping time, full-length on the ground without releasing the hand of his partner, who dances around him. At a stroke of the bow, he leaps up and again begins dancing. This display was carried out with great aplomb and agility."[39]

Few of the travelers acquired more than a smattering of the languages of the region, although some apparently made an effort in this regard. Several, however, commented on the sounds of these languages and the impressions they made of the national character of their speakers. Vittorio Alfieri spoke in 1770 of the "whining, nasal, and guttural sound of the Danish to which I was daily compelled to listen, happily however without understanding it." The Scotsman Macdonald showed a greater appreciation in claiming that the Danes talked in a "barking Buchan or Aberdeenshire accent." Küttner, as late as 1798, remarked on the widespread knowledge of German in Copenhagen, stating that "it is only within these [past] few years, that the Dane appears to pride himself in having a language of his own."[40]

The scholarly Christian Ludwig Lenz offered a more sympathetic appreciation. Both Danish and Swedish, he wrote, "sounded to me lovelier, milder, and more pleasant than the all too hard High German"—and he went on to complain that Low German (*Plattdeutsch*) had not become the literary version of his own language. Danish, he added, was "the tenderest among all the sisters of the German and daughters of the Latin [tongue]." It was, he felt, admirably suited to lyric verse. Swedish—next to modern Greek when sung by women—was, meanwhile, the most beautiful European language for singing. Carr dismissed the "*patois*" of Finland as a "barbarous and unintelligible mixture of Swedish and Russ[ian]." Clarke recognized in Swedish "the origin of my native language, somewhat corrupted in Norway." He also found "both the *Lapland* and *Finnish* languages . . . pleasing to the ear, and admirably suited to poetry, owing to their plenitude of vowels. They constantly reminded us of the *Italian*." He surmised that Lappish was related to the Eskimo languages of Arctic North America.[41]

There was also some interest in regional language usage. Clarke declared—with considerable exaggeration—that only Swedish was spoken on the Finnish Bothnian coast, the whole way from Nykarleby (Uusikaarleppyy) to Åbo. La Tocnaye, who unlike the others, had a good knowledge of the Scandinavian languages, claimed the Dalarna dialect to be more similar to English than standard Swedish and, for that reason, easier for him to understand, while Thomson noted its similarity to Lowland Scots. La Tocnaye also observed that descendants of the Finnish settlers in Orsa parish in Dalarna still spoke their ancestral tongue.[42]

The travelers had little to relate about the rich oral traditions of the Nordic peasants, the notable exception being Acerbi, who was fascinated by what he encountered of it—however obscurely—among the Finns. "Runic poetry has been from the most ancient times cultivated by the peasants in Finland," he wrote. "There is scarcely any event, public or private, which does not find a poet amongst the Finnish peasants to celebrate it."[43]

On a more prosaic level, the visitors were at times taken aback by some of the more bizarre customs they found. "Nothing could be more curious," Acerbi exclaimed, "than to describe the odd and fantastic customs of the northern nations, and the gross indelicacies practiced among them on certain occasions." As examples he gave Finnish courtship and marriage practices and mixed bathing in the sauna. He left a memorable account of the latter. After describing the bathhouse and the means of producing steam, he continued:

> Men and women use the bath promiscuously, without any concealment of dress, or being in the least influenced by any emotions of attachment. If, however, a stranger open the door, and come on the bathers by surprise, the women are not a little startled at his appearance; for, besides his person, he introduces along with him by opening the door, a great quantity of light, which discovers at once to the view their situation, as well as forms. . . . I often amused myself with surprising the bathers in this manner.

The heat, at the "70th or 75th degree of Celsius," was searing. After switching themselves with bunches of birch twigs, the bathers rushed outside to roll in the snow, sometimes at air temperatures of minus twenty or thirty degrees Celsius. "There is nothing more wonderful," Acerbi exclaimed, "than the extremities which man is capable of enduring through the power of habit." The peasants told him that "hot vapour-baths" were indispensable for keeping up their stamina and strength.

At Kemi, Acerbi was persuaded by the local pastor to join him in a sauna bath. After being stripped naked by a servant girl, the two steamed and switched themselves, following which the girl came in and vigorously scrubbed the pastor. "Meanwhile I was extremely attentive, and almost stupefied at the whole operation," Acerbi wrote, "but what astonished me most was the perfect apathy with which the minister endured this long and stimulating process. When it came to be my turn to submit, I found myself in a state of extreme embarrassment—and at last I was very glad to get on my clothes, and walk out of the bath."[44]

Certain other traits could be downright irritating. Burr complained of the habit of the Swedes, "of every sex and grade," walking straight into one's room without knocking. "Some few things must be conceded to a *Swede*; and you make him your fast friend, and the most kind-hearted and generous of men." He continued,

> He must be allowed to enter into your apartment, unbidden, and unknown, upon the moment of your arrival, without any form of introduction or ceremony; to seat himself at your table; spit all over your floor; fill your chamber with tobacco-smoke; ask your name, your rank, your profession, your age, your country, your character, your business—all your present and future plans; where you have been, what you are doing, and whither you are going—finally what you think of *Sweden*. Having answered all these questions, sometimes without his caring at all about your replies or attending to them, you will find yourself upon even terms with him. His house, his horses, his equipage, his servants, his time, his company, his advice, and very often his purse also, all are at your service, and entirely at your command. Thus, although, in viewing his character and manners, we may sometimes find a little ground of complaint, yet we cannot see any thing seriously to condemn. It is in fact, and not in morality, that the *Swedes* are deficient. Often, when they have travelled and learned more of what is called "refinement," they lose something of their more estimable qualities.[45]

The eighteenth century, in both its enlightened and romantic modes, showed a particular fascination with the "moral character" of different nations, and Clarke's evaluation of the Swedes, cited above, in large part summarizes the visitors' appraisal of the Nordic peoples in this regard. It was for their moral qualities that they—and in particular the Swedes—received the highest praise, above all for their honesty and hospitality. "Of all the European nations, Sweden undoubtedly takes the lead in point of morals," Boisgelin proclaimed. "The people are essentially good, virtuous, and attached to the religion of their king. Strict honesty, indeed, makes a part of their nature." "It is impossible not to love and admire the character of this people," Burr wrote from Sweden to his daughter in South Carolina. "Honesty is not a virtue here; it is mere habit." "Only think of a people," he noted, "the most honest and peaceable in the world, and not a lawyer!" While Lenz exclaimed, "Happy simplicity and innocence in customs!"[46]

There were, of course, exceptions that proved the rule, as Carr found when the seemingly honest Swedish noncommissioned officer he had engaged as his fore rider had picked the locks of his trunks and made off with various valuables. Thomson was indignant over instances of sharp practice on the part of some of the peasants he had to deal with on his way through southern Sweden. Moreover, considerable regional variation was observed, both within Sweden and elsewhere in the North. Boisgelin largely expressed the general consensus among the travelers regarding both the nature and the causes of these variations:

> The loyalty of the Swedish peasantry renders them superior to every other nation—though, unfortunately, this estimable quality decreases every day. The universal corruption of the times has crept into the large towns, and the change is felt particularly in those parts of the kingdom the most frequented by travelers. The inhabitants of the northern provinces, and of the most mountainous parts of the rest of the country, have alone preserved the purity of character which distinguished their ancestors. The Swedish peasant, however, even in his present state, is still a more estimable being than those of his own class in any other country in Europe, at least in any of those we have hitherto visited.

The honesty of the Swedish country folk was, according to La Tocnaye, "beyond all praise," but he noted that they became less admirable the closer one was to Stockholm; both in Sweden and in Norway, he felt, moreover that the character of the people degenerated in the coastal areas. Consett claimed that, even on the northern Bothnian coast, the inhabitants, ignorant as they might appear, were "sufficiently knowing where their own interest is concerned." Boisgelin qualified his general praise of the Swedish character by stating that it did not altogether apply to the town dwellers, particularly in the south, who were "very much in the same state of corruption as in other places." Clarke's marked preference for the northern Swedes—beyond fifty-nine degrees north latitude—and La Tocnaye's for the Norwegians of the eastern valleys have been noted.[47]

The pride, independence, and loyalty to the crown of the inhabitants of the Swedish province of Dalarna were, meanwhile, especially admired. Of them, Boisgelin wrote, "These people, nearly as wild as their native mountains, still preserve their original harsh, rigid manners, and style of character. Enjoying the same degree of freedom, they cannot bend their necks to the yoke of slavery; and though truly attached to their king, they look up to him more as a chief than a sovereign master. . . . [T]he Dalecarlians of the present times have . . . not degenerated from their ancestors."[48]

The Swedish character could, according to certain of the visitors, reveal certain faults born of its very virtues. "Nothing is more strikingly conspicuous in the disposition of a *Swede*," Clarke wrote, "than simplicity of mind and sincerity of heart; but these qualities will be found to degenerate sometimes into great credulity, and to easy confidence in the honesty of strangers. The *Swedes* are always open to imposition, and ready to follow the dictates of any leader, however sinister his designs may be." While the honesty of the Swedes was "as proverbial as that of the Highlanders of Scotland, a nation whom they resemble in many particulars," James stated, ". . . they unmistakably possess in a high degree that feeling of rude pride (I had almost said sulkiness) which distinguishes the manners of the lower class of people under a free government."[49]

According to Clarke, "A *Swede* is rarely found who is unmindful of his religion: and as it is a purer worship than that of the *Greek* and *Catholic* Churches. . . . so his principles are purer, and his heart more upright."[50] Otherwise the travelers are notably silent on the subject of popular piety in the North.

There is all the more regarding the level of public enlightenment in the region, which strongly impressed the foreign visitors. Matthew Consett was enthusiastic in 1786 over Sweden's "Education and training of the young people so as to render them useful members of Society," adding that "they are particularly attentive to the Education of the inferior classes of people." Every effort was made to identify and foster "particular marks of genius, or an uncommon assiduity in any of the walks of Science. . . . to dig the rough diamond from the mine . . . and to polish it and make it fit for use," a laudable practice "worthy of the imitation of more enlightened nations." Boisgelin in 1790 considered the Swedes "infinitely better informed than other nations," since "all of the peasantry, without any exception, know how to read." Acerbi in 1799 and James in 1813 expressed similar admiration of popular education and literacy in Sweden. La Tocnaye, however, maintained that, while most could read, few could write; and the Scotsman Macdonald, coming from one of Europe's most literate nations, also had some reservations about the degree of education among the Swedish peasantry. In Norway, Clarke considered it proof of the "excellent manner" of educating the lower orders that all could read and most could write.[51]

It is apparent that literacy in the North was largely independent of schooling, even though a small but growing number of parishes had established schools throughout the period. The progressive Saxon pedagogue Lenz, equating literacy with schooling, complained in 1796 that "many, many thousands of peasant children" in Sweden received no schooling at all and thus, in his view, grew up in "almost bestial ignorance." Where such instruction was provided, it was most frequently of the type Malthus described in Norway, by which itinerant schoolmasters made an annual circuit of their widespread districts, staying for two or three months at a time in various locations, supported by the local farmers. In 1814 the Danish government decreed that every parish in the kingdom—by now no longer including Norway—was to have its own school, the first such ordinance in Scandinavia.[52]

Literacy could at times expose Nordic peasants to what both their rulers and their visitors might consider dangerous outside influences. Gustav III sharpened censorship to prevent the spread of French revolutionary ideas. "The French revolution," Mary Wollstonecraft declared in 1795, "has not only rendered all the crowned heads more cautious, but has so decreased every where (excepting amongst themselves) a respect for nobility, that the peasantry have not only lost their blind reverence for their seigniors, but complain, in a manly style, of oppressions which before they did not think of denominating such, because they were taught to consider themselves a different order of beings." Malthus reported from Norway in 1799 that "the farmers read the gazettes & talk on Political subjects." They were, however, "at present contented; which was not quite the case at the commencement of the French Revolution." They lost their "disposition toward the French" when they heard that "the lower classes of people in France had gained nothing by the revolution. They now rejoice at the victories of the English."[53]

In the preceding chapter, I noted that there was some lack of agreement among the visitors regarding the industriousness of the inhabitants of the Northern lands. While Boisgelin, for instance, praised the Swedes' "energetic character," he still had reservations when it came to the artisans employed in manufacturing.[54]

It was, meanwhile, evident that the most fertile and productive regions of the North were frequently also the most poverty ridden. Thus the whole discussion of industriousness tended to be largely focused upon the presence or absence of oppressive manorial obligations. Here Denmark provided the test case, for varying forms of servitude had existed on Sjælland, Møn, Falster, and Lolland since the later Middle Ages and in a new form had been extended to the whole country, except for the islands of Bornholm and Amager, under the *stavnsbånd*, or Adscription Law, of 1733. Ostensibly intended to keep male peasants of military age within their districts, by 1762 it effectively bound them from their fourth to their fortieth year to the manors where they resided, to the benefit of the landlords. For eighteenth-century travelers, dedicated to the ideal of freedom in its law-bound British or more popular American or even French revolutionary versions, it was axiomatic that such feudal servitude must prove degrading and enervating, as its critics in Denmark itself energetically maintained.[55]

To William Coxe, one of the few literary travelers who visited Denmark before the abolition of the *stavnsbånd* in 1788, it was "part of the unfortunate remains of the feudal system, which, however modified and changed in the other parts of the Danish constitution, still leaves behind it that indelible mark of its former preponderancy and injustice. . . . a servitude, no less disgraceful to the government, than prejudicial to the community." If they were freed from their servitude, Consett declared in 1786, "the Cultivators of the land would then rise to a proper importance in the Scale of Subjects. Then would they feel their consequence: Agriculture would be pursued with diligence and their toil would be crowned with success." Before its abolition two years later, Lenz maintained in 1796, the Danish peasants had been "lethargic, characterless, downtrodden, and dehumanized," whereas since then they were becoming "manifestly . . . more cheerful, industrious, and active." Malthus in 1799 described the effects of the *stavnsbånd* upon agriculture:

> Before their emancipation, the farmers were still more oppressed than the labourers, as the Seigneurs had their horses & cattle at command as well as themselves. This was in general so disheartening that they exercised no kind of industry. Their cattle almost constantly died in the winter, and the lords were absolutely obliged to assist them in the spring. The farmers or boors would then have parted with their farms almost for nothing,—now they valued them most highly.

The rapid rise in land values was attributed, Malthus added, chiefly to "the emancipation of the peasants, which has rendered them so much more industrious."[56]

Lenz was at pains to point out that serfdom had never existed in Sweden, whose peasants revealed a more "manly" character. But throughout much of southern and central Sweden, as well as in southern Finland, there were extensive manorial holdings, on which peasant tenants were often subject to varying degrees of exploitation. Brougham, for instance, commented on evidence of manorial oppression on his way to Stockholm. Lenz, meanwhile, painted in 1796 a particularly grim picture of peasant conditions in Sweden, which stands in contrast to the more positive views offered by his contemporaries:

> Never shall I forget how, debased and impoverished, I saw, in these frightful holes (for rooms one can scarcely call them), one of the best parts of humanity, upon which in most countries so many burdens are almost exclusively placed, which must bear [the weight of] the entire nation. It is bitter to see how this, by far the greater part of the nation in Sweden—and so many other lands—is so totally deprived of almost all real enjoyment in life. And what a dangerous impression may it not make upon them when they first become aware of the well-being which the peasant class has attained in two great lands, on this and on the other side of the great ocean!

Lenz thereupon offered dark prophecies of future upheaval. His account is, however, clearly tendentious, part of a general polemic assault upon the evils of the manorial system wherever it still existed. It is worth noting, too, that his observations were based principally upon poverty-ridden southwestern Sweden and that he never ventured north of Stockholm. Brougham, too, was apprehensive of "some violent convulsion." Malthus considered it fortunate that Denmark had emancipated its peasantry when it did: "Had the measure been delayed a little longer, probably it would not have taken place; as the government would not have ventured upon it, after the popular commotions in France."[57]

There was widespread agreement that the main weakness of the Northern peoples was their fondness for strong drink. If ever a Swede might misbehave, Boisgelin claimed, "it is brandy alone can induce him to such an act; for their passion for that liquor is so violent." Swedish *brännvin*, Küttner warned, "is in general doubly distilled, and the strongest of its kind I ever drank." Wollstonecraft found it not surprising that, on Sweden's west coast, among those who lived so hard a life, "the churlish pleasure of drinking drams takes the place of social enjoyments amongst the poor." When the Swedish government sought to restrict distillation in 1799 due to grain shortages, La Tocnaye reported that this almost led to a peasant revolt.

Lenz—in his most polemic vein—offered the most lurid picture of the evils of drink, that veritable "scourge of the North!" *Brännvin*, together with his meager diet, he claimed, left the Swedish peasants generally "thin, bloodless, and emaciated." Both sexes had such "long, thin, ugly faces, that one could not contemplate these tall, ghostly, walking skeletons without a shudder of sympathy," while one was moved to tears by their poor, pale children, who also imbibed *brännvin*, almost with their mother's milk. Finland received more lenient treatment from Clarke, who claimed that "no people upon earth are more harmless 'in their cups' than these simple Finns," although their fondness for drink could leave them "easy prey" to artful traders. La Tocnaye, meanwhile, commented on the "mania" for smoking in Sweden.[58]

Near Stockholm, John Carr came upon "two fine female peasants from the distant province of Delecarlia [*sic*]: their sisterhood partake very much of the erratic spirit of our Welch girls." They were wandering on foot to work as haymakers.

> Their food for the road was black bread and water, and their travelling wardrobe a solitary chemise, which as cleanliness demanded, they washed in the passing brook, and dried on their healthy and hardy frame, which, how-

ever, was elegantly shaped; the glow of Hebe was upon their dimpled cheeks, not a little heightened by the sun . . . their eyes were blue, large, sweet, and expressive. . . . There was an air of neatness, innocence, delicacy, and good humour about them, which would have made even a bilious spectator happy to look upon them.[59]

With this charming vignette, we turn to a matter of obvious interest to literary travelers and their readers: the daughters of the land. In general, Nordic women won their enthusiastic praise; but beauty is proverbially in the eye of the beholder, and tastes varied according to region and country. While Küttner considered the men in Värmland better looking than the women, on the other side of Sweden, he was "particularly struck with the beauty of the females. They were not only well-grown and had a good complexion, but likewise had much more delicate features than is observed in the country-people or the labouring classes in other countries." He regarded central Sweden as the "land of beauty." However, "Between Helsingborg, Norway, and the southern shores of the lake of Wenner, the women were the reverse; from which I had been surprized that travellers could praise the beauty of the sex in Sweden." In the same region, Macdonald considered the women generally handsome, like those of the "finer Scottish counties," although they were "rather lean, and their bosoms rarely display that charming luxuriance which is so conspicuous in their sex, in Germany and France"; their dress unfortunately did nothing to remedy nature's "churlishness" in this respect. Like Carr, Miranda had particularly admired the peasant women of Dalarna, "stronger and more robust in build than in Uppland and with an energetic behavior such as is fitting for a free nation."

Malthus, who described only southwestern Sweden, found the Norwegian women more attractive than the Swedish, which may have inspired his friend Clarke—who assiduously mined his friend's then-unpublished travel diary—to the same reflection. Clarke added that, whereas in Sweden the men were handsomer than the women, the reverse was true in Norway, although he found women in the north of Sweden more appealing than in the south. Windham, on the contrary, considered the Swedish women "much more comely" than the Norwegian, "owing chiefly I believe to their taking more pains to protect their faces from the weather." Traveling overland from Bergen, he noted that the Norwegian peasant women did not cover their heads and were the "most disgustfull objects I ever saw," although they made a better impression near Christiania, where "the use of a large covering of linen began." In Copenhagen, Consett offered the high encomium: "The women are fair, well made, and not unlike the English." Malthus was not taken with the Danish peasant women, claiming that they appeared old before their time. Macdonald owned that he did not find the Jutlanders a "handsome race" and that the men were better looking than the women. Moreover, as the latter all dressed alike, it was difficult to distinguish between "a woman of six or sixty." He nonetheless found them "uncommonly good-humoured and obliging," and if they lacked "those personal attractions for which the dear sex is generally conspicuous," they possessed "what is substantially valuable, true feminine softness of manners, and sweetness of disposition." Miranda, in the meantime, was greatly impressed by the women of Kiel in Holstein.[60]

In Sweden Consett observed that "the province of Agriculture is not altogether intrusted to men as in England. Women here bear their part, and handle the plough, which on that account is made very light and small." Mary Wollstonecraft, author in 1792 of *A Vindication of the Rights of Women*, was more concerned with the condition than with the comeliness of her sex in the North. She commented in western Sweden on the harshness with which the servant class was treated, which "shews how far the swedes are from having a just conception of rational equality." "Still," she added, "the men stand up for the dignity of man, by oppressing the women. The most menial, and even labourious offices, are therefore left to these poor drudges. Much of this have I seen." In winter, when the women washed clothes in holes in the ice, their menfolk would not "disgrace their manhood by carrying a tub to lighten their burden." "Hapless women!" she sighed, reflecting on the future of her little daughter. "What a fate is thine!"[61]

Discussion of women naturally raised the question of sexual conduct among the broader masses. "The North abounds in love as well as the East," Lord Baltimore rhapsodized, "and the warmest nymphs exist in these cold waves." Peasant courtship practices attracted comment. Miranda wrote of the practice of "bundling" among young couples in Norway; he used the English word, doubtless having become familiar with the similar practice in New England. Malthus's diary gave a fuller account. In Trondheim he was informed that "much irregularity prevails among the common people before marriage, & that in some districts, it is even approved of & sanctioned by the parents. In general however it is not thought creditable to have more than one Sweetheart at a time." The girls were said usually to "have sweethearts for a considerable time before they marry. A marriage seldom takes place but when a child is about to appear." According to Wollstonecraft and La Tocnaye, similar courtship patterns prevailed in Denmark and Sweden. La Tocnaye reported, indeed, that marriage even among the Norwegian merchant class usually followed the bride's pregnancy, since they "hardly enter into commitments without being sure of the outcome."[62]

Male travelers, meanwhile, discovered that they could not simply take such liberties as they might wish with peasant girls. Acerbi left an amusing account of a girl from Kollare (Kollari), in what is now Finnish Lapland, who "immediately attracted our notice by her stature, her gaiety, and by a sharp and decided manner in her deportment." "She had such strength of arms, that when we were disposed to toy with her, and seek perhaps to be a little too familiar, she would repulse us with a blow that forced us back four or five paces. . . . [T]he girl from Kollare was so strong, and made such impression with her Herculean arm, that she had driven us to a man almost off the field." Miranda, who was not used to taking no for an answer, found the country girls on Sjælland less willing than their sisters in Copenhagen.[63]

In and around the larger towns, the case was different. La Tocnaye commented ironically that the day after the aforementioned group wedding at Drottningholm, several of the bridegrooms—after duly receiving Gustav IV Adolf's gift of forty *riksdaler*—sought separation from their brides on the plea that the latter had been debauched by the palace guards, a charge that, in view of their homeliness, he felt disinclined to believe. In Stockholm, Acerbi declared, "The same constitution which produces distance and reserve in one [the upper] class of women, is the cause of excessive licentiousness in the inferior orders. The prodigality of their kindness is in proportion to the coldness of their temperament. They seem to think they can never give enough, because they feel little even in bestowing the greatest favors." Mary Wollstonecraft wrote, surely on the basis of hearsay, that while wealthier women in Sweden engaged wet nurses for their children, "the total want of chastity in the lower class of women frequently renders them very unfit for the trust."[64]

There were many "public women" in Stockholm, Clarke observed, although they did not "swarm" in the streets as they did in London. Miranda discovered there "good girls, who are to be found here in abundance, easy to get, and cheap." As a symptom of the moral corruption of the larger Swedish towns, Boisgelin declared, "It is not an uncommon circumstance to meet with girls of only twelve years old given up to every kind of debauchery. But, what is very remarkable, these girls are frequently reclaimed at eighteen or twenty, and become good wives and mothers. They meet with men who, regardless of their former manner of life, make no scruple of marrying them, and it seldom happens that their husbands have any reason to repent their choice." Of Copenhagen, Mary Wollstonecraft wrote, "Love here seems to corrupt the morals, without polishing the manners," being informed of the "gross debaucheries into which the lower order of people fall; and the promiscuous amours of the men of the middling class with their female domestics, debases beyond measure, weakening every species of family affection."[65]

In addition to open prostitution, there was much of a more casual kind, even, at times, outside the larger towns. A particularly distasteful case was reported by Carr in 1804 from Husum in Schleswig. At an inn,

> a pretty pale and interesting girl, whose age could not have exceeded thirteen, entered with a trembling step, and presented one of the gentlemen present with a note—the contents of it unfolded such a secret as must have shocked the soul of the most depraved libertine—it was written by her mother. We detained her miserable and devoted child until we had raised a little subscription for her, and dismissed her with an involuntary exclamation of abhorrence against the parent.[66]

In a lighter vein, Burr wrote cryptically in 1809 of how, "in the evening, to my great surprise, and uninvited, tapped gently at my door Tempe. You know I never disappoint people if I can help it." This coy allusion from Burr's published letters gives only the faintest intimation of the contents of his vast unpublished diary, which shows him to have been a compulsive and well-nigh insatiable libertine. Miranda, meanwhile, discussed his amorous exploits with complete candor in the privacy of his diary, to which we owe thanks for insight in this regard. He was circumspect with ladies of the upper classes—although he did have a serious affair with a merchant's wife in Gothenburg—but was quick to make local arrangements for his pleasure. Miranda was provided before departing Christiania with a list of the "nymphs of Cythera" in Copenhagen, but he there preferred quasi-domestic relations with compliant young housemaids. During his stay in the Danish capital, he held to one he called "my girl-child"—except for an occasional visit to "my other girl-child"! He found, nonetheless, that his principal mistress had her demands as well and refused him her favors when he strayed away for too long. His other mistress was compliant to the point that, when she was indisposed, she sent for her "sweet" fifteen-year-old cousin to take her place.[67]

The propensity of the times for broad and categorical judgments on the character of nations emerges in sharpest relief in the explicit comparisons the literary travelers did not hesitate to make between the different Nordic peoples and between them and the inhabitants of other lands.

The natives of Holstein and Schleswig consistently fared well, particularly when contrasted with the Danes of the kingdom proper. Mary Wollstonecraft, for instance, noted a greater liveliness and industriousness the further south she traveled in the duchies. In German-speaking Holstein, she observed, "the robust rustics [appear] to have their muscles braced, instead of the *as it were* lounge of the Danish peasantry." Even on the isolated North Sea island of Heligoland, a "vast lofty perpendicular rock rising out of the ocean" belonging to Holstein, Carr—who alone among our travelers visited it in 1804—found three thousand inhabitants living in "health, prosperity, and happiness." To be sure, their livelihood derived largely from salvaging wrecked ships, but at least they never lured them to their destruction, as did certain "barbarians" in the west of England.[68]

Malthus considered that "our Danish ancestors were probably a stout race as their descendants here still retain a very robust make. The men had most of them very broad shoulders and good countenances; and the women were a little in the same way." He could, however, find them at times infuriatingly dull and sluggish. "In three out of four stages across Zealand [Sjælland] we had drivers that were very good specimens of Danish louts. Their countenances were completely expressive of their stupidity, & even the promise of a good Drinkgelt [tip] could not arouse them from their lethargy." When a Frenchman he met railed against the Danes in general, Malthus nevertheless protested that, at least before reaching Sjælland, "we had observed nothing of the kind, & then, nothing that could make us draw so very unfavourable an inference against the whole nation."[69]

The Danes tended in general to suffer in comparison to the Swedes, as perceived by the visitors. Macdonald considered them "neither as tall, nor of so athletic an appearance" as the latter. "We remarked on entering Sweden," Malthus wrote, "that the men were much more lively than the Danes. Our drivers, instead of hanging their heads down in stupid apathy like most of those that we had seen in Zealand, were singing and laughing all the way." Upon arriving in Helsingborg, Clarke noted that the inhabitants seemed not as cleanly as the Danes; "in many good qualities, however, they are much their superiors." They were tall and strong, though less "stout" than the Danes, with characteristically a "long and somewhat pale face, with grey eyes, good teeth, and an expression of mildness in the countenance." Though they might appear mild mannered compared, for instance, with the fiery Italians, Clarke nonetheless stated, "it is the *Italian* who possesses an effeminate character; and the *Swede* who is actuated by a manly spirit." "Coming from England, where no vigilance can secure you against fraud and theft," Burr exulted, "it is like passing to another planet to travel in [Sweden,] where you can sleep in security without a latch on your door." Thomson found striking similarities between Swedish peasants and Scottish Highlanders.

Lenz, who was sympathetic toward both the Danes and the Swedes, sought to compare them on the basis of the sound of their respective tongues: "In the language of their land, the spirit, the ways of thinking of the truly estimable and especially lovable Danish nation, this peaceable and moderate, benign and friendly, extremely soft, adaptable, and tenderly sensitive people, are clearly and genuinely revealed, as in a perfect mirror." Swedish, soft and musical when spoken by educated women, was generally "raw, frightening, and jarring, often unpleasant, indeed repellent" when spoken by men. "This is however by no means inherent in the language itself, but rather in the raw, firm, unbending, unshakable, and truly manly spirit and character which this noble, highly admirable Swedish nation has, on the whole, preserved to the present day, more than the other Northern nations. Their powerful speech bears the stamp of their spirit."[70]

Arriving from Sweden, Clarke found the Norwegians a "smaller race of men: the athletic and gigantic stature characteristic of the northern Swedes no longer appears." While he regarded the Swedes as more industrious, the Norwegians impressed him as a livelier people. Departing Norway, he re-

called, "When we entered *Sweden* through *Denmark*, we were struck with
the superior liveliness of the *Swedes*; but in entering it now from *Norway*, we
received a very different impression." Mary Wollstonecraft praised the Norwegian peasants' "rough kind of frankness," as opposed to a seemingly
greater obsequiousness among their Swedish brethren. Still, according to
Clarke, "The condition of the poor in *Norway*, and the state of morality
among the lower orders, will not bear a comparison with *Sweden*." The numerous beggars he found in Norway, in comparison with Sweden, where
there were almost none, has been noted. And others, too, besides Clarke,
found the Norwegians more covetous and mercenary than their neighbors,
due, it was generally agreed, to a more commercialized economy and greater
maritime contacts with the world beyond. The Frenchman La Tocnaye wrote
in exasperation of the avaricious inhabitants of "Surendall" (Sunnadalen) in
Norway, "These people must be the grandparents of our Normans!"[71]

The Finns seemed strikingly different in significant ways and thus caused
no small perplexity among those who encountered them. No other Nordic
people aroused such varied and seemingly contradictory reactions. Their
very appearance, according to Clarke, who was particularly interested in
them, set them apart: "their shorn features, long dark unbending hair, and
sallow countenances; eyes, extended length-ways, and half closed; a peaked
nose, frequently inclining upwards, but always pointed; sharp and square
chin; elevated cheekbones, and pinched mouth." In his view, they evidently
resembled the Lapps, perhaps even the Gaelic-speaking Scottish Highlanders. The *"Finlanders"* he held to be of a very different character than the
Swedes, with a "greater vivacity of spirit, a more irascible disposition," as
well as a greater inclination to violence. Travelers to the head of the Gulf
of Bothnia would find that

> whenever the *Finns* are mentioned in conversation, the [Swedish] inhabi-
> tants shake their heads, ascribing to them, or to their influence, all deeds of
> anger, lust, violence, and drunkenness. The *Finns* are to the *Swedes* and *Lapps*
> what the Irish are to the *English* and *Scotch*; that is to say, a nation in which
> the extremes of virtue and vice are singularly blended; haughty, impetuous,
> and arrogant, in prosperity; abject and spiritless in adversity; in all things
> given to excess, whether on the brighter or on the darker side.

The Finns in Österbotten (Pohjanmaa) Clarke found to be blonder and
more athletic in build, a "mixed race, produced by the intermarriages of

Swedish and *Finnish* families; producing a comely and healthy race, who are constantly engaged in wholesome occupations and labours of an agricultural life, and differ materially from the true swarthy and smoke-dried *Finn.*" Indeed, Clarke concluded that the Finns, like the land they inhabited, were "intermediary between the *Swedes* and the *Russians*; being nevertheless superior to the *Russians* in every amiable qualification."[72]

As discussed in the next chapter, Clarke, like Acerbi and Buch, had the highest regard for the northern Finnish settlers in Lapland and Norwegian Finnmark. He tended to be a good deal more critical of the inhabitants of southern Finland. These, in turn, still made a better impression on him than the wretched Karelians and Ingrians of Russian Finland and the St. Petersburg region. Swinton, who unlike Clarke admired the Russians, held these unfortunate Finns in utter contempt. The idea of removing them en masse to the Ukraine was even bruited about, a concept he was inclined to favor.[73]

5

Ultima Thule

Fᴏʀ ᴛʜᴇ ʟɪᴛᴇʀᴀʀʏ ᴛʀᴀᴠᴇʟᴇʀꜱ and their readers, the far northern periphery—Swedish Lapland and Norwegian Finnmark beyond the Arctic
Circle and the Atlantic islands, the Færøes (Faroes) and Iceland, far to the
west—represented the ultimate Nordic experience, expressing the most
basic motives for travels in the North: exoticism, primitivism, and escape
from Mediterranean classicism.

"What are the objects, it may be asked, which would induce any literary
traveler to venture upon a journey into *Lapland*?" Clarke asked rhetorically.
"Many!" he replied: "That of beholding the face of Nature undisguised; of
transversing a strange and almost untrodden territory; of pursuing inquiries
which relate to the connexion and the origin of nations; of viewing man as
he existed in a primaeval state; of gratifying a taste for *Natural History* . . .
to sum up all, the delight which travelling itself affords, independently of
any definite object." There, Acerbi declared, the "enlightened philosopher"
could observe "society in its most ancient and primitive form" and contemplate "nature, the order and harmony which prevail in the creation, the
fixed and unchangeable order of things, and the wisdom of Providence that
is everywhere conspicuous."[1]

Due to expense and hardship, only an indomitable few made their way
to these remote regions. Still, there is a high degree of unanimity in their reactions to what they found. This may be attributable in part to the considerable influence of certain earlier, widely read accounts: by the Icelander
Eggert Ólafsson for Iceland; by Pierre Louis Moreau de Maupertuis, Jean-
François Regnard, and Carl Linnæus for Lapland; and by the Norwegian
Knud Leem for Finnmark.[2]

The small number of published travel accounts from the Far North in
this period can nonetheless be misleading, for quite a few others also passed

that way. Carl Gottlob Küttner met in 1796 an unnamed Englishman who had spent the whole previous winter in Lapland and had ventured as far as seventy degrees north latitude. In a visitors' book in Torneå (Tornio)—now on the Finnish side of the border—Acerbi found under the year 1787 the name of "William Langhorn, an American, famous for his walking. He passed the mountains during the summer to enter Norway and returned on his way to Archangel." There was also "John Stuart, an American," the same year. Other visitors included Aubris de la Motraye, who had published his travels in English, in 1718; Johann Scheller, a German who had published an account in 1727; Maupertuis and his companions in 1736; the marquis Arconati Visconti in 1783; Mr. Marey, a Frenchman, in 1786; the Chevalier Statella, a knight of Malta, in 1787; the marquis de Tourbie, in 1787; President Vesvrotti, with Mr. Outiverou, secretary of the legation of the Spanish embassy; the duke of Orleans (later King Louis-Philippe of France) and a companion, Montjoye, who traveled under the pseudonyms Müller and Froberg in 1796; and E. D. Clarke with his pupil-companion, John Marten Cripps, in 1799. Clarke found a child allegedly fathered by the duke of Orleans at the Lapland parsonage of Muonioniska.[3] Such observations should serve as a useful reminder of the sizable numbers of foreign travelers—everywhere and at all times—who see and experience but leave little or nothing to posterity.

Travel to the subarctic regions of Sweden (including present Finland) and Norway—a region today known collectively as Nordkalotten—comprised a long northward excursion from more frequently visited areas to the south. Those who undertook it were thus already well traveled elsewhere in Scandinavia and therefore require no special introduction here. The principal literary visitors of our period were, as seen, E. D. Clarke and Giuseppe Acerbi in 1799 and Leopold von Buch in 1806. While Clarke was eventually forced by illness to turn back from Enontekis (Enontekiö) in Lapland, Acerbi had the satisfaction of claiming to be the first Italian to reach the North Cape. Matthew Consett, who traveled up the Swedish Bothnian coast as far as Torneå in 1786, also contributed some observations about the region.[4]

If travel involved hardships elsewhere in Scandinavia, they paled into relative insignificance compared with those confronting travelers in what Clarke described as the "Frigid Zone." The road—good to the last, as always in Sweden—ended a short distance north of Torneå. From there on, trav-

elers proceeded on boats, manned by hardy Finns, up the Torne and Muonio Rivers, far into the interior. Clarke considered this boat traffic well organized, like the post stations on the roads to the south. The boatmen
could, moreover, cover remarkable distances: as much as five or six Swedish
(33 to 45 English) miles a day, upstream, according to Clarke, who nonetheless considered this rather slow going!

None of these visitors traveled in winter, with its legendary cold. On the
contrary, Clarke complained of entering the "Frigid Zone" amid almost
"tropical" summer heat and held that winter was the "festival time of all
the inhabitants of these Northern latitudes," the time for their travel, fairs,
and high spirits. Summer, however, meant that the travelers were unrelent-
ingly plagued by what Consett called the "Mosqueto-fly." Houses were
"filled with dense smoke" to drive them out, according to Clarke, which was
"scarcely more tolerable" than the insects themselves. Outdoors, he continued, he was ultimately forced to follow the natives' practice of covering
exposed skin with a mixture of cream and tar. "However revolting this may
appear to persons who judge of a *mosquito scourge* by the gnats and summer-
flies of *England*, it is a penance that all will gladly endure who visit *Lapland*
during this season of the year."[5]

Despite inconveniences that could arise due to the sparsity of settlement,
accommodation proved less of a problem than it might first appear—at least
outside the mountainous border region. Both persons of quality, in particular parish pastors, and Finnish settlers hospitably offered the travelers surprisingly good lodgings.

The physical environment encountered in the northern interior was awe-
inspiring. There, Acerbi declared, with some exaggeration, one could sometimes travel four hundred miles without seeing a single house. Clarke found
that, "when removed from the noise of the cataracts, there is sometimes a
stillness which is quite awful; it is the unbroken silence of Nature left entirely to herself. . . . Man seems to be an intruder, for the first time, into
the midst of solitudes that have never been trodden by any human foot: the
very path which he pursues has not been traced by the footsteps of men, but
of animals."[6]

According to Clarke, the inhabitants of the Far North consisted of "peasants, colonists, and Laplanders." Swedish and Norwegian peasant farmers
and fishermen were restricted to the coastal areas, and conditions among
them have, in general, already been considered in previous chapters.

The mainly nomadic indigenous population roamed over a vast area, extending from the more mountainous parts of Swedish Jämtland and Norwegian Trøndelag to the south, up to the North Cape, and eastward to the White Sea. No small confusion results from the fact that, while they were called "Lapps" or "Laplanders" in Swedish and other European languages, they were known as "Finns" in Norway, where settlers originally from Swedish Finland were known as *Kvener*. Malthus, who visited an encampment of them near Røros, called the aboriginal people "Lapfins."[7] My practice here—admittedly anachronistic—is to refer to them by their own term, *Sámi*, except in direct quotations.

"Ignorant of all the improvements of Life, unknowing in the several embellishments of society," Consett wrote of the *Sámi* in 1786, "they live, in the interior parts of Lapland, as much as possible in a state of Nature." He and those who followed after reflected a venerable tradition with literary antecedents going back at least as far as the sixteenth-century Swedish savant Olaus Magnus. Linnæus, who had actually traveled widely in Lapland, delivered a lengthy encomium in his *Iter Lapponicum* from 1732, surely known to interested foreigners, beginning: "O fortunate Lapp, who in the remotest corner of the world thus lives well, content, and innocent in obscurity. . . ." In a passage quoted at length by Consett in his account, James Thomson's "Winter," in the revised version of 1744, rhapsodized over the undefiled virtues of the simple "Sons of *Lapland*," who wisely

> Despise th' insensate barbarous trade of war;
> They ask no more than simple nature gives
>
> . . . .
>
> Thrice happy race! by poverty secur'd,
> From legal plunder and rapacious pow'r:
> In whom fell Interest never yet has sown
> The seeds of Vice. . . .[8]

Direct confrontation with the *Sámi*, however, put the romantic conception of the "noble savage" severely to the test. Their appearance was unprepossessing, to say the least. Consett, who encountered some of them in Torneå, wrote that they "in general are below middle stature, with flat faces, high cheek bones, long black hair, and their complexions of a mahogany hue." They were "perfectly pacific in their tempers." The women he nonetheless declared to possess "so gentle and complaisant a manner that their behavior removes a prejudice which their first appearance does not fail to excite." His aristocratic patron was so taken with them that he took two young "female Laplanders" back to England, where they were received as "great curiosities and visited by all ranks of People," remaining "graceful and unaffected" until sent back to their native land. La Tocnaye, who encountered some of the southern *Sámi* in Jämtland, likewise received a generally favorable impression of them.[9]

Others, who had closer contact, particularly with the northern *Sámi*, judged them less charitably. They were, in Clarke's view, a "pigmy swarthy race, of stunted growth and most diminutive stature." Describing a woman whose features seemed to him Chinese, he commented, "A more unsightly female, or with less of the human form in appearance, can hardly be conceived. Indeed both man and woman, if exhibited in a *menagerie* of wild beasts, might be considered as the long-lost link between man and ape."

Clarke remarked, too, on the *Sámis'* "mild and pacific disposition." They were "the most timid of the human race." In their cups they might become boisterous, but never showed "anger, malice, or cruelty." "When sober," Clarke continued, "they are gentle as lambs; and the softness of their language, added to their effeminate tone of voice, remarkably corresponds with their placable disposition." It might be imagined that they took after their reindeer.[10]

The reindeer-herding *Sámis'* nomadic way of life seemed to the visitors depressingly squalid. Acerbi complained of their "stupidity, laxness, and beastliness," their "sloth and dirt." "There did not appear to be any kind of rule or order among these people," he wrote, "no beginning of any thing, and no end. Their only regulator and guide seemed to be appetite and instinct." He nonetheless acknowledged their hardiness and agility. According to Buch, the *Sámi*, like the "Iroquois or the Esquimaux"— or indeed the improvident Norwegian fishermen of the northern coast—lived only for the moment, without looking or planing ahead. Consett considered their *kota*, or reindeer-skin tent, as "not unlike [the dwellings] described in Cook's Voyage of the inhabitants of Kamschatka." Buch held that the *Sámi* "sinks in the struggle with necessity and climate."[11]

If the *Sámi* were "savages," they seemed far from "noble." "One would think," Clarke wrote, "that to a wild *Lapp*, living in tents, poverty or riches would be almost indifferent; but there is no people more prone to avarice. Their sole object seems to be the amassing of treasure, and for the strange purpose of burying it afterwards." Some, he maintained, possessed, in addition to hundreds of reindeer, rich hoards of silver plate. Their greatest fault was, meanwhile, a fatal weakness for strong drink, which permitted their exploitation by the merchants they dealt with. Buch called this the "scourge," through which "all the little intellect" their minds "may be supposed to possess, every spring of activity, and every incentive to improvement, are destroyed and eradicated."[12]

The nomadic *Sámi* could also, on occasion, reveal what seemed to the travelers startlingly primitive customs. Clarke described how one, upon visiting Pastor Eric Grape at Enontekis, "pointed to his wife and to the bed, made a free tender of her person and charms, in the most unequivocal manner." The clergyman explained that "the *Lapps* consider it as a great honor and as a propitious event, when any stranger will accept an offer of this kind." Quite aside from moral implications, such an offer scarcely seemed appealing to the Cambridge don, considering the appearance of the women.[13]

The folk culture of the *Sámi* was baffling and bizarre to outsiders. Acerbi declared that they knew nothing of poetry, music, or musical instruments and later that their singing consisted of "hideous cries." Clarke described it as "a most fearful yell . . . the usual howl of the *Laplanders*, consisting of five or six words repeated over and over. . . . During their singing, they strained their lungs so as to cause a kind of spasmodic convulsion of the chest, which produced a noise like the braying of an ass. In all this noise there was not a single note that could be called musical." In an appendix, Acerbi nonetheless provided specimens of "Lapland Music," with texts and notations on provenance and performance.[14]

"With respect to religion," Consett wrote, "I'm afraid the Laplanders have yet much to learn." The "high Laps" of the mountains had not yet abandoned their old beliefs, despite the efforts of the clergy. "Many superstitious customs still remain to proclaim the darkness of their minds. Augury and witchcraft make a part of their belief." They were widely assumed by other inhabitants of the North, Clarke pointed out, to be witches and magicians, capable of "committing injuries to the persons of those whom they do not see, and even upon those whom they never have seen." Both Acerbi and Clarke were interested in the original heathen practices, such as remedies for illness and the use of the "divining drum," described by the latter.[15]

Clarke, in fact, undertook to demonstrate some "magic" of his own. He had once constructed and sent aloft a hot-air balloon from the courtyard of Jesus College, Cambridge. He undertook the same experiment at Enontekis, to the astonishment and delight of the natives.[16]

For all their repugnance with the life of the *Sámi* as they found it, the visitors were not lacking in sympathy for them, as becomes evident not least in their discussion of religion. Acerbi, inspired by the revolutionary idealism of the time, declared,

> One general remark may, I believe, be made of polytheism; that it has little tendency to influence its votaries with apprehensions, terrors, or intolerance. The gloom and darkness which almost incessantly hang over Lapland, has not communicated to the religion of its inhabitants either that moroseness or dejection, which too much pervaded the perversion of our most holy system of divine faith and worship during the dark ages. Though the Laplanders were habituated to sacrifices, yet they appear not to have been subject to rigid ceremonies, or severe mortifications. . . . Where societies are not operated upon by the terrors of superstition, there seems little probability that their natural religion will be much tinctured with those frightful apprehensions of eternal punishments, which are repugnant to humanity and common sense.

"The kings of the North, animated by a spirit of religion and piety," Acerbi went on, had sent Christian missionaries into the region, which the natives were obliged both to support and to obey. Thus, although the "poor ignorant Laplanders paid with tolerable patience the contributions required by the missionaries, who promised them happiness in another world. . . . In fact, they look upon rulers and their commissaries in no other light than that of robbers, who like to live in ease and luxury, at the expense of others, without taking the trouble, like themselves, of following the rein-deer, or even being at pains either of fishing or hunting." This, to Acerbi, explained their extreme reserve and evasiveness toward him and his companions, who found it difficult to get them to believe that they were "neither kings, commissaries, nor priests, but only private individuals who were traveling from mere curiosity."[17]

Buch was particularly critical of the exploitation by "iniquitous and avaricious merchants" in Finnmark and Torneå of both the nomadic *Sámi* and the Norwegian fishermen on the Finnmark coast. For all his skepticism, he too was not without sympathy toward the *Sámi*. Encountering a friendly and hospitable family near Kautokeino, he reflected: "Without a doubt, the nature of Laplanders varies as well as that of other beings. Why should kindness and benevolence be strangers to these people alone?"[18]

"A notion prevails in *England*," Clarke wrote, "that all the natives of the regions beyond the *Arctic* are so many *wild Laplanders*; whereas the *wild Laplander* is almost as rare an animal as the *rein-deer* his companion." Although they were generally despised by the Swedes and Norwegians, some of the *Sámi* had settled down as farmers and fishermen. Without their herds of reindeer, they no longer enjoyed the freedom of the nomads or even their wealth. Clarke nonetheless found them of greater stature and strength, although "they work harder and fare worse." In contrast to the reindeer herders, he found the "*agricultural Laplanders*" to be "so thoroughly insensible . . . to the passion of avarice, and so little disposed to take advantage of a stranger, that we could never, without difficulty, prevail upon the poorest of them to accept our offer of payment." Acerbi, indeed, tended to idealize the simple and unspoiled life of the settled, coastal *Sámi* in Finnmark.[19]

It is evident that the visitors were little capable of appreciating the native folkways and culture of the *Sámi*, so remote from their own. Yet a curious ambivalence appears in their accounts, showing the persistence of the concept of the "noble savage," even in the face of disagreeable realities. This ambivalence is nowhere more evident than in Acerbi's account. No one expressed greater disgust with the *Sámi* as he actually found them; yet he looked—as seen—to outside oppressors as the cause of their degradation and in a lengthy appendix provides a notably sympathetic description of their life and ways, drawn principally from the work of the Norwegian scholar Knud Leem. Myth and reality stand in clear relief.[20]

Among those Clarke classified as "colonists" in the region, the great majority were relatively recent settlers from northern Finland or their descendants. Buch reported in 1806 that they seemed to come mainly from the Kaajani district, beginning around the time of the Russian invasion of Finland during the Great Northern War a century earlier. Their area of settlement extended from the head of Bothnia Gulf to Alta Fjord in Finnmark. Here Finnish served as the vernacular. At Enontekis, Clarke learned that among the female population of that vast parish only two could speak Swedish. Traveling down the Swedish coast in 1806, Buch found that Finnish first gave way to Swedish at Landjärv, some twenty English miles west of Torneå.[21]

Compared with the native *Sámi*, the Finns (or *Kvener*, as they were called in Norway) made a very favorable impression. Clarke offered one of his typically facile characterizations: "Even the *Finlander*, who is supposed to be a sort of *cousin-german*, differs, in many respects, from the *Laplander*. The hair of the *Finlander* is of a fair colour; either pale yellow, flaxen, or almost white: and the honest *Swede*, of nobler race than either, is a giant, in whose person and manner there is nothing of the *cat-like* flexibility of the *Asiatic*, nor any resemblance to the Orient complexion and form of countenance which assimilates the *Laplander* to the natives of *Japan*." Proceeding up the Torne River, he commented, "we perceived a change in the manners of the people; the noisy, turbulent, and mirthful disposition of the *Finns* being substituted for the mild gravity of the *Swedes*."[22]

The visitors in particular admired the hardiness and industriousness of the Finns in the Far North. Their strength, endurance, and cheerfulness as boatmen could not fail to impress. Acerbi described them as a "sober, ro-bust, active race of people." Buch enthusiastically attributed to them the spread of agriculture to the Far North.

> The Quäns [Finns] are the most civilized inhabitants of Finmark, not even excepting the Norwegians. They are distinguished by their understanding: their comprehension is easy and rapid, and they do not dislike to work. Hence they easily learn all the trades which are necessary for ordinary estab-lishments; and the progress they are capable of yet making in agriculture, and, consequently, in the arts of life, is proved by the peasants of Torneo, Uleoborg, and Cajaneborg. Even the pernicious influence of sea life, the expectation of profit, without laying by anything for times of want, never manifested itself among the Quäns to the extent which it has among the Norwegians or Finns [*Sámi*].

Everywhere their farms and villages gave evidence of good husbandry and even prosperity. Of the Torne Valley in Swedish Lapland, he wrote, "This is a rich country. Where is there any thing, in Norway or even in the south of Sweden, equal in point of cultivation?"[23]

The travelers were surprised and delighted by the homes of the Finnish settlers, in which they commonly lodged. According to Buch, "There are great numbers of a much worse description in the most cultivated coun-tries"; the cottages in the Torne Valley, he declared, would "shame those of the best districts of Germany." Clarke commented frequently on their cleanliness. "The walls, the floor, the tables, the beds, were all of white deal," he wrote of one such cottage, "pure and spotless as the interior of an *English* milk-pail."

Life was hard, to be sure, in such northerly latitudes. Buch noted the Finns' sobriety, compared with Finnmark's Norwegian fishermen and the *Sámi*. He further attributed their good health to their well-heated dwellings and use of the sauna, which provided "such a temperature as nature requires for the development and advancement of the functions of life in the physical man." Clarke commented that an Englishman would hardly regard their diet of "sour *milk*, raw *salmon*, or dried *flesh*," as nutritious.

> Yet how feeble did the stoutest among us appear, when opposed to them! We never saw stronger or healthier men anywhere. . . . The food of an *Englishman*, and without which he fancies he cannot work, would enervate and destroy an *Arctic* farmer; who labours more, when it is necessary, than any of the *London* coal-heavers; taking no other sustenance, for days together, than a little biscuit[,] half of which consists of the bark of trees, washed down with *pïma* [sour milk].[24]

The Russians from the Murman Coast, who traded with northern Norway and fished off Finnmark, also attracted the attention of Buch, who regarded them as more sober, industrious, and enterprising than either the Norwegian fishermen or the *Sámi* of the region.[25]

To foreign travelers of genteel origins, it was naturally a relief to meet, on occasion, persons of their "own kind" amid the wilds of the Far North. Acerbi found at Muonioniska in Lapland Pastor Matthias Kolström, "the most clownish parson I ever saw in my various travels," who nonetheless possessed much common sense and "violently declaimed against the manner in which the aristocracy and high clergy abused their riches." He was a "determined enemy to every thing despotic" and had "infinite respect for Bonaparte." "Sometimes," Acerbi added, "he would discourse on the abuses of birth and hereditary succession, in a manner which I was altogether astonished to hear from a man, who had nothing in the world but a shirt, a pair of breeches, and the shoes on his feet."

Clarke, meanwhile, extolled the hospitality of the cultivated pastor and his daughters at Övertorneå. "With these companions," he wrote, "we sat down to rather an elegant supper; in the midst of so many unexpected *agrémens*, we were disposed to imagine the parsonage, *Parnassus*, the minister's daughters the muses." On the pianoforte, he found a song composed by Acerbi, who had recently passed that way, dedicated to one of the young ladies. Spending the night there, Clarke was nonetheless plagued by large bedbugs! Acerbi, Clarke, and Buch were greatly impressed by the scholarly Pastor Eric Grape, whose parish of Enontekis Clarke held to be as large as Yorkshire, of which he had written a learned account, giving much attention to its natural history. At Rebvog, near the North Cape, Buch found "polished and cultivated men," while at the remote ironworks at Kengis in Lapland, he was put up in a room that appeared to have been "transported from one of the best houses of the capital."[26]

Certain of the visitors speculated over the development of this northern frontier. "In some future period," Clarke observed, "posterity may perhaps read descriptions of the provinces watered by the *Aunis* [Ounas] and the *Muonio*, as the granaries [of] the *North* of *Europe*." He was moved to hear at Enontekis hymns that, "notwithstanding what has been said of the vocal music of *Lapland*, were devoutly chanted" by the congregation, appearing to presage the "triumph of Religion over the most wretched ignorance and superstition" of a "savage people." Buch, meanwhile, envisioned a more relentless onward march of civilization. Of Lapland he wrote, "Scarcely a country in Europe can be named which has made such rapid progress in cultivation and population as this very northern part of Sweden." In Finnmark it appeared to him that the enterprising Finnish *Kvener* would in time drive out not only the *Sámi* but even the Norwegians themselves: "The prosperity of the country will lose nothing by it."

> The unfortunate race of Laplanders is driven higher and higher up the mountains, cut off from communication, and in some measure destroyed for want of subsistence. This is the fate of every people who set themselves against cultivation, and are surrounded by a people making a rapid progress in civilization. The cultivation of the wastes of Baraba in Siberia, and the wonderful growth of Kentucky and Tenesee [*sic*] in America, have in our times driven out nations of nomade shepherds, and extinguished almost the very names of many of them.

The only hope for the unfortunate *Sámi* would be for them to learn civilized ways from the Finns, so that they would be "at last raised to men and to citizens; and we shall finally be convinced that nature never exclusively destined one people to serve, and another to command."[27]

To the Italian Acerbi, the lesson learned in the Far North was to love and seek to improve his own country, "anxiously cherish that science and civility which have so close a connection with virtue and humanity, and teach and assure his countrymen, that they are the happiest people in the world." But Clarke and his companions, while feeling exultation upon leaving the "Frigid Zone," were "not insensible of a contending emotion of regret," knowing they would not see those scenes again.[28]

Foreign visitors to the Atlantic islands, Iceland and the Færøes—almost all of them Britons—formed a group apart, drawn to these remote destinations above all by Iceland's geological curiosities and rich medieval saga literature. Although some also visited continental Scandinavia, they left little or no account of it. Thus it seems appropriate to introduce them here, separately from the main group of travelers discussed in chapter 1.

Yves-Joseph de Kerguélen-Trémarec (1734–97), commander of a French naval expedition in 1767–68, skirted the coasts of Greenland, Iceland, and "Ferro," or Færø, but left only brief topographical, scientific, and navigational observations.[29]

The most renowned visitor to Iceland was celebrated English naturalist and later president of the Royal Society Sir Joseph Banks (1743–1820). After participating in Captain James Cook's first voyage to the South Pacific in 1768–71, he was preparing to join Cook's second expedition when he backed out, due to a dispute with the Admiralty. Having already engaged his assistants, including Carl Linnæus's Swedish disciple Daniel Solander, who had been with him in the Pacific, he hired a ship to undertake a voyage of their own, to the Hebrides, Orkney Islands, and Iceland, in the summer of 1772. Banks kept only a brief and fragmentary diary of this expedition, first published in 1973, containing nothing that would not be better covered by later accounts from our period. A member of his party, the young Swedish scholar Uno von Troil from Uppsala, later archbishop of Uppsala and Sweden's primate, wrote a general description of Iceland, published in English in 1780, consisting largely of information gathered from local clergymen.

Banks's journey of 1772 would nevertheless be of great importance in arousing interest in Britain, in large part inspiring those who came after. James Boswell claimed that Samuel Johnson himself planned a visit to Iceland, while the well-known visit of the two to the Hebrides undoubtedly owed much to Banks. The latter, moreover, gained great popularity in Iceland, paving the way for the hospitable reception the later British visitors received from those who held him in grateful memory.[30]

In 1789 John Thomas Stanley, a wealthy English enthusiast with both sci-entific and literary interests, organized at his own expense an expedition to the Færøes and Iceland, aboard a chartered ship from Edinburgh. He was accompanied by James Wright, a medical student, and John Baine, a teacher of mathematics, both from Edinburgh, as well as by Isaac Benners, son of an English planter's family on St. Croix in the West Indies and thus a Dan-ish subject, although his knowledge of Danish seems to have been scanty. All three were charged with keeping diaries of the expedition for Stanley, who later added his own commentaries to them. Only recently have they come out in print.[31]

Following the British attack on Copenhagen in 1807, Denmark and Britain were at war until 1814. Cut off from Denmark, Iceland became during this period a de facto British protectorate, allowing access to traders and other visitors from Britain. Thus William Jackson Hooker (1785–1865), a wealthy former brewer who with Banks's encouragement had become a dedicated botanist, visited Iceland during the summer of 1809, inspired by Banks's and Troil's accounts. The visit produced a stout work in two volumes, dedicated to Sir Joseph Banks, giving, in addition to the actual account of his travels, extensive information on Iceland's natural history, government, and folk-life, much of it from existing sources, including Banks's then-unpublished diary.[32]

Iceland was visited the following year, in 1810, by an expedition headed by wealthy Scottish laird and amateur geologist Sir George Mackenzie, Baronet (1780–1848). The result was a large volume in which Mackenzie, who comes across as a good-natured, sympathetic traveler, concentrated pri-marily upon the narrative of the journey, natural history, agriculture, and commerce. Several sections, however—on history, folklife, culture, and health conditions—were the work of the young scholar Dr. Henry Holland (1788–1873), whose own travel diary has only lately come out in print.[33]

The Reverend Ebenezer Henderson (1784–1858), likewise a Scot, spent over a year on Iceland in 1814–15—a far longer time than any of his prede-cessors—as a representative of the British and Foreign Bible Society. He covered almost all the inhabited areas, as well as many of the uninhabited parts of the island, much of which, he claimed, had never before been vis-ited by a Briton. From 1805 to 1813, he had served as a mission pastor in both Denmark and Sweden, organizing Bible societies, and in 1808 had traveled widely through Lapland and Finland. Henderson knew Danish and Swedish well and had studied Icelandic prior to his sojourn in Iceland. His two large volumes, published in 1818, provide a wealth of information on natural history and offer the fullest and most sympathetic foreign account of Icelandic folklife during our period.[34]

Among the foreign travelers to the region, only the members of the Stanley expedition in 1789 left any account of the Færø Islands, after first stopping at the Orkney and Shetland Islands, which had also been Old Norse colonies.[35]

The rugged islands had their own somber beauty. Upon ascending Sjælingfjeld on Nólsoy, Wright was rewarded with a "fine prospect of all the Faroe Islands, not one of which but appeared entirely mountainous. The evening was remarkably clear—& the sun was near setting—his beams which were become very faint added more Gloominess to the far distant blue mountains."[36]

The inhabitants gave a favorable impression. According to Wright, "The men in general are comely, Stout & well made. The Women in general small in proportion to the size of the Men—More dark complexions among them than I had expected—They have the character of being Honest—Cheerful, Hospitable & obliding we found them, to a great degree."[37]

The party was welcomed at Tórshavn on Streymoy, the only town on all the islands, by what seemed like its entire population. Stanley described it as consisting of "a hundred or more well built houses, the inhabitants of which are almost all well clad, well behaved and rather handsome than otherwise." Its "aristocracy" consisted of a few merchants and officials. Here he nowhere saw "any thing like poor people struggling in hovels for their Lives as in Orkney." The town's prosperity had derived since the 1760s largely from a thriving smuggling trade with the British Isles, especially during the War of American Independence, and Stanley saw "two or three large Warehouses still remaining full of West Indian produce." This had, in turn, led to depredation by British privateers, causing, Stanley noted, initial apprehensions upon the arrival of his vessel. When he explained that he came "mere for the Pleasure of seeing them, they seemed to think we were making fools of them."[38]

"The pastoral Life on the whole is the most followed in the Faroe Islands," Wright reported. "Altho' every one manufactures his own wearing apparel, & fishes at certain seasons. The No. of sheep may be about 100,000."

The human population was at the time only about five thousand. Agriculture he judged to be in a "very imperfect State." Neither plow nor harrow was used, only the spade; and the only grain cultivated was barley, which was harvested by pulling it up by the roots. Fishing was done with lines, seldom with nets. Still, the inhabitants seemed reasonably well-off. A tenant farmer he visited paid an annual rent to the king of Denmark of "250 Sheeps Skins, one Barrel of Butter & another of Tallow—& some dozens of Coarse Stockings for the use of the Army—for this he lives in a comfortable house, has as much hill as feeds between 6 & 700 Sheep a number of Cows &c. Mr. Stanley and him played a Game at chess, at which the latter was greatly superior." Such substantial farmers, Stanley commented, should rightly be called country gentlemen, for "they have no body above them in rank in the Islands."[39]

Stanley and his companions were everywhere received with great hospitality. Visiting the neat cottage of a widow and her beautiful daughter on Stómoy, Baine wrote, "the good Woman . . . had prepared for us the nicest Supper I ever eat in my Life, consisting of dishes I cannot describe, but all of them very grateful to the taste. . . . [N]othing surprised me more than to find in a Country that I expected to find the very *Dominions of Famine, cold and fogs,* good eating and drinking, comfortable neat houses, and the best Beds upon earth." The coffee, too, was "the best I ever tasted." The English visitors could not, however, prevail upon the women to violate local convention and sit at the table with them. On remote Vágoy, a farmer, after hosting Wright, offered him as a parting gift "a handful of Danish Crowns from his strongbox," this being the ancient custom, and when refused said "he was very much disappointed, as I was the first Englishman . . . that had been on the Island in the memory of man."[40]

Entertained by the leading citizens of Tórshavn before their departure, the British visitors witnessed a traditional Færøese long-dance: "They Joined hands all round," as Wright described it, "& then began to dance to their own singing, Moving 4 steps forward & 2 back, & thus round without the smallest variation, changing the Tune occasionally untill they tired. All our Party joined in it, but I did not relish it much, as the music is detestable, & no variety in the measure." In return, the Britons summoned a Scottish fiddler from their ship, "& we found the Faroes could dance Country dances Minuets &c. extremely well."[41]

Iceland's awesome grandeur produced a powerful impression upon those foreigners who reached its shores, with its grassy coastal slopes; its jagged, snow-covered mountains; its great *jökulls*, or glaciers; its lava beds and vast interior "deserts"; its volcanoes, hot springs, and geysers. "The spectacles presented," Henry Holland wrote to Maria Edgeworth, ". . . are probably as magnificent as any on the surface of the globe."

They could also appear forbidding and desolate, as they did to John Baine, who wrote dejectedly, "Færöe is a paradise to this horrid country, where nothing can live but codfish, ravens and fox's." Speaking of the lava beds around Mount Hekla, Mackenzie declared, "The rivers, lakes, streams of lava, all the horrors of nature combined, oppose very desire to penetrate into these unknown districts; and the superstitious dread in which they are held by the natives is readily excused, the instant they are seen, even from afar."[42]

It was this unique natural environment that in large degree attracted these adventurous travelers, and their accounts are mainly filled with voluminous observations of its geology, fauna, and flora. They also provide details concerning Iceland's recent natural disasters, such as the devastating volcanic eruptions of 1783 in the Skaptarjökull massif in the southwest and the earthquake of 1784, both of which had devastated its livestock and small human population.[43]

Travel in such a setting was far more arduous than anything encountered by travelers in continental Scandinavia, outside the mountains of the Far North. Lacking roads, almost all land travel was on the backs of sturdy ponies of local breed. On an expedition to Mount Hekla in pouring rain, Wright—who was not inclined to complain—described his party as "a Parcel of half drowned Shivering Creatures having undertaken a Journey of 120 miles," of which they had that day, "with the greatest difficulty," covered no more than twenty. Henderson, who experienced one, claimed that during winter travel was altogether impossible, as sledges were "almost wholly unknown."[44]

There were, moreover, no public accommodations. Visiting remote localities, Holland and his companions were invited to put up at turf-walled farmsteads, where "the dirt & smell within were so intolerable, that we gladly availed ourselves of the church as our place of habitation for the night." Earlier visitors had done the same. When a peasant offered Henderson the same opportunity, he remarked that "in my native country it was not reckoned any honour to sleep in church," to which the former replied that "it was deemed equally disgraceful among them to do so in day-time; but he was certain there could be no harm in sleeping there during the night." On occasion, Mackenzie's party spent the night under the open sky. "Previous to leaving England," Holland noted in his diary, "scarcely could we have conceived it possible that we should sleep on the ground among the mountains of Iceland, with snow not more than a hundred feet above us." Like the Icelanders themselves on their summer travels, Henderson preferred a tent of traditional design.[45]

The Icelanders—who then numbered fewer than fifty thousand—created, upon first encounter, mixed impressions. The men were, according to Holland, in general "tall & well made, their hair light coloured and very long with ruddy complexions," and showed "much curiosity & observation, without impertinence or awkward intrusion." Henderson described them in similar terms. The Stanley party had, meanwhile, reacted less favorably. "I have not been nearly so much pleas'd with Iceland as with the Faroes," Stanley wrote in 1789 to a friend in England. "The inhabitants of Iceland are a dirty, insolent & unamiable set of beings. Those of the Faroes obliging, cleanly & because they will be so, happy—here they disdain every thing that could add in the least to the Comfort of Life." Baine, who was most unhappy on Iceland, described his first meeting with Icelanders at Bessastaðir, near Reykjavík: "Had several of the natives on board, who came out of curiosity to see the Ship. They Stunk abominably of Fish. The Women very ordinary, indeed worse than those of Færoe by a great deal so are the Men. . . . I wish I had not got the Itch by shaking hands with them." Hooker was equally uncomplimentary.

In time, however, they inspired greater respect. Looking back in the 1840s, Stanley reflected,

> The Icelanders are really kind & hospitable & we had no reason to complain . . . of any thing like Ungraciousness. . . . [W]e considered to[o] much the Owners of the Farms we came to as a lower Class of the Inhabitants of the Country and claimed Respect as their Superiors whereas, however humble their dwellings & coarse their apparent mode of Life, many of them were the descendants of the Earls & Barons, the Jarls and Herskers of the Norwegians of the 9th Century & constituted in fact the real Gentry of Iceland.[46]

To the natives, meanwhile, the visiting Britons must have seemed strange indeed. On the Snæfjell Peninsula, Mackenzie wrote,

The curiosity of the people manifested itself no where in such a degree as in this place. We could not move without being closely observed; and when we applied our hammers to the lava, with the view of collecting specimens, it seemed to excite no small surprise among the group of people, who watched our motions. But this changed to astonishment, when following us into the house, they saw us carefully wrapping our specimens in paper. Whether they thought us very wise or very foolish, we could not ascertain.[47]

Iceland was a harsh environment in which to provide for life's basic needs. Because of its climate, grain could not really be cultivated there. The island was practically treeless, except for occasional thickets of willow, dwarf birch, and mountain ash, which at most attained a height of ten to fifteen feet; the Danish governor at Bessastaðir had in his garden a forty-foot mountain ash, of which, Wright noted, "he is as proud as he could be if it was a Sugar Cane." The right to gather driftwood was thus a valued asset for farms along the shoreline.[48] The mountainous interior of the island was uninhabitable, the population being thinly scattered in the coastal areas.

Still, there were resources to be exploited. Lush grass for grazing and haymaking grew in the settled regions, so that agriculture consisted almost entirely of the raising of livestock, mainly sheep. Henderson spoke of "wild corn" (*Arundo arenaria islandica*) which grew in places and was used to make porridge and flat cakes like Scotch bannocks.[49] Fish abounded in Icelandic waters. Myriad sea birds provided eggs, feathers, and down.

Henderson described the varied round of work in the peasants' year. During the short summer, there was much moving about. Except during the haying and when making their annual trek to the often far-distant trading stations, the men during this season were largely engaged in fishing, while the women gathered lichen as fodder in wild areas, living in tents. This was the happiest time of the year. During the winter, all were largely occupied with domestic crafts.[50]

There were, as the visitors noted, possibilities for further development. The Stanley party was greatly impressed in 1789 with the governor-general's garden at Bessastaðir, where a surprising number of vegetables thrived. Wright, meanwhile, noted that "few if any of these are cultivated by the natives, & as for Potatoes, which grow extremely well in the Governors gardens no persuasions will induce them to make a trial of them." Henderson was similarly impressed with the Danish factor's garden at Húsavik in northern Iceland, which "shews how much the ungenial influence of climate may be subdued by the energy of persevering and indefatigable industry." By this time, 1814, Henderson observed that local peasants were going to the factor for seeds. He was pleased to note that a fine herd of reindeer had recently been brought over from Norway.

Sir George Mackenzie, who gave the fullest account of Iceland's primitive agriculture, was convinced that much good land for haying could be reclaimed by draining the extensive boglands, which he believed would also improve the climatic conditions. "Though there is little encouragement from the climate, yet there are some parts of Iceland where experiments might be made in cultivating barley, potatoes, and turnips. Along the shores, where the soil is sandy, and where sea-weeds can be procured in abundance, something in this way might be done. "But," the laird added, surely mindful of the Scottish Highlands, "nothing can be effected without the superintendence of some active and intelligent person, able to combat the prejudices, and to encourage the exertions of the natives."

Baine remarked on the scrawny appearance of the Icelandic sheep, which struck him as surprisingly few in number and "resemble goats," with coarse wool and meat lacking the "fine flavour of Scotch mutton." Henderson observed that the wool was torn, rather than shorn, off of the sheep. Little else was produced on Iceland, except by the cottage industry of knitting woolen stockings, although Baine did write of a "Manufactory of Woolen cloth" near Reykjavík, and Henderson found a sulfur mill at Húsavik in the north. Mackenzie noted the Icelanders' primitive method of weaving, using no shuttle, the threads of the woof instead being weighed down with stones, hanging on a perpendicular frame. It surprised him that the Icelanders made no use of the "natural source of comfort" offered by nearby hot springs. Obviously, there was much room for future economic improvement.[51]

The visitors were particularly critical of the crown's trade restrictions, which until 1789 had kept the island the monopolistic preserve of privileged Copenhagen merchants. This "plunder of the poorest people upon Earth," Baine declared, had been "enough to raise the Indignation of Job." Before its abolition, Henderson wrote, "the natives were in a state of absolute slavery to foreign merchants. . . . It is chiefly to these circumstances that we are to ascribe the comparative want of spirit, inactivity, and poverty, which characterize the present race of Icelanders. Under the iron yoke of oppression, the nobler features of the human mind contract and decay; the spirit of enterprize is damped; and a degree of constitutional apathy and indolence necessarily ensues." Hooker too was impressed by the impassive fatalism of the Icelanders. Stanley later commented that, while the Danish government could on the whole not be accused of "either oppressing or neglecting the Icelanders," it "ought to estimate so valuable a Set of men higher than it appears to do. They are allowed to linger away their lives in the most discouraging & heart breaking State of Poverty."[52]

A brief but dramatic revolution in miniature took place in Iceland in the early summer of 1809, when a renegade Dane, Jørgen Jørgensen (Jürgen Jürgensen), supported by a London merchant named Phelps, seized control of the island and organized his own government, until he was taken in hand two months later by the Royal Navy. An interesting aspect of Hooker's visit is that he had arrived in Iceland on the same ship as Phelps and Jørgensen (whom he admired for his courage and good intentions) and witnessed various incidents in this episode, including the arrest of the Danish governor by Jørgensen's British tars. Jørgensen titled himself "His Excellency, Protector of Iceland, Commander-in-Chief by Sea and Land"; raised an army of eight men and a new flag, featuring three white split codfish; and devised a republican constitution, which was, according to Hooker, "similar to that which existed before the country was united with Norway in the thirteenth century." Hooker provides a detailed narrative of events. That the natives offered no resistance—and indeed frequently expressed their satisfaction with the new order—he attributed to the long-standing unpopularity of the Danish regime and hopes of permanent British protection.[53]

Despite a state of war with Denmark since 1807, Britain thus protected the local Danish administration on Iceland and the Færøes. A British Order in Council dated 7 February 1810 declared Denmark's Atlantic dependencies neutral to permit necessary trade and to protect against British privateering. This was doubtless above all thanks to the interest and influence of Sir Joseph Banks. Since 1801 he had, moreover, vainly urged his government to annex Iceland, for which he claimed there had been widespread sentiment on the island already at the time of his own visit in 1772.[54]

Iceland's only actual town in this period was Reykjavík, which would not until 1944 become a full-fledged national capital. During the eighteenth century, it was scarcely more than a village. Wright held in 1789 that it consisted of "one short street of wooden houses, which have been all built since 1783 & entirely inhabited by Danes & Norwegians." As Henry Holland described it in 1810:

The approach by sea to the metropolis of Iceland, for such is Reikiavik, by no means prepossessed us in its favour. A few habitations, constructed of wood and scattered along the beach, with an awkward edifice, called a cathedral in the back ground, were the only objects in the first instance presented to our eyes. The country around the town wore the appearance of complete barrenness—a rude, irregular surface, covered every where with moss or fragments of rock. Such was the first impression of the place.

Nevertheless, this was the closest equivalent to an urban center to be found on the island. Returning to Reykjavík after an excursion into the interior, Holland exclaimed,

> The impression with which we now entered the latter place was widely different from that which attended our first arrival there. Then every thing appeared mean, miserable & desolate—At the present moment, the contrast with what we had lately seen in the interior of the country was sufficient to give to the place a certain semblance of magnificence—something of life, population & activity to which our eyes for the last fortnight had been little accustomed.

Henderson noted in 1814 that Reykjavík had grown greatly over the past fifty years and now consisted of two streets.[55]

Living conditions among the Icelandic peasantry seemed primitive in the extreme, even if adapted to climate and available resources. Several detailed descriptions of their building style are to be found. According to Henderson,

> In general, the Icelandic houses are all constructed in the same manner, and, with little or no variation, exhibit the plan of those raised by the original settlers from Norway. The walls, which may be about four feet in height [above ground level] by six in thickness, are composed of alternate layers of earth and stone, and incline a little inwards, when they are met by a sloping roof of turf, supported by a few beams which are crossed by twigs and boughs of birch. The roof always furnishes good grass, which is cut with the scythe at the usual season. In front, three doors generally present themselves, the tops of which form triangles, and are almost always ornamented with vanes. The middle door opens into a dark passage, about thirty feet in length, by five in breadth, from which entrances branch off on either side, and lead to different apartments, such as the stranger's room, which is always the best in the house, the kitchen, weaving room, &c. and at the inner end of the passage lies the Badstofa [*baðstofa*], or sleeping apartment, which also forms the sitting and common working-room.

Small windows on the roof, usually covered by the "amnion of sheep," admitted light, while smoke went up through a smoke hole. Beds were arranged around the walls, with mattresses filled with "sea weed, feathers, or down, according to the circumstances of the peasant." Interior walls were sometimes paneled with boards, but usually they were bare "and collect much dust, so that it is scarcely possible to keep any thing clean. It is seldom the floor is laid with boards, but consists of damp earth, which necessarily proves very unhealthy." At a distance, Holland reported, an Icelandic farmhouse "looked as if a number of grassy eminences had been irregularly heaped up, a door placed in one—a window in another. . . . The whole has much resemblance to a rabbit warren on a large scale." Elsewhere he described one as a group of "mole-hills of large size." Stanley, meanwhile, recognized that houses thus constructed "would bid defiance to a Hurricane, and no slight Earthquake could do them any Mischief."[56]

Hygiene seemed abominable, resulting in various health problems. The young people of both sexes, Henderson wrote, were "generally of a very weakly habit of body," due to the "poorness of their living; yet it is surprising what great hardships they are capable of enduring in after life." However, seldom did any of them reach a very advanced age. "Owing to the nature of their food, their want of personal cleanliness, and their being often obliged to sit long in wet woollen clothes," he continued, they were prone to skin ailments and to frequently fatal pulmonary diseases, conditions also observed by others. He noted, too, four modest "establishments" on the island for the care of incurable lepers. Hooker noted as well "lowness of spirits."

Baine offered, as a "specimen of the cleanliness of these people [that] one of them yesterday offer'd Mr. Crawford a chew of Tobacco—out of his own mouth—which assuredly is not the cleanest in the world if one can judge from the dirtiness of their faces and their beards are I believe seldom or never Shaved." When a hospitable peasant family offered Holland and his companions an "abundance of milk," the latter quickly lost their appetite when they discovered that spoons were cleaned "by the simple process of passing them through the mouth, & afterwards wiping them upon a dirty wadmal gown."

As in Norway and Sweden, the swaddling of infants seemed appalling. Wright, the Stanley party's acting physician, visited in 1789 a house in which a woman had just given birth.

The husband made us sit down in a Close confined Room where the poor woman was lying covered wt. a thick bed & as thick a Coverlet panting for air. I ordered the latter to be removed & the Cranny (for it was not a window) to be opened—the Child was tyed up with cords in coarse woolen Stuffs—so amazingly tight that its face was become perfectly livid. After stripping it, at my request, of 2 blankets it still [had] a sufficiency in an under Jacket & 2 or 3 lamb Skins in which it was rolled—this I endeavoured to demonstrate to the Father who seemed to agree with what I said.[57]

"Foreigners always complain of the insupportable stench and filth of the Icelandic houses," Henderson wrote, "and not without reason." Still, he doubted whether such evils were not equally bad in the Scottish Highlands, the hamlets of Ireland, and peasant huts in Germany. Much as Holland deplored such conditions, he admitted that a greater state of cleanliness seemed to prevail away from the coasts. Henderson found the most prosperous farms and most decent conditions in northern Iceland, an area not visited by the other travelers of the period.[58]

Regarding the moral character of the Icelanders, opinion was greatly divided. Baine—as might now be expected—took a particularly dark view. They were "very meagre[,] dirty and greedy. Either money is of far less value here than one can imagine or else those people are the most avaricious creatures that can be." Even the usually sanguine Wright had his misgivings about their "Honesty & Fidelity."

Holland was of a very different view. To his friend Maria Edgeworth he wrote in 1811:

There is a singularly disparity between their physical & moral condition; such as is probably found in no other community. They have little good turf & no good potatoes—they live amidst all the asperities of soil & climate, the face of nature is to them everywhere dreary & desolate—they are deprived not merely of all the luxuries, but even of what are deemed the essential comforts of life—yet these people have good temper & cheerfulness of mind, they have warm social & domestic affections, they have a high sense of moral rectitude, and an admirable observance of moral restraints.

Although the widely traveled Henderson admitted he encountered only one peasant "that I could not, by any means, prevail on to accept payment for his services," he considered the Icelanders generally a "very moral and religious people." Like many of the visitors to continental Scandinavia, he was convinced that morality was strongest where there was least contact with commerce and the outside world, particularly on Iceland's northwestern peninsula and north coast. It was most corrupted in areas strongly involved in fishing and especially in Reykjavík, where "the tone of society is the lowest that can well be imagined," due to the presence there of foreigners avid only for gain. Their corrupting influence upon the native Icelanders, in and about Reykjavík, he lamented, was all too apparent. He thus deplored the government's dissolution of the ancient Icelandic *Allthing* at Thingvellir and the holding of an annual market at Reykjavík, which "as a poor substitute" now provided the only opportunity for persons from all parts of the island to meet and mingle.[59]

Far from the town, however, Henderson encountered touching—and even amusing—evidence of venerable traditions of hospitality to strangers. On one occasion, when he needed to replace his exhausted horses, a peasant immediately traded a "strong fresh horse against one of my lean ones, without so much as expecting a single shilling to the bargain. This the natives call *Hesta-kaup*, and regard it as a duty they are indispensably bound to discharge towards travellers who may stand in need of their assistance in this way." Another time, when he was a guest in a rural home,

> a ceremony took place, which exhibits, in the strongest light, the hospitality and innocent simplicity of the Icelandic character. Having wished me a good night's sleep, [the host couple] retired, and left their eldest daughter to assist me in pulling off my pantaloons and stockings, a piece of kindness, however, which I would a thousand times rather have dispensed with, as it was so repugnant to those feelings of delicacy to which I had been accustomed. In vain I remonstrated against it as unnecessary. The young woman maintained it was the custom of the country and their duty to help the weary traveller. . . . Such I afterwards found to be universally a custom in Icelandic houses. Where there are no daughters in the family, the service is performed by the landlady herself, who considers it a great honor to have it in her power to shew this attention to a stranger.[60]

In one respect, the Icelanders could not but greatly impress those who visited them on their remote, subarctic island: their remarkable level of literacy and learning. Holland was convinced in 1810 that the rate of literacy in Iceland was the highest in Europe, except possibly for Scotland; indeed, couples there were not permitted by the church to marry "if the woman is not able to read—this being deemed indispensable to the proper education of the future children of the family." On Iceland there were, in fact, no elementary schools whatsoever, and training in literacy was entirely a family responsibility. What particularly impressed Henderson was "not so much the literary fame of a few select individuals, who have enjoyed superior advantages . . . as the universal diffusion of the general principles of knowledge among its inhabitants."[61]

The only educational institution on the island was the Latin school at Reykjavík—for a time at nearby Bessastaðir—recently established by moving and combining the old episcopal schools at Skálholt and Hólar; the two bishoprics were at the same time merged into one in Reykjavík, in keeping with the Danish government's centralizing policies. Several of the travelers visited Skálholt and Hólar, which were never more than small villages, and which they found falling into melancholy decay.[62]

The new Latin school, the usually skeptical Baine conceded in 1789, "would not disgrace the capital of a more flourishing country." Still, Holland found there, in a building "by no means in good repair," only three masters and twenty-three scholars in 1810, "the funds for the school not allowing for the reception of a greater number." Henderson in 1814 regretted the loss of the old schools at Skálholt and Hólar, which had provided a "good classical education," and their replacement with a new school in a shabby locale in Reykjavík, where the young men were, moreover, "exposed to contamination from the immorality of foreigners." It was far preferable, in his view, for clerical candidates to prepare for ordination in their home localities under the guidance of their local pastors.[63]

Looking back in the 1840s, Stanley reflected, "I doubt whether out of any Compass of Country in Europe containing no more than the Population of Iceland would be found any where a greater proportion of Men of superior Spirit than that produced at this Moment by Iceland." Those who eagerly sought remnants of a proud Nordic antiquity were not disappointed. "In the persons, habits, and customs of the present inhabitants of Iceland," Henderson declared, "we are furnished with a faithful picture of those exhibited by their Scandinavian ancestors. They adhere most rigidly to whatever has once been adopted as a national custom." "Their language, dress, and mode of life, have been invariably the same during a period of nine centuries," he continued, "whilst those of other nations have been subjected to numerous vicissitudes."

The inhabitants of the northwestern peninsula, being the most isolated, were not only particularly tenacious in preserving their traditions, "but they apply themselves with greater diligence to the transcription of the written or printed sagas, the greater part of which many of them have learned by heart, and they are almost all capable of expatiating on the excellence or turpitude of the leading actions in the story." Because of the archaic nature of their language, he claimed, any peasant could read the "most ancient documents extant on the island." Hooker, Holland, and Henderson described the tradition of reading or reciting the old sagas in peasant households while their members worked at their handicrafts on long winter evenings. Hooker held that this amusement was "not of a kind calculated to dispel the gloomy habit which continually hangs about them" and that the sagas were "replete with absurd stories." While painting a more idyllic picture of such evenings, Henderson was nevertheless gratified that household devotions seemed now to be largely replacing this old custom. "The Sagas are certainly of great value," he reflected, "and, in the hands of the learned, may be turned to a good account; but to encourage their perusal by the common people, would only be to nourish those seeds of superstition and credulity which they are but too prone to cultivate, and which, in their vegetation, cannot but have a baleful influence on their sentiments and conduct of life." On occasion, too, the travelers met rural parsons of great erudition in Nordic antiquities.[64]

From the saga literature, "a thought suggested itself" to the Stanley party that, had it succeeded, according to Wright, "would have immortalized [Stanley's] name & celebrated the names of those who accompanied him, & even tho' it failed it still would have had the merit of being one of the boldest attempts that was ever undertaken." A colony of Norwegians had once existed on Greenland. Several attempts by the Danish crown to find descendants of "these unfortunate people" had hitherto failed, most recently the year before. Wright held high hopes that the Stanley expedition might succeed in such an enterprise, but "this glorious attempt was smother[ed] in Embryo by the *Prudence* of our Capt." I might add that some of the foreign travelers in continental Scandinavia were likewise aware of the Norse discovery of the New World; the Danish scholar, P. H. Suhm assured Miranda in 1788 that Columbus had initially been inspired to undertake his first expedition after learning of this on a visit to Iceland.[65]

As for recent literature, Baine noted the existence of two printing presses on Iceland in 1789, whereas there was only one in 1809 when Mackenzie found two printers who made their own ink out of "oil and lamp-black." Baine declared in his categorical manner,

> They have no Poets at present. No Wonder, In such a Climate where Apollo seldom deigns to shew his face and seldom to communicate his fire to the imagination—and where Cupid's wings are clipt, his arrows tipped with lead and . . . [where] there are neither Woods nor groves, nothing but the ever-lasting sameness of Mounts and Hrinnas except here and there a spot of grass. What in the name of all that is musical should a Poet find to Sing about or if he does who will regard him. To get dinner and a warm bed is of far greater importance.

As might be expected, Holland was of the opposite view. "The cultivation of poetry," he wrote, "though by no means so general as in ancient times, still forms a striking feature in the literature of the country." "The days are indeed past," he went on, "when the bard 'poured forth his unpremeditated lay' to the assembled and admiring multitude; but in exchange for these irregular effusions of fancy, a more classical style has been acquired, and greater selection and taste are exercised in poetical compositions." He thereupon discussed a number of contemporary Icelandic poets, as well as two learned and literary societies, established in 1779 and 1794, respectively.[66]

Learning among the Icelanders was, meanwhile, by no means limited only to their own literature and past. Henderson in particular met numerous persons, often in remote places, who revealed an astonishing knowledge of the outside world:

> It is no uncommon thing, to hear youths recite passages from the Greek and Latin authors, who have never been farther than a few miles from the place where they were born. Nor do I scarcely ever recollect entering a hut, where I did not find some individual, or another, capable of entering into a conversation with me, on topics which would be reckoned altogether above the understanding of people in the same rank of society in other countries of Europe. On many occasions, indeed, the common Icelanders discover [i.e., reveal] an acquaintance with the history of literature of other nations which is perfectly astonishing.

Holland, too, was impressed with widespread knowledge of classical antiquity and languages, even among farmers and fishermen. "While traversing the country," he declared, the traveler "is often attended by guides who communicate with him in Latin; and, arriving at his place of nightly rest, he not infrequently draws forth from the labours of his little smithy, a man who addresses him in this language with the utmost fluency and elegance."[67]

At Saurbæ on Hvalfjörður, Henderson met a man who had "read more of the Hebrew Bible than hundreds of the more opulent clergy in Great Britain," although he had only begun studying the language on his own at the age of sixty. Near Akureyri on the northern coast, he found a clergyman who was highly versed in French, German, and especially English literature. Another, nearby, had translated John Milton, Alexander Pope, Friedrich Gottlieb Klopstock, and other European poets into Icelandic. At Hliðarendi he encountered a peasant remarkably knowledgeable regarding Britain's history and geography: "He gave me a long detail of the events that transpired during the usurpation of Cromwell, and proposed several questions relative to the *Thames*, *Tay*, *Forth*, &c." Recently he had discovered a book in German that interested him and was now learning that language "in order to make himself master of its contents."[68]

Surely expecting to arouse the lively interest of the local people, the members of the Stanley expedition in 1789 anticipated Clarke's experiment in Lapland by constructing and attempting to launch a hot-air balloon at Reykjavík, but "alas!" Wright reported, "there is no sublunar certainty. The Balloon instead of ascending found it more convenient to fall into the sea, where it was soon torn to pieces by the waves." Such scientific interests notwithstanding, Stanley was induced by his crew to ensure fair weather on their return voyage by making a small payment to an old woman reputed to have occult powers. "Let us make what philosophical Remarks we please on the weakness of human Nature & its submission to superstition," he later reflected, "but it is not perhaps one Man in a thousand that frees himself as to be under the Influence of his Reason only."[69]

The literary visitors left Iceland with mixed feelings. Baine, no doubt, felt pure relief. Stanley later recalled his party's departure at the end of August 1789:

> All that the Icelandic summer could be was then. What days following days were to bring with them! Now winter appear'd almost set in, and we had for our Contemplation, of what was to be Life of the People of the place, and any people forced to stay here, eight months of Cold, Snow, Storms and all

the wretchedness & dreariness of an Arctic Winter Season. All my thoughts were Southwards, & I pitied the poor Icelanders who could not like Swallows gather themselves together for a flight to Climates less hostile to the Comforts of human Existence.

"Mankind cannot thrive & multiply any more than plants, when Climate is always at war with his Nature," he reflected. He could not help but consider what wonders the capable Icelanders, in view of the feats of their ancestors, might accomplish if all forty thousand of them could be moved to Canada or Australia. Throughout the remainder of his long life, meanwhile, Stanley, like Sir Joseph Banks, continued to take a particular interest in Iceland and its people. Mackenzie reflected soberly upon departing in 1810 that, "having nothing to rouse them into a state of activity, but the necessity of providing means of subsistence for the winter season; nothing to inspire emulation; no object of ambition; the Icelanders may be said merely to live."

Hooker upon leaving in 1809 reassured himself with Troil's theory that Providence wisely decreed that attachment to one's native soil seemed to be "in inverse proportion to the natural blessings it has received." "This is," Hooker marveled, "indeed, most justly applicable to the patient and contented Icelander; who, happy in the lot that Providence has assigned to him, is scarcely ever known to leave his cold and barren mountains for all that plenty and comfort can offer him in milder regions."

Henderson departed with "strong feelings of regret, which not even the anticipations necessarily connected with my return to the continent of Europe were fully able to repress," having witnessed "some of the more sublime displays of the wisdom and power of God in the operations of nature" and having come to know a people of high "moral worth" and "superior intellectual abilities."[70]

6

The Rise and Fall of a New Arcadia

DURING THE YEARS COVERED BY THIS STUDY, as travel literature increased in volume and popular interest, there was a constant search for new motifs, as well as for new meaning, in the travel experience, both direct and vicarious.[1] From this perspective, Scandinavia offered new and unfamiliar vistas.

Charles L. Batten, Jr., has aptly defined the ideal of the eighteenth-century travel account as "pleasurable instruction," following Horace's classic prescription for balancing the *utile* with the *dulce*. Henry Fielding, at the beginning of his *Journal of a Voyage to Lisbon* wrote, for instance, in 1755 of the great value of travel accounts, "if they be writ, as they might be, and ought to be, with a joint view to the entertainment and information of mankind." The *Critical Review* declared in 1759, "There cannot be an easier or more wholesome diet for boundless curiosity, than the mental entertainment" in travels, "where pleasure and instruction go hand in hand."

In introducing his account of the North, Andrew Swinton summarized his version of this ideal in 1792:

It is not, however, long details, biographical, historical, or philosophical, that are expected by every Reader to form the principal parts of books of travels. What the Traveller himself observed, inferred, suffered, or enjoyed—but above all, manners, customs, dress, modes of life, domestic oeconomy, amusements, arts, whether liberal or mechanical, and, in a word, whatever tends to illustrate the actual state of society, and that not only among the great, but the body, and even the very lowest of the people: all this, in the opinion of those who read rather for amusement, than for the study of either politics or natural philosophy, should enter into those narratives which are supposed to hold a kind of middle rank between the solidity of studied discourse and the freedom of colloquial conversation.[2]

145

During the later part of the century, however, this classic balance shifted, as the "philosophic traveler," concerned with the conveying of useful information, increasingly gave way to the "sentimental" or the "picturesque traveler." The former, under the powerful influence of Laurence Sterne's *Sentimental Journey through France and Italy* (1768), saw as the true purpose of travel the inner voyage of self-discovery. The latter, inspired largely by William Gilpin's accounts from the British Isles, viewed the passing scene with the idealizing eye of the artist and portrayed it, in both text and illustrations, "not as it is but as it ought to be," in Batten's words. The decline of the idea of pleasurable instruction reflects, Batten maintains, the increasingly technical nature of science: "No longer could the knowledgeable gentleman be master of all natural and experimental sciences."[3]

Foreign visitors' accounts of Scandinavia in this period reflect this gradual transformation. Nathanael Wraxall declared in 1775, "Mankind are become more skeptical, and refuse to be amused with superstitious legends, or the wanton sallies of a luxuriant and fertile imagination. The refinement and civilization of modern manners has rendered it no difficult matter to inspect kingdoms and provinces, to which access was formerly barred by bigotry, barbarism, and want of all police. Even Spain herself is not impervious to curiosity." Of the Northern kingdoms—among which he included Russia—Wraxall wrote,

> Covered during many months with snow, and wrapped in all the horrors of a polar winter: unpolished in their manners, and still retaining the vestiges of Gothic ignorance, they present not many charms to tempt the traveller. The Roman arms never penetrated into these inhospitable climes, nor is the Antiquarian allured to pass their snows by venerable remains of amphitheatres, temples, and naumachiæ. Yet even in these remote and inclement kingdoms, are the seeds of knowledge scattered; and if the mind receives no pleasure from the reflection of their past greatness or refinement, yet may it be enlarged and improved from the consideration of their present comparative power and importance in the scale of Europe.

How different Mary Wollstonecraft, who in introducing her letters from Scandinavia in 1795 denies that they were "designed for publication . . . but in proportion as I arranged my thoughts, my letters, I found, became stiff and affected: I, therefore, determined to let my remarks and reflections flow unrestrained, as I perceived that I could not give a just description of what

I saw, but by relating the effect different objects had produced upon my mind and feelings, whilst the impression was still fresh." La Tocnaye, although ironically critical of most other literary travelers in his time—not least Wollstonecraft—revealed much the same attitude when he expressed his impatience with the encyclopedic cataloging of information and stated, "As for me . . . I content myself with speaking of those things that strike me, having frequently enough noted that what bores me also makes others yawn." "My purpose," the French émigré wrote, "is, after all, only to pass my time in the best way I can and in eventually printing my reveries, to allow others to pass time in the same manner."[4]

The shift away from the philosophical toward the sentimental or picturesque travel account reflects more than just the competitive search for novelty to attract a growing reading public avid for accounts of faraway places. It also reveals the rising preromantic spirit during the late decades of the century.[5]

In the philosophic spirit of the Enlightenment, travelers looked at nature in terms of the material resources it provided to meet human needs, as discussed in chapter 3. From the romantic viewpoint, nature was significant for its relationship to human emotions, with which it was in constant intercommunion, both forming and reflecting the inner world of the imagination. From at least the 1770s, travel accounts dwell with ever greater intensity upon the beauties of nature, in both its idyllic and its grander aspects, to engage readers' sentiments and enthusiasm.[6]

The preromantic mind was particularly drawn to nature in its wilder and most "sublime" aspects. Edmund Burke best expressed this fascination in 1757: "Whatever is fitted in any sort to excite the ideas of pain, and danger . . . is a source of the *sublime;* that is, it is productive of the strongest emotion which the mind is capable of feeling. . . . When danger or pain press too nearly, they are incapable of giving any delight, and are simply terrible; but at certain distances, and with certain modifications, they may be, and are delightful."[7]

Accounts of Scandinavia by foreign travelers during our period are increasingly filled with lengthy descriptions of natural wonders, frequently described as "awful," "terrible," or "horrible"—capable, that is, of inspiring awe, terror, or horror. Wraxall, to be sure, could only regard the surround-

ings of Stockholm in May 1775 as "uncommonly savage and inhospitable.
. . . Even in this lovely season . . . every thing is joyless and infertile." Uppland he found "chiefly a horrid desert, covered with shapeless stones, or
with impenetrable woods, incapable of cultivation, and devoid of inhabitants." He was not surprised that Queen Christina, in the seventeenth century, should have flown from "these uncivilized and unlettered kingdoms,
to the abodes of art and elegance," and he would "rather reside in a cottage
beneath a temperate and genial heaven than in a palace invested so many
months with ice and darkness." Yet even Wraxall, by the Dal River at Älvkarleby, was forced to admit that the "woods of aspen, birch, and fir, which at
this season of the year are very beautiful . . . spread a gloom and awfulness
not unpleasing to a contemplative mind."[8]

Others were more attuned to the mood of the times. Already in 1770, five
years before Wraxall's visit, Vittorio Alfieri traveled by sleigh in midwinter
from Copenhagen to Stockholm over deep snow and frozen lakes and was
altogether enchanted. "The novelty of this spectacle," he recalled, "the majestic and wild aspect of the immense forests, lakes, and precipices, filled my
mind with wonder and delight. Though I had never read Ossian, yet I experienced many of those romantic images rising in my mind." Had he then
known how, the future poet wrote, "I should have turned it all into poetry."

The changing mood was captured in 1798 by Küttner, who wrote, "Mr.
Coxe, indeed, came [through Sweden] from Norway, by the same road as
we; but his attention is so entirely occupied with mines, canals, and statistical details, that he takes very little notice of the beauties which nature presents." And traveling through thinly populated Småland, he mused, "However dreary such a country may appear in the eyes of the politician, to the
painter and the lover of nature it is exquisitely beautiful."

Yet even the often prosaic Coxe, contemplating the majestic Dal River
four years after Wraxall, exclaimed that "neither pencil nor poetry are adequate to the description." Attempting to depict the environs of Christiania, Küttner similarly confessed, "I never was more in want of words,
though my mind overflows with ideas." James was more articulate, as well
as characteristic, when he described the falls at Trollhättan in 1813 as a "scene
of stupendous horror" as "the whole body of this majestic river, hurried over
four mountainous precipices in rapid succession."

Vivid depictions of Nordic nature abound in the travel accounts of the time: to mention only some of the more memorable, Coxe and Malthus described idyllic landscapes on Sjælland and in eastern Norway, respectively; Boisgelin and Wollstonecraft, together with James, left stirring accounts of the mighty Trollhättan falls; Windham and La Tocnaye, of western Norway's deep fjords and towering mountains; Acerbi, of the North Cape in its desolate grandeur; Wright, of the sweeping view from the lofty Snæfjellsjökull on Iceland's western coast.

Reflecting on the reactions of the traveler to the wild Norwegian landscape, Clarke wrote,

> the mind is never more disposed towards sublime reflexions, nor ever more elevated towards his Creator, than in the midst of so much awful, solemn, and terrific grandeur; where Nature always assumes a frowning aspect; where, instead of the gladness which is inspired by views of human labor in milder and more cultivated scenes, a deep sense of seriousness bids him regard the manifestations of supernatural power, as teaching him that "there are yet greater things than these."[9]

It was regarded as self-evident in the eighteenth century—as it largely remains today—that nature and climate affected not only the emotions of the solitary viewer but the basic character of entire peoples, or "nations," as they were generally called at that time. This view was developed upon, each in his own way, by such varied thinkers as Montesquieu, Rousseau, and Herder.

Deriving from this concept was the idea that those who lived in closest communion with nature, not least in its grander and more inspiring manifestations, preserved their virtue, as opposed to those who were removed from such natural surroundings and corrupted by the overrefinement and artificiality of civilization. This message was most strikingly stated during the eighteenth century by Jean-Jacques Rousseau in his *Discours sur les arts et sciences* in 1750, thereafter reinforced by his *Julie, ou la Nouvelle Héloïse*, in 1761 and *Émile, ou Traité de l'éducation*, in 1762. It was, however, by no means novel, dating back at least to the Hellenistic age with its yearning for Arcadia, the abode of simplicity and innocence, a dream that recurred constantly in the literature and arts of the eighteenth century. This *fin de siècle* primitivism provided one of the strongest attractions drawing foreign travelers to Europe's northern periphery.[10]

From a concern with nature there thus followed a strong interest in the distinctive "character" of "nations" formed within their procrustean beds in different regions of the world. With none of these, however, did the second half of the eighteenth century show a greater fascination than with the "Goths" of yore and their latter-day descendants in the Scandinavian lands.

The terms *Goth* and *Gothic* bore strangely contradictory meanings during the eighteenth century, revealing the cultural crosscurrents of the time. In the classical-humanistic tradition, the *Goths* were the destroyers of the civilization of antiquity and *Gothic* was taken to be synonymous with "ignorance and superstition," the enemies of all that the Enlightenment stood for.

Yet the "Goths" exercised a growing fascination for the preromantic imagination. Building upon a tradition traceable back to Tacitus's *Germania* from the first century A.D., they seemed to embody primitive virility, vitality, valor, and hardihood, in contrast to the effete and degenerate Romans of the late Empire, heirs of an overrefined and dying civilization. The "despised 'Gothick' of Addison," according to Henry A. Beers, "was fast becoming the admired 'Gothic' of Scott."

With the appearance of the first of James Macpherson's "Ossianic" odes in 1760, a veritable anticlassical counterculture came to the surface. "Ossian," Johann Wolfgang von Goethe's young Werther declares in 1774, "has replaced Homer in my heart." The publication in Copenhagen of the Swiss scholar Paul Henri Mallet's *Introduction à l'histoire de Dannemarc* and *Monumens de la mythologie et de la poésie des Celtes, et particulièrement des anciens Scandinaves*, in 1755 and 1756 soon aroused widespread enthusiasm in Europe. "History has not recorded the annals of a people who have occasioned greater, more sudden, or more numerous revolutions in Europe than the Scandinavians," Mallet proclaimed in the preface to his *Introduction*, "or whose antiquities, at the same time are so little known." They were, he continued, the "chief origin and source" of "our own manners and institutions."[11]

Thomas Percy in England translated and adapted in 1761 examples of Old Norse epic verse provided by Mallet, which he published two years later as *Five Pieces of Runic Poetry*. This in turn moved Thomas Gray to write his celebrated "Norse" odes—"The Fatal Sisters" and "The Descent of Odin"— which in following decades inspired a host of eager imitators. In 1782 William Hayley extolled Gray's influence in his *Essay on Epic Poetry*:

Thy modest GRAY, solicitous to pierce
The dank and distant source of modern Verse,
By strings untried first taught his English Lyre
To reach the Gothic Harp's terrific fire:
The North's wild spectres own his potent hand,
And Hell's nine portals at his voice expand;
With new existence by his Verse endued,
See Gothic Fable wakes her shadowy brood,
Which, in the Runic rhymes of many a *Scald*,
With pleasing dread our Northern sires appall'd.

Such writings, Margaret Omberg holds, strongly appealed to the Briton's particular fascination with "supernatural terror and sanguinary horror"—thereby indicating what perhaps came to be the most characteristic literary usage of the term *Gothic* at the time and since. The Nordic vogue was fully and fairly launched with the publication in London of Thomas Percy's translation and adaptation of Mallet's two volumes, under the title *Northern Antiquities*, in 1770.[12]

As the full title of Mallet's *Monumens* from 1756 indicates, its author regarded the "ancient Scandinavians" as "Celts," a confusion that made it all the easier for contemporaries to assimilate them into the world of Ossianic fantasy. In the introduction to *Northern Antiquities*, Thomas Percy sought to correct this error and in his text replaced "Celt" with "Goth," but it long persisted, even in the minds of serious scholars. This association emerges in the foreign travelers' accounts of Scandinavia. Malthus described in 1799 the "stoutest & strongest man I ever saw" in Norwegian Gudbrandsdal, who had "light long hair, & put us in mind of some of Ossian's heroes." Clarke the same year purported to find the remains of a "*Celtic* coemetery" in Swedish Västergötland, with a circle of upright stones "like what we should call, in *England*, a *Druidical* Circle," arousing fantasies of "*Valhall* (that future state of happiness where all the Northern nations expected to carouse with full goblets of ale with the Gods)." In what was probably a later addition, he decided that Celts had been in the region long before the arrival there of the Goths from the south but had never settled down in Sweden and had had "no connexion" with the Goths.

"Perhaps it was [John Thomas] Stanley's exposure to such a world," Andrew Wawn has written, "which led him to enact what was arguably as 'gothic' a gesture as the late eighteenth century produced—namely, to ride on horseback through the swirling mists of a Faroese morning reading aloud to his companions from that most arch-typical of gothic novels, Horace Walpole's *Castle of Otranto!*"[13]

Both Britons and continental Anglophiles, meanwhile, found further cause to extol the warlike "Goths": their alleged love of freedom, an idea that derived, in large part, from the myths surrounding their origins. As early as the first century B.C., Tacitus had praised the rude democracy of the Germanic tribes. The sixth-century historian Jordanes, drawing upon a now-lost history of the Goths by Cassiodorus, proclaimed the "island of Scandza" to have been the *vagina gentium*, or "womb of nations," the ancient home, above all, of the "Gothic" peoples. Scandinavian antiquarians ever since the later Middle Ages had thereafter assiduously cultivated the myth of the Nordic origins of the freedom-loving Goths, a trend that reached its apogee in the *Atlantica* of Olof Rudbeck and the work of his disciples at Uppsala in the late seventeenth century. Tradition in Sweden still identifies with the Goths the provinces of Östergötland ("East Goth-Land") and Västergötland ("West Goth-Land"), as well as with the island of Gotland; in Denmark, the Teutons, Cimmerians, and Vandals are commonly associated with specific districts in Jutland, as are the Angles and Jutes, the Burgundians with Bornholm, and so on.[14]

These beliefs, in turn, came to be combined with the legend, set forth by the thirteenth-century Icelandic historian Snorri Sturluson at the beginning of his *Heimskringla*, or chronicle of the Norwegian kings, that the *Æsir*, or Asa folk, in the remote past had migrated from their original home, "Great Svithiod," supposedly somewhere near the Black Sea, to Scandinavia, led by their warrior chieftain, Odin. As further elaborated upon by the eighteenth century, it was widely held that they had migrated to the North after being defeated by the Roman general Pompey, causing Odin to swear eternal enmity against Rome. To keep this flame alive, he established a warlike religion for his people, among whom he came to be revered as a god. In due course, the Goths, breaking out of their northern fastness, carried out the "Revenge of Odin" by destroying tyrannous Rome and making themselves masters of its former territories.[15]

Already during the contentions of the seventeenth century between the crown and Parliament in England, political freedom had become associated with the "Gothick" Anglo-Saxons, as opposed to Norman despotism. Indeed Kent, traditionally settled by the Scandinavian Jutes, was long regarded as the stronghold of English liberties, even after the Conquest. The theme of "Gothic" liberty ultimately received its classic formulation from Montesquieu in his *L'Esprit des lois* from 1748, in which he described the North as the home of European liberty, the "factory of those instruments which broke the shackles forged in the South," an idea that in turn pervades Mallet's volumes on ancient Denmark. In 1782, William Hayley characteristically extolled the "Gothic" nations as "Ye brave Progenitors, ye vigorous Source / Of modern Freedom and of Europe's Force."[16]

Literary visitors to the North could, at times, question aspects of this mythic past. Swinton, while he gave a particularly vivid account of the Revenge of Odin, was not altogether convinced that this had brought the blessings of liberty to the inhabitants of the former Roman lands. Responding to Scandinavian antiquarians' fanciful accounts of the thriving condition of the ancient North, the skeptical La Tocnaye wondered why "those immense hordes, known by the names of Cimbrians, Goths, Visigoths, etc.," should ever have departed to establish themselves elsewhere. Similarly, Clarke was convinced that Scandinavia, "thinly-peopled" as it was, had never been more heavily populated in the past, for which reason he considered the idea of its having been the "storehouse of nations" to be one of the most "ridiculous fables ever imposed upon a credulous world." In Sweden, La Tocnaye also found it strange that the Goths, to whom Gothic architecture was attributed, had hardly cultivated it in their own homeland.[17]

Foreign visitors were nonetheless strongly attracted to the North by nostalgia for a past far removed from the Mediterranean origins of civilization. In the Angeln Peninsula in Schleswig, Coxe recognized the home of his forebears. On Sjælland, Swinton exclaimed, "I am not treading here upon classic, or upon holy ground, but I am treading upon the tombs of heroes: the very dust of my shoes has possibly pointed the spear of Canute." This glorification of rude "Gothic" virtues reveals, in turn, contemporary apprehensions of the degenerate and enervating effects an overrefined and luxury-loving civilization, what James Thomson in his *Brittania* from 1729 had called the "soft penetrating plague." "Liberty," in Thomson's poem by that name from 1735–36, meanwhile extolled the hardy Swedes:

By keener air
Their genius purged and tempered hard by frost,
Tempest and toil their nerves, the sons of those
Whose only terror was a bloodless death,
They, wise and dauntless, still sustain my cause.

Nor were such sentiments limited to Britons only. Even the Latin American Miranda—with evident reference to Spain's Visigothic conquerors—could exclaim, upon reading Mallet, "I really do not know how it can be that we are so ignorant of the history of those peoples to whom we owe our origins, and who must necessarily be our forefathers."[18]

In the Nordic lands, foreign travelers could, they were convinced, recognize an ancient way of life, now sadly departed in their homelands. In Trøndelag in Norway, Clarke exclaimed, "If any one wishes to see what *English* farmers once were, and how they fared, he should visit *Norway*." In Gudbrandsdal he found that "the customs are so strictly those of former times in *England*, that . . . an *Englishman* would call to mind the manners of his ancestors, as they are still preserved in some part of our country," carrying him in memory to the "golden days of good *Queen Bess*." The Frenchman La Tocnaye, who was well acquainted with the British Isles, was fascinated by the Nordic origins of their heritage.[19]

The legendary migration of Odin and his following to the North, meanwhile, gave rise to a good deal of imaginative speculation about their ultimate origins and *Urheim*. Among the travelers, Swinton in particular was fascinated by this question. While he took exception to Georges-Louis Leclerc de Buffon's *Histoire naturelle*, which claimed a physical similarity among all the inhabitants of the subarctic zone throughout the Northern Hemisphere, he nonetheless maintained that the Scandinavians, together not only with both the Lapps and Finns but also the Russians and the various native peoples of Siberia and central Asia, were of "Scythian" origin, from "Tartary." In Ingria, near St. Petersburg, he mused in 1789, "In this country of Scythia, I imagine myself a thousand years old, and nearly related to Odin." Among the various "Tartars" assembling in the Russian capital to take part in the then-ongoing war with Sweden, he found the ragged "Kirgees," whom he regarded with veneration as "our Scythian fathers." He thereafter considered them poorly employed in the war, which he viewed as a disgrace for the "children of our ancestors."

Swinton offered, perhaps, a way out of his seeming confusion when he astutely observed, "Difference in language is not always, however, a certain proof of different origin; nor, on the contrary, is similarity of customs proof of the same original. The Russians, Swedes, and Danes, are as unlike the natives beyond the Arctic Circle, as the other inhabitants of Europe." He nonetheless believed that "the Esquimaux, who dwell on the dreary coasts of Labradore," were descended from Icelandic and Norse Greenlandic settlers.

La Tocnaye equated Odin's *Æsir* with "Asiatic," suggesting the "Goths'" descent from the "Tartars" of "Scythia." He believed the Finns (or the related Lapps) to have been the first inhabitants of Scandinavia, before Odin "conquered" the area, which would seem to agree with Snorri Sturluson's mention of the *Vanir*, who predated the *Æsir* in the North. Hooker held that Icelandic, "the most ancient, and most pure of all the Gothic and Teutonic dialects," had been called "the Cimbric, from its having been the one which chiefly prevailed among those tribes who inhabited the Cimbrica Chersonesus"—that is, the Kherson Peninsula on the Black Sea. "Could any one expect to find such a field of antiquity in Lapland!" Clarke wrote to William Otter from Stockholm in December 1799. "A view of mankind in their origin opens before me, so extensive, and so glorious, that human vision cannot bear it. It comprehends all the descendants of Japheth, spreading their colonies and language over the north-western world."

In Åbo Clarke was informed by Professor Henrik Gabriel Porthan that "the *Finns* are the second colony of *Tàrtars* who settled in *Scandinavia*; the old and original colony, or first-comers, being the *Lapps*." He noted too the similarity of Finnish to Hungarian. Buch in 1806 was inclined to believe that the Finns descended from the "Hunns," while James speculated that they derived from the "ancient Ouigres of Siberia" and were thus related to the Huns, Samoyeds, Ostyaks, Cheremis, and Laplanders, among others.[20]

In all this picturesque confusion, one may discern a groping for some viable conception of race and ethnicity—between the environmental determinism of Montesquieu and Buffon, on the one hand, and Herder's concept of distinct and immutable folk-types, on the other.

In addition to valor, hardihood, and fierce love of freedom, later eighteenth-century enthusiasts for Nordic antiquity found other admirable qualities in their "Gothic" forebears. One of these, ultimately traceable back to Tacitus, was respect for womanhood, which they saw as foreshadowing medieval chivalry. The very rigors of their way of life was, furthermore, credited with fostering in them a true poetic vein, whose stark and vivid imagery—in contrast to the classical canon—profoundly appealed to pre-romantic *Sturm und Drang*. As Henderson expressed it,

> Accustomed, indeed, as we are from our school years, to hear the Roman historians expatiating on the barbarism and ferocity of the northern nations, and taught to regard the terms "Goth" and "Gothic," as synonymous with savage and barbarous, we naturally deem it in a high degree paradoxical to assert, that those very nations, whose furious ravages extinguished the poor remains of expiring genius among the Romans, should cherish the art of poetry with all possible care among their own countrymen; but . . . it must not be forgotten that effeminacy and excessive politeness are even more hostile to some of the principal beauties of poetry—enthusiasm, boldness, and sublimity—than the fierce and martial spirit which generally characterizes the ruder and more ancient stages of society.[21]

Iceland's rich saga literature, recorded in written form during the thirteenth century, meanwhile, encouraged the ahistorical view that Iceland had remained a refuge of learning during the European "Dark Ages." It was there, according to Swinton in 1789, that a "chosen band of god-like spirits chose to retire" from the oppression of early Norwegian kings and there, following the fall of Rome, "as to a fortress of heaven, the peaceful philosopher retreated, bringing with him the wrecks of learning saved from the wide ruin." At a time when Europe was sunk in darkness and ignorance, Iceland was the "nurse of the muses." Both Holland and Henderson, who visited the island, held warmly to the same golden vision of its past.[22]

In 1732 the Swiss scientist Albrecht von Haller extolled in *Die Alpen* the majesty of his native mountains and the simple virtue of their inhabitants. "Here has Nature taught right living To the heart of Man, and not the mind," he wrote—thereby anticipating William Wordsworth. But it was above all during the 1760s that Rousseau revealed to Europe as a whole—above all in his immensely popular *Nouvelle Héloïse*—the unspoiled Arcadia in Switzerland, which thereafter loomed large on the preromantic map. The region that had previously appeared to travelers a vexatious mountain barrier between France and Italy, was now discovered in all its natural grandeur and its poverty-ridden peasantry as touching examples of uncorrupted mankind. That this moral was not lost in Scandinavia is shown by the young Swedish Count Hans Axel von Fersen, the younger, who, visiting Switzerland on his Grand Tour in 1771, not only marveled at its Alpine scenery but moralized in his diary: "Here the philosopher will find men who are the least degraded and who hold most strongly through the simplicity of their manners and usages to the primitive existence of the reasonable being."[23]

The Swiss idyll faded during the 1790s with the French Revolution, the resulting European wars, Switzerland's invasion and reorganization by republican France, and the growing disillusionment of preromantic enthusiasm for the progressive ideals of the Enlightenment. "O, wretched land, trodden underfoot by pride and despicable deeds of violence!" lamented the German Heinrich Reichard in 1803, "O, Switzerland, once happy and prosperous, now desecrated by the atrocities of war, ravaged by discord!"[24] In its nostalgic search for an unspoiled haven of peace, simplicity, and innocence, preromantic sensibility now found a new Arcadia, still accessible to travelers in a time of revolution and war—in Scandinavia.

The connection emerges clearly in the accounts of the literary travelers around the turn of the century. Vejle in east Jutland "would be reckoned romantic in Upper Austria or Switzerland," wrote Macdonald, "and that is no trifling compliment any place." Küttner enthusiastically described Norway as the "*Switzerland of the North*." Clarke, who had earlier visited Switzerland, fondly compared landscapes in Swedish Ångermanland and Norwegian Trøndelag with Swiss scenery and declared a Swedish farmhouse in Uppland as conspicuously clean as "in any part of *Switzerland*." He wrote to his mother that "Switzerland must yield the palm to Norway, in beauty and grandeur of scenery." The home of a wealthy Trondheim merchant enjoyed a "situation . . . such as *Rousseau* might have chosen for the place of his residence." In remote Finnmark, Acerbi found a landscape that to him embodied "all that is most romantic and delightful in the natural scenery of Switzerland."[25]

As they had in the Alps, romantic souls above all sought in the new Scandinavian Arcadia a sturdy peasantry living in uncorrupted simplicity amid sublime natural surroundings. Idyllic scenes abound in the travel accounts. Carr was moved in 1804 to depict "A Swedish Cottage" in verse:

Here, far from all the pomp ambition seeks,
Much sought, but only whilst untasted prais'd;
Content and Innocence, with rosy cheeks,
Enjoy the simple shed their hands have rais'd.
. . . .
Oh! in my native land, ere life's decline,
May such a spot, so wild, so sweet, be mine.

"How silent and peaceful was the scene," Mary Wollstonecraft mused upon arriving in Swedish Bohuslän. "I gazed around with rapture, and felt more of that spontaneous pleasure which gives credibility to our expectations of happiness, than I had for a long, long time before. I forgot the horrors I had witnessed in France, which had cast a gloom over nature. . . . [C]are took wing while simple fellow feeling expanded my heart."[26]

Acerbi repeatedly contrasted rustic simplicity with worldly vanities. "In the very rudeness of the natural elements, and in their poverty," he declared, "the Swedes have a pledge and security for civil freedom and political independence." Of the hardy Finns of pastoral "Yervenkyle," he wrote, for instance:

> Such examples, but too rare and too little known in the polished circles of great towns, are not so in those places which are far removed from a metropolis, where morals have become the victim of selfish and corrupt passions. It is the traveller, who, constantly carrying about with him his ideas of civilization (which is often only a different name for a system of refined selfishness), introduced his degenerated notions into the bosom of a simple people, obliging from instinct, and generous and beneficent from nature.

Speaking of the Laplanders and their simple life, Lord Baltimore — echoing his revered Linnæus — had declared that they "lead uncriminal, a pastoral life. When there was no Gold, then was the Golden age." How fortunate it would be, Acerbi moralized, for the "disturbed and afflicted mind," the "victim of those vices and passions which riot in great towns, and countries highly civilized and refined," to escape to the "innocence and simplicity" of Lapland. And while he was not sparing in his depiction of squalid conditions among the *Sámi*, he enthused that those who had adopted a settled life on the fjords of Finnmark "all live in the most perfect innocence. Here the necessity of government, for the distribution of justice, the equal protection of the people exists not." Visiting Enontekis (Enontekiö) shortly after Clarke's departure, Acerbi found the latter's "apostrophe" in the pastor's guest book: "Stranger, whoever thou art, that visiteth these remote regions of the North, return to thy native country, and acknowledge that philanthropy is taught among civilized nations, but practiced where theories of science never come."[27]

Intimately connected with such sentiments was the visitors' eager search for the artifacts and survivals of the heroic Nordic past. Miranda, Clarke, La Tocnaye, and Porter, among others, devote much loving attention to stone circles and burial mounds. Macdonald was struck by the "immense number" of "tumuli," or "hillocks," he saw in Jutland, about which the local people seemed to know little but which conveyed a "high idea of the population and power of this country in ancient times." Acerbi was moved to meet, at Mamola in Finland, a venerable blind fiddler with a long beard, "white as snow, "who had the look of those bards who are described with so much enthusiasm in the history of the North." Henderson wrote of the reading or reciting of the old sagas in Icelandic peasant households during long winter nights.[28]

For all their preromantic enthusiasm for the ancient North, educated travelers could not at times refrain from drawing parallels to classical antiquity. In Swedish Västerbotten, for instance, Clarke wrote, "In our road, we met with a group of wood-nymphs, the real *Dryades* and *Oreades* of these forests and mountains, wild as the daughters of *Phoroneus* and *Hecate*," who regaled the party with blasts on their birch-bark horns. Clarke's fancy took him even further. Of a wedding decorated with "garlands suspended upon upright poles," he was moved to speculate,

> There are few remains of *Heathen* customs which have a higher claim to antiquity than this of the *garlanded May-pole* and its festive *choir*; and to these *nuptial dances*, as they were celebrated by the *Athenians* and by other collateral branches of the original family whence the *Goths* and *Greeks* were severally deduced, we find allusions in *Homer* and *Theocritus*; but it is only in the *rural* sports of such countries as *Denmark*, *Norway*, and *Sweden*, and perhaps in a few provinces of *England* and *Germany* where old customs have not been superseded by later refinements, that some of the popular ceremonies alluded to by those antient poets may now be observed.

"We have found occasion, in former parts of our journey in *Scandinavia*, to allude to the curious remains of customs which belonged equally to the *Hyperboreans* and the *Greeks*," he later commented, after himself having visited Greece. "Whoever attends to the rites and ceremonies of a *Dalecarlian* wedding, will be struck by their resemblance to the manners of the antient Greeks."[29]

The travelers to the North before the 1790s, such as Wraxall, Coxe, Consett, Miranda, and Swinton, were generally persons comfortable with the world they lived in, despite their occasional flights of rhetoric. If they criticized polite society, it was for its shortcomings when measured against the established standards of Paris or London.

The more restless souls who arrived during the turbulent years that followed tended rather to criticize the upper classes for attempting too slavishly to hold to those same standards. None was more outspoken in this regard than Mary Wollstonecraft in 1795. "The politeness of the north seems to partake of the coldness of the climate, and the rigidity of its iron sinewed rocks," she wrote. "Amongst the peasantry, there is, however, so much of the simplicity of the golden age in this land of flint—so much overflowing of heart, of fellow-feeling." She found the "lower class of people," who showed a picturesque "simple gracefulness of deportment," far more appealing than the "middling, with their apish good breeding and prejudices." While Swedish persons of quality "pique themselves on their politeness," this consisted "merely of tiresome forms and ceremonies. . . . a caricature of the french." In Norway she was apprehensive of the inroads of the commercial spirit of gain. Upon meeting a group of lawyers at Laurvig, she declared, "My heart grew sick, as I regarded visages deformed by vice; and listened to accounts of chicanery that were perpetually embroiling the ignorant."[30]

La Tocnaye was no less critical of the Swedish upper classes in his description of the rude peasant democracy he found in Dalarna. The province, he claimed, belonged entirely to its peasantry, who kept outsiders from acquiring land there and were stoutly opposed to any genteel pretensions in their midst. One need only wear buttons, he wrote, to be suspected of being a ""*Knapt herre*," or petty squire, the object of their greatest contempt. Comparing the idle, drunken members of the official class in Dalarna with its proud peasantry, La Tocnaye vastly preferred the latter. The peasants were "ignorant, but good people, plain and unpolished in manner, but active and laborious, of extraordinary stature and strength," while the "*Knapt herrar*" knew how to read and write but were rendered by their artificial needs and pretensions "soft, weak, and lazy." Expanding his view to Sweden as a whole, he reflected that the nation seemed indeed to consist of "two very distinct peoples," of whom the peasantry were "the most respectable mortals one could find." Even the worldly Lady Sarah Lyttelton noted that her visit to Dalarna had "strangely lowered our opinion of the Capital circle."

Clarke was, meanwhile, amused to find how quickly polite society in Christiania avidly followed every change of fashion in London; while James in 1813 deplored that the upper classes in Stockholm strove to imitate a "particular style of refinement, which is not congenial to their constitution."

As seen in previous chapters, the travelers were inclined to credit a more virtuous character to the inhabitants of the more remote rural areas than to those of the towns and coastal districts and to believe that morality improved the farther north one proceeded.[31] Sturdy peasants living amid sublime scenery and the legends of a heroic past confirmed the preromantic Utopian dream. *Petits-maîtres*, mincing courtiers, self-important bureaucrats, pretentious hostesses, obsequious flunkies, nymphs of easy virtue, beggars and thieves, flinty merchants, quibbling solicitors, and crabbed pedants—disturbing symptoms of alien corruption—did not fit into their fond ideal.

Enlightened sense and preromantic sensibility went separate ways following the onset of the French Revolution, but the ensuing conflict of values took place not only between the proponents of each but within the minds of individuals formed by what had until then been a tightly interwoven complex of ideas and sentiments.

Upon first acquaintance, it would appear that Leopold von Buch and Mary Wollstonecraft represented the opposite poles of Enlightenment and romanticism. Certainly Buch expressed in his travel account from 1806 a strongly rationalist and utilitarian point of view. Buch, the dedicated proponent of the ideal of material progress and the onward march of civilization, had no patience with picturesque survivals from the past. He noted with approval how peasants in the Christiania region were submitting to progressive urban influences, shedding their local peculiarities, and becoming "part of a nation."

> That the towns have so powerful an influence on the surrounding country, and render the Norwegian a quite different being from what he was in the time of *Snorro Sturleson*, is lamented by many, and those among the most exalted characters, as a national calamity; and they earnestly wish that it were possible to arrest the further progress. But why? Are men to remain for ever stationary like insects? . . . Through social institutions, a still higher freedom may be acquired. Virtue has no national physiognomy, but belongs to all men, and to all ages. . . . Though evils formerly unknown may follow in the train, let them be weighed against the mass of newly developed good, and let us never forget that a free and happy man is a much more respectable and distinguished being than a free and happy *Samoiede*.

Considering the degraded condition of the *Sámi* in Finnmark, he exclaimed,

> No doubt many a philanthropist will here break out in complaints and wishes (and how often do we not hear them?) that this people had never been incited to have any connexion with trade, and that they might have continued to live happily and unnoticed in their former innocence. Would be to God, that neither the Norwegians nor the brandy, had ever found their way to these Fjords! This might be all very well, if a troglodite life of this sort were either the happiness or destiny of a people; if men were not to keep pace with nature in their career.

He looked forward to the day when Scandinavia's Far North would be settled by the "maximum of inhabitants which the polar lands are capable of supporting," which to him represented "true conquests." To regret that the industrious Finnish settlers were driving out the native *Sámi* was like "lamenting, that in the free States of America, instead of the indigenous, wandering, and scalping Iroquois and Chippiways, many millions of foreign husbandmen are living on the produce of the soil, and that many thousand spots are now inhabited by emigrants in regions formerly peopled by the wild beasts of the forest and the rattle-snake."[32]

Yet even Buch was not altogether impervious to the romantic currents of his time, as shown by some of his descriptions of landscapes. Of the fertile and prosperous Guldal in southern Trøndelag, he wrote: "The views down the valley, over numerous and considerable hamlets and churches, with the broad and glittering stream in the middle, are altogether enchanting. Fertility and cultivation smile upon us from every hill. The whole antiquity of the nation is crowded together in this valley: it is the cradle of the land. . . . Pure and hospitable valley! Here I again took courage, and began to live. I had escaped from winter, and was once more among men."[33]

Mary Wollstonecraft was more clearly torn between the impulses of the head and heart. "My very reason," she held, "obliges me to permit my feelings to be my criterion. Whatever excites the emotions has charms for me; though I insist that the cultivation of the mind . . . produces taste, and an immense variety of sensations and emotions." "You have probably made similar reflections in America," she wrote (ostensibly) to Gilbert Imlay, "where the face of the country, I suppose, resembles the wilds of Norway."

> I am delighted with the romantic views I daily contemplate, animated by the purest air; and I am interested by the simplicity of manners which reigns round me. Still nothing so soon wearies out the feelings as unmarked simplicity. I am, therefore, half convinced, that I could not live very comfortably exiled from the countries where mankind are so much further advanced in knowledge, imperfect as it is, and unsatisfactory to the thinking mind. . . . My thoughts fly from this wilderness to the polished circles of the world, till recollecting its vices and follies, I bury myself in the woods, but find it necessary to emerge again, that I may not lose sight of the wisdom and virtue which exalts my nature.

She regretted that the advancing season would prevent her from traveling into the interior of Norway, north of Christiania, whose uncorrupted inhabitants "despise the arts for which those traders who live on the rocks [along the coast] are notorious."

> The description I received of them carried me back to the fables of the golden age: independence and virtue; affluence without vice; cultivation of mind, without depravity of heart; with "ever smiling liberty", the nymph of the mountain.—I want faith. My imagination carries me forward to seek an asylum in such a retreat from all the disappointments I am threatened with; but reason drags me back, whispering that the world is still the world, and man is the same compound of weakness and folly, who must occasionally excite love and disgust, admiration and contempt.

She owned that her "favourite subject of contemplation" was the "future improvement of the world." Indeed, Wollstonecraft anticipates Buch by a decade when she holds that "the increasing population of the earth must necessarily tend to its improvement, as the means of existence are multiplied by invention." She was impressed by the "advantages obtained by human industry" with the constant clearing of forests for new settlement in Norway. "The world requires, I see, the hand of man to perfect it; and as this task naturally unfolds the faculties he exercises, it is physically impossible that he should have remained in Rousseau's golden age of stupidity. And, considering the question of human happiness, where, oh! where does it reside? Has it taken up its abode with unconscious ignorance, or with the high-wrought mind?" This not withstanding, she showed an ecological awareness far beyond her time when, three years before Malthus published his *Essay on the Principle of Population*, her imagination carried her "a million or two years" forward, to the point when the earth might be cultivated to full capacity, and "pictured the state of man when the earth could no longer support him. Where was he to fly from universal famine? Do not smile."[34]

Like Wollstonecraft, Lenz and Acerbi show the persistence, in some circles, of prerevolutionary romantic enthusiasm for the humane ideals of the Enlightenment and the principles of the Declaration of the Rights of Man and of the Citizen, although they do so with less self-revelatory soul-searching. The other travelers from the 1790s and first years after the turn of the century—Boisgelin, Fortia, Küttner, Brougham, Malthus, Clarke, and the rest—although disillusioned with the French Revolution and, in varying degree, with the rationalism of the Enlightenment, show the same tension between sense and sensibility.

Clarke, who met La Tocnaye in Trondheim, described him as an irascible French émigré who later wrote an ill-tempered account of Scandinavia. La Tocnaye, for his part, dismissed Clarke and his companions as a "typical English expedition to the Far North," moving quickly and comfortably. He doubtless sought to distance himself in the eyes of his readers both from those pedantic travelers, who copying from existing sources, listed "the numbers of clocks and lamp posts that adorn the capital of Sweden," and from those who sought to titillate their readers with "*picturesque* and *romantic* episodes"; he considered both of these types self-indulgent and superficial.

La Tocnaye was particularly ironic toward the late Mary Wollstonecraft:

She makes frequent use of those new terms which are called *sentimental*, grotesquely decked out in the manner of Sterne and the new craze for spectres, and moonlight; thus it is the cow bell that rings—the mortal music of the murmuring of the waters—the spirits of peace who wander abroad—eternity in such moments—the light-footed sylphs who surely have danced their airy dance—who is it who fears the falling of the dew?—good night to the crescent that hangs suspended before the ethereal vault and which lures me to far wanderings, etc.—this is the style à la mode, which the lady amateurs of Great Britain employ *rather too frequently*. They here lavish sublime sentiments willy-nilly upon the most simple object, and the first that presents itself. Thus Madame Wollstonecraft is moved and thinks of her daughter in watching a calf gamble on the meadow.

"Poor Sterne!" he added in a footnote, "He would not have imagined, in writing his *Sentimental Journey* . . . that his amiable style would thus be profaned by people who imagine they resemble him."

And yet, in reading La Tocnaye's vivid descriptions of the sublimities of Nordic nature—above all the awesome grandeur of the western Norwegian fjords—and his solitary reflections on life and the world, there can be no mistaking the preromantic mood. Unlike other travelers, who had set goals and timetables, the exiled La Tocnaye prided himself for being able to ramble—or "promenade," as he called it—wherever the spirit moved him, immersing himself at leisure in the languages and cultures he encountered.[35]

An examination of the views of foreign travelers to the Nordic lands during the half century from 1765 to 1815 thus reveals much about the complex transition from the Enlightenment, through preromanticism, to the full-blown romanticism of the early nineteenth century.

Like Rousseau's ideal Switzerland a decade before, the new Arcadia of the North could not survive unscathed in a world ravaged by revolution and war. Already during the 1790s, Boisgelin, Wollstonecraft, Clarke, La Tocnaye, and others feared that its innocence was being eroded by the lure of lucrative wartime trade, legal and contraband, and the seduction of outside ideas.

In 1800 a British fleet attacked the Danish navy at Copenhagen Roads to break up the threatening League of Armed Neutrality formed that year that included both Denmark and Sweden. The Danes fought valiantly, for which they were much admired throughout Europe, but this was the fateful harbinger of things to come. In 1805 Sweden entered the conflict as a member of the Third Coalition against Napoleon, leaving it Britain's only remaining continental ally when France and Russia made peace and concluded the Tilsit alliance in 1807.

The Tilsit alliance brought in its train a second British attack on Copenhagen in 1807, to prevent the Danish fleet from falling into French hands. This brought Denmark into Napoleon's camp in his war against Britain. Soon thereafter it led to the invasion and annexation of Finland in 1808–9 by France's Russian ally. Sweden's disasters precipitated a revolution in March 1809, which deposed the unfortunate Gustav IV Adolf, placed his uncle, the duke of Södermanland, on the throne as Karl XIII, and created a new constitution. The Swedish Riksdag in 1810 elected as the childless Karl XIII's successor the French field marshal Jean-Baptiste Bernadotte as Crown Prince Carl Johan, who after a brief respite brought Sweden back into the war against his former master, Napoleon, in return for the annexation of Norway from Denmark. In 1814, following a spirited resistance, Norway was joined in a dynastic union with Sweden, although under its own constitution.[36]

The travelers' accounts from these years offer few comments on the effects at the time of the Napoleonic Wars in the North, the principal exception being Macdonald in 1808 who noted how Aalborg's once thriving trade was then languishing. He wrote of his encounter with privateers in North Jutland and Sjælland who preyed upon British and Swedish shipping. He described the indignation of the inhabitants of Fyn over the ill behavior of the French troops who had been bivouacked there some months ago and the greater popularity of their Spanish auxiliaries. He also speculated over the feasibility of possible British operations against Denmark. Macdonald noted too that, although the Danes felt great bitterness over the attack on Copenhagen the year before, British prisoners—himself included—were treated humanely and considerately, while he was surprised by the hostility between Swedes and Danes, considering how long they had been at peace.[37]

From 1805 the North was thus no longer an unspoiled idyll, an almost miraculous haven of peace and innocence, free from the ills that flesh is heir to. Perhaps, too, by that time Scandinavia as a fresh and exciting new source of travel accounts was becoming overworked. Certainly the number of such published works fell off by the end of the Napoleonic Wars from their high point at the end of the 1790s. Margaret Omberg has likewise noted a decline in the vogue for "Gothic" verse with Old Nordic themes during the same years.[38] Romantic yearning took wing to remoter regions, across the seas or out of the world of here and now altogether into a shining vision of high medieval chivalry and faith.

"Is it not glorious," Robert Ker Porter wrote upon visiting Sweden, then battling against Napoleon's Russian ally in 1808, to see the "enthusiasm of virtue" ready to stand up against the "fury of ambition"? The wily and over-weening "Briareus" could be withstood by principle and enthusiasm alone. "The Swedes seem to have both; and I trust they will stand their ground."

Others among the visitors took a darker view during the final years before the Congress of Vienna. Norway, Clarke wrote in a footnote added probably around 1809—when he was at last preparing his volumes on Scandinavia for publication—"remains as it was, and as it ever will be—the most beautiful and fertile country in the world, full of the grandest scenery in Nature"; but its commerce and prosperity now lay in ruins. Surely also in retrospect he soberly reflected,

> Much may yet be expected from the *Swedes* . . . but it must be owned the prospect is a bad one. The spirit of the people remains yet unbroken: but where the liberty of the press is annihilated—and *Russia*, like one of those moving bogs of which we read, in *Ireland*, comes slowly but surely on, threatening to overwhelm the country, and to extinguish all that remains of genius and heroism in the land—he must indeed be sanguine who can hope to see *Sweden* regenerated and her glory restored.

Clarke perceived already in 1799–1800, in fact a troubled time in Sweden, a "gloomy prospect in the State, seeming to foretell the bursting of a storm, which was gathering fast around the throne. . . . Such was, at this moment, the abject and deplorable state of this land of heroism, honesty, and benevolence." And still, with greater prescience than he could have realized in his lifetime, he added, "It seemed to every reflecting mind as if *Sweden* awaited one of those tremendous moral revolutions, which, by tearing to atoms the constitution of the country, offers, amidst its ruins, the materials of a more solid structure." His words would well summarize the rebirth of a new Scandinavia, which would arise out of the ashes of the Napoleonic *Ragnarök*.[39]

Conclusion: "The Eye of the Beholder"

THE ACCOUNTS OF SCANDINAVIA by foreign travelers offer an illuminating example of the basic trends in travel writing during the pivotal half century between 1765 and 1815. Characteristically they tell us as much about the travelers themselves, and about their attitudes toward their own homelands and toward life in general, as they do about the lands they visited. They reveal, too, the gradual shift from the cosmopolitan urbanity of the High Enlightenment to the visionary primitivism of the preromantic mood. The "philosophic" increasingly gives way during these years to the "sentimental" and the "picturesque."

It would, meanwhile, seem that the widely read accounts of explorations in remote parts of the world by such celebrated explorers as Cook, Bougainville, and Kerguélen-Trémarec—of whom the last named also appears among Scandinavia's foreign visitors—stimulated a growing interest in Europe's own wilder and more remote fringe areas and their inhabitants, from the Highlands and Isles of Scotland to the Nordic lands and Russia. In this connection, it seems not irrelevant to mention that La Tocnaye once whiled away his time in Christiania by reading the Scotsman Mungo Park's just-published account of his explorations in the African interior.[1]

The travel accounts of this period from Scandinavia demonstrate the uses of such source material for later historians. Although there is much writing of this nature by native Scandinavians as well during this time, the foreign visitors observed and described for their unfamiliar readers much that the former naturally took for granted and therefore considered needless to relate. A literary Dane would, for instance, hardly feel called upon to depict the polite usages of Copenhagen society, a Swede to write about the traditional construction of rail fences, or a Finn to describe the sauna. Not only did the foreigners see different things, they also saw them in different contexts, based on their own cultures and experiences. Conversely, lacking the natives' cultural and historical background, there were important things they were often unable to perceive.

The travelers were a highly varied lot with regard to nationality, class, and personality. As regards origins, Lady Sarah Lyttelton, for instance, derived from the highest English peerage, whereas Ebenezer Henderson had begun life as a Scottish plowboy. However, few foreign women, let alone those who left any account of the region, visited the North, which is not surprising under the conditions of the time. Aside from Mary Wollstonecraft— who was truly important—there was, in effect, only the lighthearted and at times irreverent young Lady Sarah Lyttelton.

Lady Sarah noted in 1813 much talk in Stockholm of Madame de Staël's sojourn there the previous winter. That redoubtable literary lady's uncompleted memoirs end, frustratingly enough, in the midst of a stormy crossing of the Baltic from Åbo in Finland to Sweden, after noting that Tsar Alexander was treating his new Finnish subjects well and musing on the harshness of the climate upon their "firmness of character." Regrettably, the publication of Madame de Staël's collected correspondence has not yet reached the years 1812–13, and the only published letters from her months in Stockholm are to Madame Récamier in Paris, in which she says of her surroundings only that she found herself in "a very dull country."[2]

The travelers' findings naturally varied, often quite widely. Their writings sometimes seem superficial, if not downright wrongheaded, and they reveal personal quirks, prejudices, and preconceptions. Still, upon studying a broad and representative selection of these works, the more insubstantial aberrations tend generally to cancel each other out, leaving a high degree of consensus, decade by decade through the period.

Historians are concerned with the processes of continuity and change through time, and these travel accounts from two centuries ago illustrate both. Again and again, the reader well acquainted with present-day Scandinavia feels a sense of déjà vu in reading their descriptions of landscapes, traditional building styles, social customs, and the appearance and characteristics of the Nordic peoples.

Yet the changes are even more striking, when one compares relatively poor, backward, and underdeveloped agrarian societies with the prosperous, highly industrialized, urbanized, and cosmopolitan Nordic lands of today. More than that, who would recognize the jovial, quick-witted Danes of our time in their loutish, dull-witted, and apathetic forebears, as described by a number of foreign travelers? Or the orderly, peace-loving

Swedes in their politically volatile and at times violence-prone countrymen of the Gustavian period, whose history from early times James in 1813 believed revealed a certain "cold-blooded obduracy" and "sanguinary turn of mind"?[3]

As most of the travelers visited more than one Nordic country, they naturally found comparisons and contrasts between them. Their accounts offer a number of surprises in contrast to generally established presuppositions today. It seems hard to imagine that the duchies of Schleswig and Holstein should have been so much more prosperous and progressive than Denmark proper, even after several years of vigorous social and economic reform in the kingdom; that the southern provinces of Sweden, now its agricultural and industrial heartland, still remained poor and unproductive in contrast not only to the Mälar provinces but especially to Norrland and Finnish Österbotten; that Norway should seem so much better off economically than Denmark or Sweden; that Scandinavian economic development as a whole should lag so far behind not only that of Great Britain—the usual yardstick—but that of much of continental Europe as well. Yet despite differences in detail, this is essentially the composite picture the foreign travelers give at the end of the eighteenth century.

Such observations in turn suggested comparisons with other parts of the world, most often across the Atlantic. Clarke, who characterized the Swedish realm as largely "one contiguous unbroken forest, as antient as the world," considered that the only region with which it could be compared was "*North America*; a land of *wood* and *iron*, but very few inhabitants," and like America a society in a "state of infancy." It has been seen that Buch likened the Finnish settlers in the Far North with the pioneers in the Ohio Valley. By the Skagerrak in southern Norway, Mary Wollstonecraft mused, "I could almost fancy myself in Nootka Sound, or on some of the islands on the north west coast of America."

Such comparisons often culminated in reassuring declarations of gratitude and loyalty to the travelers' own homelands. Acerbi ended his account by maintaining that travel should above all inspire the returning voyager to "teach and assure his countrymen, that they are the happiest people in the world." A poverty-stricken village in southern Finland prompted Clarke to the rhetorical outburst—doubtless calculated to satisfy his British readers—"Oh, *England!* decent abode of comfort and cleanliness, and decorum!—Oh blessed asylum of all that is worth having upon earth! Oh sanctuary of Religion, and of Liberty, for the whole civilized world!—It is only in viewing the state of other countries, that thy advantages can be truly estimated."[4]

"O wad some Pow'r the giftie gie us / To see oursels as others see us," to invoke Robert Burns's oft-quoted lines.[5] To study outsiders' views is to be made aware of how differently from insiders they may perceive a given situation. For Scandinavians and for those who have studied the late eighteenth century in the North from an inside perspective, myself included, the years between 1765 and 1815 were a time of dynamic, exciting, and often surprisingly rapid development in virtually all areas of life.[6] To outsiders, especially in the 1790s, this seems hardly to have been evident, viewed against a turbulent European background and in the light of their particular concerns.

Scandinavians could, on occasion, take exception to loosely grounded observations by foreign visitors, as in the case of Acerbi's Swedish traveling companion in the Far North, Anders Fredrik Skjöldebrand, who after falling out with Acerbi sharply criticized a number of the young Italian's statements. They could also make very different comparisons with other regions, as did the Dane Henrik Steffens. "In the most fertile districts the villages, as well as the small towns [in Denmark], have an altogether cheerful appearance," he wrote in his memoirs, "I was startled when I first saw a Brandenburg village, [one of] those dirty clusters of tumble-down mud huts. Certainly one may find on Sjælland relatively poor villages, but such crudity of construction. . . . dirt and filth . . . I had heretofore never known."[7]

Mary Wollstonecraft declared in 1795 that in Denmark there were "some respectable men of science, but few literary characters, and fewer artists. They want encouragement."[8] Taking the North as a whole, several of the travelers noted that the great era of Nordic natural philosophy was past, even as early as the mid-1760s. The visitors were, however, better prepared to judge the state of the sciences than of literature. It is true that, after the death of Frederik V of Denmark in 1766 and the assassination of Gustav III of Sweden in 1792, the literati no longer enjoyed the same royal largesse as before. But this by no means precluded a previously unprecedented blossoming of imaginative literature in the Nordic lands around the turn of the century, which still unfortunately remains largely unknown outside the region itself. The same was true in the realm of painting and sculpture in the era of Sergel, Martin, and Thorvaldsen.

Thus James offered sage advice when he reflected in 1813, "The just discrimination of national character is a task of infinite difficulty: it is denied to the native from prejudice, to the resident from too great familiarity, to the visitor from too little means of observation; it is imperious, therefore, on every one to contribute to whatsoever he may be able towards the illustration of such a point, and to leave it to those persons who may succeed better in forming abstract views on the subject."[9]

What the travelers sought out and described depended upon shifting criteria of value. The philosophic travelers of the 1760s, 1770s, and 1780s were, for the most part, comfortable with their world. In the rational, cosmopolitan spirit of the Enlightenment, they looked above all for the common attributes of an elite, cosmopolitan civilization with classical antecedents. Those who came during the following decades were, in large part, no longer at home in the times in which they lived. Their preromantic spirit yearned for an escape from the constraints of that very civilization to an imagined state of simplicity and virtue, especially by the turn of the century. Coming from lands torn by revolution and war and eroded, in their view, by dry rationalism and vain materialism, their ideal North was the projection of their *mal de siècle*.

The values and viewpoints of this complex transitional period cannot meanwhile be neatly separated out. The travel accounts show the authors' own ambiguities between enlightened rationalism, which resulted in realistic and often critical observation of actual, specific details, and romantic idealization, which led to characteristically positive generalizations. But this tension also illustrates the literary travelers' appraisal of what the reading public expected. By the turn of the century, travel literature had become a largely, if not a predominantly, romantic genre of an escapist nature. Thus the public wanted picturesque or sentimental idealization. It also welcomed a measure of implied rebuke—albeit only in generalized terms—to their own overrefined civilization. This not withstanding, they also craved ultimate reassurance that, for all its faults, home was best after all.[10]

The authors' preconceptions and prejudices largely explain variations in their interest in and sympathy toward the different Nordic lands. It should now be apparent that Denmark fared least well in this regard, which calls for some examination. Before entering more deeply into this matter, it might be suggested that much of the explanation is provided by Clarke, who candidly admitted that his predilection for the Swedes was based perhaps on the fact that "they so strongly resemble *Englishmen* in all they do and say."[11] He had felt much the same about the Norwegians. Others, too, imply similar preferences for those they perceived to be most like themselves.

The duchies of Schleswig and Holstein seem to have provided a commendable example of a region whose resources were effectively exploited to provide comfortably for the needs of a numerous and industrious population. Denmark, although a civilized European country, was not yet "civilized" enough to meet the same rational, utilitarian criteria, yet to the preromantic mind it was too civilized, too close to the corrupted continental European pattern. Norway and Sweden, meanwhile, were moving ahead on the road to progress—while still preserving much of their unspoiled, Old Nordic simplicity. Iceland, while offering little to recommend itself to the enlightened philosopher, held that much more fascination for the romantic imagination. Denmark thus largely failed to appeal to either camp.

The travel accounts, meanwhile, make clear how profoundly European— and particularly British—opinion reacted against the brutal treatment of Denmark's Queen Caroline Mathilde, the sister of George III, by the cabal that seized power from her lover, Johann Friedrich Struensee, in 1772.[12] The almost routine detailed accounts of this lurid episode and exclamations of high-minded indignation over it show well what the literary travelers knew their readers expected of them and the depth of feeling that lay behind it.

As damaging as the fate of the unfortunate queen was to Denmark's international reputation, its impact built in turn upon underlying prejudices extending back over the previous century. The establishment in Denmark of Europe's (theoretically) most absolute monarchy after 1660 had aroused profound misgivings. This reaction received its most influential expression in *An Account of Denmark as It Was in the Year 1692*, by Robert Molesworth, after his return from Copenhagen, where he had served as English minister under William III. A staunch Whig supporter of the Glorious Revolution of 1688 and of John Locke's principles of government, the Irish-born Molesworth was bitterly critical of Danish royal absolutism. This established him as an "important forerunner of 18th century ideas," according to Thor J. Beck, who holds that practically every French work touching upon Danish history during the first half of the century, including those of Voltaire and Montesquieu, cited Molesworth as a valuable source. This influence would seem evident in the case of Paul Henri Mallet, whose *Introduction à l'histoire de Dannemarc* (1755) and *Monumens de la mythologie* (1756) had aroused the preromantic fascination with the ancient North. A Swiss republican strongly influenced by Montesquieu, Mallet was engaged by the Danish crown to counteract Molesworth's still powerful influence and rehabilitate Denmark in European opinion. Mallet, while accepting this commission, took refuge by concentrating his attention upon the allegedly free society of Nordic antiquity, which in actuality was a veiled rebuke to the absolutism he was charged with justifying. Molesworth remained unexorcised and was cited as an authority during our period by various of the visitors to the North.[13]

This in turn reinforced the venerable tradition of the North as the ancient home of European liberty, which made Denmark's royal despotism appear a rank betrayal of its historic heritage. This idea crops up repeatedly in the travelers' accounts, most notably in Swinton's, published in 1792:

> In speaking of the character of the modern Danes, it is necessary to consider their ancient and present situation, to prevent drawing an unjust likeness from a figure of which little more than the skeleton remains. They were formerly free; — they are now slaves. That nation which first pulled down Roman tyranny, and spread the flame of liberty throughout Europe, now behold every other European nation free, or attempting to be free; while they, driven back into their northern provinces, are again deprived of the natural as well as the political sun. That flame was as suddenly extinguished as it was raised.

Still, Swinton wrote, "The modern Danes have not forgot their former name; and the recollection occasions sullen pride, or, frequently, despondency, as the various tempers of men receive the impression." They had "transferred their liberties from the Nobility to the Sovereign." Now, however, "revolutions are kindling over Europe," and the monarch would do well to restore to the Danes their lost liberty "with a good grace, before the period arrive when he must do it with a bad one. The world at last turns wise, and will no longer submit to be ruled by one, nor by one thousand tyrants, which was frequently the only choice left to a nation." Although later travelers, such as Malthus, Wollstonecraft, and Carr, disillusioned with the French Revolution, were prepared to credit the Danish crown's benevolence, it was clearly in spite of, rather than because of, its absolutism.[14] The Swedish monarchy, with its strong constitutional and parliamentary traditions, was, meanwhile, in keeping both with the philosophy of Montesquieu and William Blackstone and with the venerable tradition of "Gothic" liberty.

Finally, it must be recalled that Great Britain was at war with Denmark from 1807 to 1814, which did nothing to assuage prejudices against its form of government and effectively barred Britons from the Danish domains—save only the exposed Atlantic islands—during those years.[15] The Swedish kingdom, as Britain's ally and Napoleon's foe during most of that time, naturally fared better in both respects.

Although the romantic vision of a Northern Arcadia was beclouded after the Scandinavian kingdoms' precipitation into the Napoleonic maelstrom, the images of natural grandeur, simplicity, and sincerity it had created would remain long-lived, to a remarkable degree down to our own time. In 1848, during a new era of revolution and turmoil, Piotr Aleksandrovich Pletnev, rector of the University of St. Petersburg, wrote to a friend, the Finnish poet Johan Runeberg:

> What could be more pleasant and useful than to travel in a country where the beauty of Nature is in harmony with the customs and civilisation of the people. Switzerland had something similar earlier. But now natural beauty has been spoilt by the horror stories of the Revolution. Yes, I am ready to believe that there is only one country in the world for you and me in which we can find our idea of happiness, and that is Finland. If I mastered the two languages spoken there, I would not hesitate to adopt that country as my fatherland.

"To an American," Charles Loring Brace wrote in 1857, "a visit to the home of the old Northmen is a visit back to his forefather's house. A thousand signs tell him he is at the cradle of the race which leads modern enterprise and whose Viking power in both hemispheres has not ceased to be felt."[16]

The visits of foreigners to Scandinavia and their accounts between 1765 and 1815 did not fail to have an impact upon the region they visited. In part this would seem to have meant some degree of corruption of its innocence by outside influences and alien practices—including those introduced by foreign travelers—particularly in more exposed areas, as various of the travelers themselves feared.

There were, however, some more concrete cases. Miranda's diary indicates that he himself played an important role in bringing about badly needed penal reforms in Denmark. In the sphere of international relations, Britain's consistent interest in the region and strong support for Sweden during the Napoleonic Wars may have reflected something more than simply strategic considerations. Britain's benevolent, de facto protectorate over Iceland and the Færø Islands during its conflict with Denmark would appear to offer a particularly apt case in point. Madame de Staël, widow of a onetime Swedish ambassador to Paris, whose testimony on her only visit to his country is sadly lacking, in 1813 intrigued vigorously in Stockholm to sway Swedish opinion in favor of an alliance with Russia and to place the new Swedish Crown Prince Carl Johan—the former Napoleonic Marshal Bernadotte—on the throne of France. Perhaps most notably the great upsurge of sympathy for Norway during its brief attempt in 1814 to assert its independence, above all in Great Britain, was well prepared by decades of highly sympathetic travel accounts. Even though the British government was by then committed to transferring Norway to the Swedish crown, Crown Prince Carl Johan was prepared to accept a purely dynastic union, in which it preserved its own, previously drafted Eidsvold constitution, government, and laws.[17]

The European discovery of Nordic antiquity and the vogue for travel to the North that it so strongly promoted, meanwhile, opened the eyes of the Scandinavians themselves to the glories of their past. It was largely through the influence of Mallet, of the German Friedrich Gottlieb Klopstock—who likewise lived several years in Copenhagen—and of the Schleswig German H. W. Gerstenberg that Johannes Ewald and his successors in Denmark took up Old Norse themes in their poetry. From Denmark, such influences spread to Sweden and Norway. Similarly, Scandinavians were inspired to look at their own homelands with new eyes. The poet, later bishop, Frans Mikael Franzén prefaced a travel account he wrote of his native Finland in 1800: "I was strengthened all the more in my resolve, as I became aware that it has nowadays become a baroque mode for wealthy and distinguished foreigners, especially for Englishmen, whose whims we are long familiar with, to see the North, and there even Lapland and Finland."

Küttner was surprised in 1796 to find so little material on Sweden in the Copenhagen bookstores, causing him to "remark, how very little connection there is between the neighbouring kingdoms of Denmark and Sweden." That Scandinavians were still, a decade later, surprisingly ignorant of each others' countries is attested by a review from 1817 of the Dane Christian Molbech's "Breve fra Sverrige" (Letters from Sweden) in *Dansk Litteratur-Tidende*: "The ideas we had of that land were received, so to say, second-hand and we saw as though through foreign spectacles, since we did not have any guides to rely upon other than the travel accounts of Germans, Frenchmen, Italians, and Englishmen. The standpoints from which these foreign authors regard land and folk, customs and usages, art and literature, are either national or cosmopolitan, but not Scandinavian." Swinton complained in 1788 that "Odin's domains are still divided among brothers; and these brothers still divided against themselves." Surely foreign views of the region as reflected in the travel literature played no small part in the creation of a new sense of a common "Scandinavian" heritage and destiny, despite the tragic conflicts of this period.[18]

In studying the reactions of the various literary travelers to the Nordic lands, not only their views but their personalities emerge in the reader's mind. Thus, before taking leave of them, it may be of interest to learn something of their later lives. Beckmann, Coxe, Malthus, Carr, Buch, and Thomson continued to enjoy comfortable, successful, and in some cases very prominent careers as scholars or publicists. Vittorio Alfieri, who claimed to have been inspired to write verse in Sweden but not yet to have known how, would become Italy's foremost preromantic poet, an outspoken enemy of the French invaders of his homeland, and the lover of the countess of Albany, consort of the late Charles Stuart, the Young Pretender. Although Andrew Swinton arrived in St. Petersburg just in time for the funeral of his influential kinsman, Admiral Samuel Greig, his account suggests that he nonetheless obtained some appointment in Russia. John Thomas Stanley spent the rest of his long life on his lavish estate at Alderley, fondly cultivating memories of remote Iceland. His companion, James Wright, died in India in 1794. Mary Wollstonecraft, married the philosopher William Godwin but died in 1797, after giving birth to the future Mary Shelley, author of *Frankenstein*. Henry Brougham, eventually Lord Brougham, and William Windham went on to enjoy prominent political and ministerial careers at Westminster and Whitehall. Francisco de Miranda, after further wanderings, would become a general in the French revolutionary army before leading the first uprising against Spanish rule in his native South America in 1812 and dying in a Spanish prison four years later.

Edward Daniel Clarke and his companions, after further extensive travels in Russia and the Near East, returned to England with a vast collection of artifacts, much of which, including a large Greek statue, was shipwrecked off Beachy Head in the English Channel—practically within sight of the home of his companion Cripps's father, who managed to salvage most of the imperiled treasures. Clarke was appointed Cambridge University's first professor of geology but struggled with penury as he turned out volume after volume of his travels until his death in 1818, before the last one appeared. Aaron Burr soon returned to the United States and his beloved daughter Theodosia. John Thomas James, after taking holy orders and becoming the Anglican bishop of Calcutta, died on an expedition to the South China Sea in 1828. Giuseppe Acerbi eventually became a diplomat in Austrian service. Lady Sarah Lyttelton would serve as lady-in-waiting to Queen Victoria and as governess to her children. As for Jacques-Louis de La Tocnaye, he wrote in Norway that if he should ever again be fortunate enough to have a home of his own, he would never travel beyond the sight of its chimney, a promise he seems to have kept—at least until the completion of his account. As for the others, they have fallen into regrettable obscurity.[19]

It seems fitting to end this study with the concluding lines of Matthew Consett's account from 1786, which may speak both for his contemporary colleagues and for me.

> We have beheld human nature under her rudest appearance: we have seen her in a State very different from that which appears in cities or at courts, and have been enabled to draw conclusions from the varieties of Life. Pleasure too, has not been wanting in our Excursion. Prospects pleasing and romantic, the roaring cataract and high projecting cliff, the large and beautiful lakes, the mountains stretching to the clouds, and the extensive forests, like the shifting Scenes in a Theatre, appeared in an agreeable succession before our Eyes. And if we have sometimes encountered dangers, and been deprived of comforts, the Lesson we have been taught by this Excursion is, always to be contented with such Enjoyments as we actually possess.

END OF TOUR[20]

Notes
Select Bibliography
Index

Notes

Introduction: Travel and Travel Literature in the Eighteenth Century

1. See Sverker Sörlin, "Scientific Travel — the Linnean Tradition," in *Science in Sweden: The Royal Swedish Academy of Sciences, 1739–1989*, ed. Tore Frängsmyr (Canton, Mass., 1989), 96–123; Erik Pontoppidan, *The Natural History of Norway*, 2 vols. (London, 1755), and *Den danske Atlas*, 7 vols. (Copenhagen, 1763–81); Ludvig Holberg, *Memoirer*, ed. F. J. Billeskov Jansen (Copenhagen, 1943), first published in Latin in 1728, 1737, and 1743, in an anonymous Danish trans. from 1755, plus a posthumous epistle in Danish from 1754, also *Memoirs of Lewis Holberg, Written by Himself in Latin and Now First Translated into English* (London, 1827); Jens Baggesen, *Labyrinten*, ed. L. L. Albertsen (Copenhagen, 1976), first published in Copenhagen, 1792–93; Frans Mikael Franzén, *Resedagbok 1795–1796*, ed. Anders Hernmarck (Stockholm, 1977); [Adam Oehlenschläger,] *Oehlenschlägers Levnet, fortalt af ham selv*, 2 vols. (Copenhagen, 1850), also Oehlenschläger, *Meine Lebenserinnerungen*, 4 vols. (Leipzig, 1850); Erik Gustaf Geijer, *Minnen. Utdrag ur bref och dagböcker* (Uppsala, 1834), also trans. in part by E. Sprigge and C. Napier as *Impressions of England, 1809–1810* (London, 1932).

2. Joseph Acerbi, *Travels through Sweden, Finland, and Lapland to the North Cape in the Years 1798 and 1799*, 2 vols. (London, 1802), I:vii, x.

3. See Geoffrey Treese, *The Grand Tour* (London, 1967); Christopher Hibbert, *The Grand Tour* (London, 1987). For an example, see H. Arnold Barton, *Count Hans Axel von Fersen: Aristocrat in an Age of Revolution* (Boston, 1975), ch. 1.

4. [Nathanael Wraxall, Jr.], *Cursory Remarks Made on a Tour through Some of the Northern Parts of Europe, Particularly Copenhagen, Stockholm, and Petersburgh* (London, 1775), 38–39.

5. William Combe, *The Tour of Dr. Syntax in Search of the Picturesque* (New York, 1903), 4 (original, London, 1812); [Henry Holland,] *The Icelandic Journal of Henry Holland*, ed. Andrew Wawn. Issued by the Hakluyt Society, 2d. ser., 168 (London, 1987), editor's introduction, 36–37.

6. Acerbi, *Travels*, I:x. See Edward Daniel Clarke, *Travels in Various Countries of Europe, Asia, and Africa*, 6 vols. (London, 1810–23), V:1–2; Jacques-Louis de Bourgrenet de La Tocnaye, *Promenade d'un français en Suède et en Norvège*, 2 vols. (Brunswick, 1801), I:1–2, II:137; Åke Davidsson, *Med utländska resenärer i svenska bibliotek* (Stockholm, 1975), 7–8.

7. See, for example, Charles L. Batten, Jr., *Pleasurable Instruction: Form and Convention in Eighteenth-Century Travel Literature* (Berkeley, 1978); Barbara M. Stafford, *Voyage into Substance: Art, Science, and the Illustrated Travel Account, 1760–1840* (Cambridge, Mass., 1984); Eric Leed, *The Mind of the Traveller* (New York, 1991); James

Buzard, *The Beaten Track: European Tourism, Literature, and the Ways to Culture, 1800–1918* (New York, 1993). A basic bibliography of travel accounts is Edward Godfrey Cox, *A Reference Guide to the Literature of Travel*, 3 vols. (Seattle, 1935–46).

8. The most useful Scandinavian bibliography is Samuel E. Bring, *Itineraria Svecana. Bibliografisk förteckning över resor i Sverige fram till 1950* (Stockholm, 1954), which is arranged chronologically. Hjalmar Pettersen, *Utlændingers Reiser i Norge*, Universitets-Bibliothekets Aarbog for 1895 (Christiania, 1897), and Eiler H. Schiøtz, *Utenlendingers reiser i Norge. En bibliografi* (Oslo, 1970), while indispensable, are rather more difficult to use, being organized alphabetically. See also Yrjö Hirn, "Finland i den utländska reselitteraturen under slutet av sjuttonhundratalet," *Skrifter utgivna av Svenska litteratursällskapet i Finland*, 36: *Förhandlingar och uppsatser*, 11 (1898): 149–74. Similar bibliographies are lacking for Denmark and Iceland, but the above mentioned are useful for them as well.

9. See Arvid Julius, *Sverige med främlingsögon. Utdrag ur utländska resenärers skildringar före 1800* (Stockholm, 1930); Carl Huitfeldt, *Norge i andres øine. Utdrag av utenlandske reisebeskrivelser gjennem 2000 år* (Oslo, 1932); see also Henrik Sandblad's valuable study, "Edward D. Clarke och Giuseppe Acerbi, upptäcktsresande i Norden 1798–1800," *Lychnos* (1979–80): 155–205. Brief discussions of some foreigners' observations in Sweden during this period are provided by Carl Grimberg, *Svenska folkets underbara öden*, ed. A. Åberg, 10 vols. (rev. ed., Stockholm, 1959–63; first published 1913–24), VIII:253–69, 473–79; and Gustaf Utterström, *Jordbrukets arbetare. Levnadsvillkor och arbetsliv på landsbygden från frihetstiden till mitten av 1800-talet*, 2 vols. (Stockholm, 1957), I:81–96.

10. Bring, *Itineraria Svecana*, 81–156. It should be noted that, in a few cases, attribution of nationality is somewhat uncertain.

11. This includes German subjects of the Scandinavian monarchies, such as the Holsteiners Johann Christian Fabricius, who wrote *Reise durch Norwegen* (Hamburg, 1779), and August Hennings, the anonymous author of *Reise eines englischen Geistlichen durch Schweden* (Berlin, 1784), or the Swedish Pomeranians Ernst Moritz Arndt, author of *Reise durch Schweden im Jahre 1804*, 4 vols. (Berlin, 1805–6), and Friedrich Rühs, *Finnland und seine Bewohner* (Leipzig, 1809), the latter a descriptive work rather than a travel account per se. Note also, for example, Johann Wilhelm Schmidt, *Reise durch einige schwedische Provinzen* (Hamburg, 1801), by a corrector of the German school in Stockholm; Jean Pierre Guillaume Catteau-Calleville, *Voyage en Allemagne et en Suède*, 3 vols. (Paris, 1810), by a longtime pastor of the French Reformed congregation in Stockholm.

1. Travelers and Travel in the North, 1765–1815

1. See C. Bullo, *Il viaggio di M. Piero Querini e le relazioni della repubblica Veneta colla Svezia* (Venezia, 1881); Robert Kerr, "Voyage and Travels of Pietro Querini into Norway, in 1431," in *A General History and Collection of Voyages and Travels*, I (Edinburgh, 1811), 485–501; *Il viaggio settentrionale di Francesco Negri, nuovamente publicato*

à cura di Carlo Gargiolli (Bologna, 1883); Ludvig Daae, "Italieneren Francesco Negris Reise i Norge 1664–1665," *Historisk Tidskrift* (Norw.), 2d. ser., 6 (1887): 85–158; Charles Ogier, *Caroli Ogerii Ephemerides, sive iter danicum, suecicum, polonicum* (Paris, 1656), and Sigurd Hallberg, trans. and ed., *Från Sveriges storhetstid. Franske legationssekreteraren Charles Ogiers dagbok under ambassaden i Sverige 1634–1635* (Stockholm, 1914); Sir Bulstrode Whitelocke, *Account of His Embassy to Sweden, Deliver'd to the Parliament in the Year 1654* (London, 1714), and *A Journal of the Swedish Embassy in the Years 1653 and 1654*, ed. H. Reeve (rev. ed., London, 1855); Carl Magnus Stenbock, *Sverige under år 1674* [F. Magalotti's account] (Stockholm, 1912); Robert Molesworth, *An Account of Denmark as It Was in the Year 1692* (London, 1694); Pierre Louis Moreau de Maupertuis, *Rélation d'un Voyage fait dans la Lapponie septentrionale* (Berlin, 1747).

2. Except where otherwise noted, information about these travelers derives from the standard biographical reference works, such as the *Dictionary of National Biography*, *Allgemeine deutsche Biographie*, *Dictionnaire de Biographie française*, *Dizionario Biografico degli Italiani*, *Dictionary of American Biography*; from Bring, *Itineraria Svecana*; from editorial commentary in published accounts; and from internal evidence in the accounts themselves.

3. Johann Beckmann, *Schwedische Reise in den Jahren 1765–1766. Tagebuch*, ed. Th. Fries (Uppsala, 1911).

4. Vittorio Alfieri, *Memoirs*, ed. E. R. Vincent (London, 1961). See also Alfieri, *Vita di Vittorio Alfieri, scritta da esso con panegirico di Plinio a Trajano* (Milano, 1818).

5. Robert Wyndham Ketton-Cremer, *The Early Life and Letters of William Windham* (London, 1930).

6. Wraxall, *Cursory Remarks*.

7. William Coxe, *Travels into Poland, Russia, Sweden and Denmark*, 4th ed., 5 vols. (London, 1792). This celebrated work appeared in several editions, from 1784, and was translated into a number of languages. Three years earlier, Coxe had brought out his *Account of the Prisons and Hospitals in Russia, Sweden and Denmark* (London, 1781).

8. Matthew Consett, *A Tour through Sweden, Swedish-Lapland, Finland and Denmark* (Stockton, 1789). I have been unable to determine Consett's birth and death dates.

9. [Francisco de Miranda,] *Miranda i Sverige och Norge 1787. General Francisco de Mirandas dagbok från hans resa september–december 1787*, trans. and ed. Stig Rydén (Stockholm, 1950); [Francisco de Miranda,] *Miranda i Danmark. Francisco de Miranda's danske rejsedagbog 1787–1788*, trans. and ed. Haarvard Rostrup (Copenhagen, 1987). The present definitive edition of the Spanish original is Josefina Rodriguez de Alonso, ed., *Colombeia* (1978–), VI: *El viajero ilustrado 1787–1788* (Caracas, 1983).

10. Andrew Swinton, *Travels into Norway, Denmark and Russia in the Years 1788, 1789, 1790 and 1791* (London, 1792). I have been unable to determine his birth and death dates. Despite his title, he did not actually visit Norway on this occasion.

11. Alphonse Fortia de Piles, *Travels in Sweden*, in *A General Collection of the Best and Most Interesting Voyages and Travels in All Parts of the World*, ed. John Pinkerton, VI (London, 1809), 373–569. See also Fortia, *Voyage de deux français en Allemagne, Dane-*

marck, Suède, Russie et Pologne, fait en 1790–1792, 5 vols. (Paris, 1796). [Pierre Marie] Louis [de] Boisgelin [de Kerdu], *Travels through Denmark and Sweden*, 2 vols. (London, 1810), esp. I, pt. 1, v.

12. Mary Wollstonecraft, *Letters Written during a Short Residence in Sweden, Norway and Denmark* (London, 1796). I use the facsimile edition, ed. and introduction by Sylvia Norman (Fontwell, 1970). See also the edition brought out by C. Poston (Lincoln, Nebr., 1976).

13. Christian Ludwig Lenz, *Bemerkungen auf Reisen in Dänemark, Schweden und Frankreich*, 2 vols. (Gotha, 1800–1801). His account had previously been serialized in part in the periodical *Der neue teutsche Merkur*, vols. 1–3 (1797–98).

14. Carl Gottlob Küttner, *Reise durch Deutschland, Dänemark, Schweden, Norwegen und einen Theil von Italien, in den Jahren 1797, 1798, 1799*, 4 vols. (Leipzig, 1801). My references are to the English translation, *Travels through Denmark, Sweden, Austria and Part of Italy in 1798 & 1799* (London, 1805).

15. Acerbi, *Travels*. See Sandblad, "Edward D. Clarke och Giuseppe Acerbi." Acerbi traveled in Lapland with a Swedish colonel, Anders Fredrik Skjöldebrand, who wrote his own account, *Voyage pittoresque au Cap Nord* (Stockholm, 1801–2), in English, *A Picturesque Journey to the North Cape* (London, 1813), and who criticized Acerbi's account in his *Premier supplément du voyage pittoresque à Cap Nord, contenant des remarques sur le premier cahier de cet ouvrage et sur le voyage de Mr. Joseph Acerbi* (Stockholm, 1802).

16. La Tocnaye, *Promenade*. This valuable work, printed for some two hundred subscribers, both Scandinavian and foreign (who are listed at the beginning of vol. I), is naturally very difficult to obtain; I was unable to locate a single copy of vol. II using interlibrary loan in North America. The part of vol. II dealing with Norway has meanwhile come out in a Norwegian translation; see La Tocnaye, *En franskmann i Norge i 1799*, trans. Axel Amlie (Oslo, 1980).

17. [Henry Peter Brougham,] *The Life and Times of Henry, Lord Brougham. Written by Himself*, 3 vols. (London, 1871), I:88–160.

18. [Robert Malthus,] *The Travel Diaries of Thomas Robert Malthus*, ed. Patricia James (Cambridge, 1966). The preserved diaries deal mainly with Norway. It is known that, on his subsequent travels in Sweden, Malthus kept a diary, which he eventually lent to Edward Daniel Clarke, after which regrettably it has not been found (see P. James's introduction).

19. Clarke, *Travels*, esp. VI:i–iv. Clarke's accounts of other countries had appeared in earlier editions, from 1810. Various later editions and foreign translations also came out. On Clarke and his traveling companions, see Malthus, *Travel Diaries*, 1–23. See also William Otter, *The Life and Remains of the Rev. Edward Daniel Clarke, LL.D.* (London, 1824); this volume was sold by subscription to provide assistance to Clarke's family (notice from "friends of the deceased," in Clarke, *Travels*, VI:n.p.; see also Sandblad, "Edward D. Clarke och Giuseppi Acerbi").

20. John Carr, *A Northern Summer; or, Travels round the Baltic through Denmark, Sweden, Russia, Prussia, and Part of Germany in the Year 1804* (London, 1805). Thomas

Thomson in 1812 (*Travels in Sweden during the Autumn of 1812* [London, 1813]), for instance, would appear to have been much influenced by Carr, to say nothing of others after 1815.

21. Leopold von Buch, *Reise durch Norwegen und Lappland*, 2 vols. (Berlin, 1810). My references are to the English edition, *Travels through Norway and Lapland during the Years 1806, 1807 and 1808*, trans. John Black (London, 1813). Several editions and translations appeared.

22. Robert Ker Porter, *Travelling Sketches in Russia and Sweden during the Years 1805, 1806, 1807, 1808*, 2 vols. (London, 1809).

23. James Macdonald, *Travels through Denmark and Part of Sweden, during the Winter and Spring of the Year 1809*, 2d ed. (London, 1810). The first edition came out in two volumes in London in 1809, but, the editor of the abridged second edition explains (p. 88), as the additional general information on the "social and commercial intercourse of the Swedes and Danes" provides no facts beyond those found in "the excellent works of sir John Carr and Kuttner," he chose to omit this material. I have been unable to determine Macdonald's birth and death dates.

24. Aaron Burr, *The Private Journal during His Residence of Four Years in Europe*, ed. M. L. Davis, 2 vols. (New York, 1838).

25. Thomson, *Travels*.

26. [Sarah Lyttelton,] *Correspondence of Sarah Spencer, Lady Lyttelton, 1787–1870*, ed. Mrs. Hugh Wyndham (London, 1912).

27. John Thomas James, *Journal of a Tour in Germany, Sweden, Russia, and Poland during the Years 1813 and 1814* (London, 1816). See also his *Views in Russia, Sweden, Poland, and Germany* (London, 1826), published in a very limited edition with hand-colored lithographs. In Miranda, *Miranda i Sverige och Norge*, Rydén (ed.) reproduces a number of James's pen and wash drawings from Sweden, preserved in the Gothenburg Art Museum.

28. Carl Linnæus's works were published as *Iter Lapponicum* (1732) and *Iter Dalicarlicum* (1734); see [Carl Linnæus,] *Linné i Lappland*, ed. Bertil Gullander (Stockholm, 1969); Erik Pontoppidan's as *Det første Forsøg paa Norges naturlige Historie*, 2 vols. (Copenhagen, 1752), in English, *Natural History*. See also Clarke, *Travels*, V:675.

29. See Batten, *Pleasurable Instruction*, 59–61; Johann Georg Canzler, *Mémoires pour servir à la conoissance des affaires politiques et économiques du Royaume de Suède, jusqu'à la fin de la 1775ᵐᵉ année*, 2 vols. (London, 1776), in German, 1778; John Williams, *The Rise, Progress and Present State of the Northern Governments; viz. the United Provinces, Denmark, Sweden, Russia and Poland*, 2 vols. (London, 1777), also in French and German translations. See also Anton Friedrich Büsching, *Neue Erdebeschreibung*, 5 vols. (Hamburg, 1767–1771); Joseph Marshall, *Travels through Holland, Flanders, Germany, Denmark, Sweden, Lapland, Russia, the Ukraine and Poland, in the Years 1768, 1769, and 1770*, 3 vols. (London, 1772).

30. Coxe, *Travels*, IV:328; Consett, *Tour*, 3; Miranda, *Miranda i Sverige och Norge*, 45, 96; Swinton, *Travels*, v–vi; Lenz, *Bemerkungen*, I:129; Küttner, *Travels*, 67, 71; Acerbi, *Travels*, I:4–5; Malthus, *Travel Diaries*, 25; Boisgelin, *Travels*, I, pt. 2, iii–iv, II:vii–xx.

31. La Tocnaye, *Promenade*, II:138; Pinkerton, ed., *General Collection*, esp. vol. I; Susie I. Tucker, "Scandinavica for the Eighteenth-Century Reader," *Saga-Book of the Viking Society for Northern Research* 16 (1963–64): 233–47.

32. Clarke, *Travels*, V:498–508, 680, VI:222–23; Brougham, *Life and Times*, I:137, 159.

33. Swinton, *Travels*, 1–2; Acerbi, *Travels*, I:x.

34. Wollstonecraft, *Letters*, 235; Buch, *Travels*, 8, 409–58, passim, esp. 458; Macdonald, *Travels*, 5–7, 12, 19; Miranda, *Miranda i Danmark*, 195; Otter, *Life and Remains*, 372, 374–76.

35. Malthus, *Travel Diaries*, 82, 148; Clarke, *Travels*, V:82; Otter, *Life and Remains*, 348, 350, 370; Consett, *Tour*, 14–15, 137; Burr, *Private Journal*, I:312; Lenz, *Bemerkungen*, I:145, 148–49; La Tocnaye, *Promenade*, I:46–47, 228–29. See also Ketton-Cremer, *Windham*, 123; Macdonald, *Travels*, 55, 81; Brougham, *Life and Times*, I:104; Küttner, *Travels*, 47; Wraxall, *Cursory Remarks*, 99; Compare Utterström, *Jordbrukets arbetare*, I:90–92.

36. Acerbi, *Travels*, I:8; Küttner, *Travels*, 41–42, 47; Lenz, *Bemerkungen*, I:147; Macdonald, *Travels*, 82; La Tocnaye, *Promenade*, I:233; Thomson, *Travels*, 19, 246.

37. Ketton-Cremer, *Windham*, 103–21; La Tocnaye, *Promenade*, II:179–84, 211–20. I am unsure what kind of "miles" La Tocnaye intended in this passage.

38. La Tocnaye, *Promenade*, I:82; Alfieri, *Memoirs*, 99; Miranda, *Miranda i Sverige och Norge*, 166; Clarke, *Travels*, V:452, VI:320, 334–35; Otter, *Life and Remains*, 379, 381; Coxe, *Travels*, IV:18.

39. La Tocnaye, *Promenade*, I:71, II:89. Again, I am uncertain what type of "miles" La Tocnaye meant.

40. Wraxall, *Cursory Remarks*, 35, 89; Lenz, *Bemerkungen*, I:150–52. See also Clarke, *Travels*, V:142–43; Burr, *Private Journal*, I:312.

41. Acerbi, *Travels*, I:4–6, 364; Wraxall, *Cursory Remarks*, 93, 106–7; Clarke, *Travels*, VI:269, 377–78; Küttner, *Travels*, 56, 66; Miranda, *Miranda i Sverige och Norge*, 57, 69, 72, 74, 75, 165, 251, 252; Lyttelton, *Correspondence*, 143, 148, 149, 157.

42. Clarke, *Travels*, V:129; Acerbi, *Travels*, I:264–66, 275; Wraxall, *Cursory Remarks*, 86–87.

43. Lyttelton, *Correspondence*, 147; Clarke, *Travels*, V:502; Acerbi, *Travels*, II:101.

2. The Public Visage: Culture, State, and Polite Society

1. H. Arnold Barton, *Scandinavia in the Revolutionary Era, 1760–1815* (Minneapolis, 1986), 101.

2. Acerbi, *Travels*, I:6.

3. Coxe, *Travels*, V:126–27; Boisgelin, *Travels*, I, pt. 2, 10–12; Wollstonecraft, *Letters*, 197–99; Clarke, *Travels*, V:63; Küttner, *Travels*, 18–20; Brougham, *Life and Times*, I:93–94. See also Swinton, *Travels*, 25; Miranda, *Miranda i Danmark*, 140n.; Malthus, *Travel Diaries*, 54.

4. Wraxall, *Cursory Remarks*, 105, 123–24; Coxe, *Travels*, IV:31; Boisgelin, *Travels*, II:47–48; Brougham, *Life and Times*, I:110–11; James, *Journal*, 112; Miranda, *Miranda*

i Sverige och Norge, 94. See also Küttner, *Travels*, 77–83; Clarke, *Travels*, V:150–51n., VI:264–65; Buch, *Travels*, 403; Porter, *Travelling Sketches*, II:126.

5. Clarke, *Travels*, VI:264; James, *Journal*, 113–14; Küttner, *Travels*, 80–81. See also Consett, *Tour*, 19; Boisgelin, *Travels*, II:47–48; Porter, *Travelling Sketches*, II:119.

6. Clarke, *Travels*, V:742; Brougham, *Life and Times*, I:155; Wollstonecraft, *Letters*, 164. The populations of Norwegian towns given here are from 1801 and derive from Buch, *Travels*, appendix (n.p.).

7. La Tocnaye, *Promenade*, II:185–207; Yves-Joseph de Kerguélen-Trémarec, *Relation of a Voyage in the North Sea*, in Pinkerton, ed., *General Collection*, I:765; French original, *Rélation d'un voyage dans la mer du Nord, aux Côtes d'Islande, de Grönlande, de Ferro, de Schettland, des Orcades & de Norwège; fait en 1767 & 1768* (Amsterdam, 1772); Clarke, *Travels*, VI:2. See also Huitfeldt, *Norge i andres øine*, 87–90; Ketton-Cremer, *Windham*, 97–102. For a detailed description of Bergen from a slightly later period, see Wilhelm von Reinöhl, "Beschreibung der Stadt Bergen in Norwegen und ihrer Umgebung," *Neue Allgemeine Ephemeriden*, 5 (Weimar, 1819): 17–58; in Danish translation, "Om Staden Bergen i Norge," *Journal for Politik, Natur- og Menneskekundskab* 4 (Copenhagen, 1822): 148–64, 215–24.

8. Clarke, *Travels*, V:623–26, 663, 742; Buch, *Travels*, 109. See also La Tocnaye, *Promenade*, II:102.

9. Boisgelin, *Travels*, II:15; Küttner, *Travels*, 47–50; Acerbi, *Travels*, I:13–16; Brougham, *Life and Times*, I:145; Burr, *Private Journal*, I:290–92; James, *Journal*, 2; Thomson, *Travels*, 6–11; Anne-Marie Fällström, "Kontinentalblokaden och de sociala förhållandena i Göteborg," in *Historia kring Göteborg*, ed. Hans Anderson (Stockholm, 1967), 132–57.

10. Wraxall, *Cursory Remarks*, 194; Clarke, *Travels*, VI:407–31; see also Boisgelin, *Travels*, II:300.

11. Boisgelin, *Travels*, II:302–3; Clarke, *Travels*, VI:460–65.

12. Küttner, *Travels*, 12; Kerguélen-Trémarec, *Relation*, 765; Macdonald, *Travels*, 47; La Tocnaye, *Promenade*, II:192.

13. Clarke, *Travels*, VI:96–97. See also Burr, *Private Journal*, I:257; James, *Journal*, 114.

14. Miranda, *Miranda i Danmark*, 197; Küttner, *Travels*, 59–60, 75–76, 91; Burr, *Private Journal*, I:257; Clarke, *Travels*, V:519, VI:389–90; Buch, *Travels*, 213; Wraxall, *Cursory Remarks*, 95; James, *Journal*, 95.

15. Clarke, *Travels*, V:67.

16. Miranda, *Miranda i Danmark*. Most of this diary deals with Copenhagen and its environs.

17. Boisgelin, *Travels*, II:47, 56–58, 142–53; Küttner, *Travels*, 81, 83–84, 88; Thomson, *Travels*, 97; Porter, *Travelling Sketches*, II:118; Lyttelton, *Correspondence*, 148–49; Wraxall, *Cursory Remarks*, 118–19; Clarke, *Travels*, VI:265; La Tocnaye, *Promenade*, I:94.

18. Wraxall, *Cursory Remarks*, 27, 63, 123; Boisgelin, *Travels*, I, pt. 2, 22; Küttner, *Travels*, 19–20; Clarke, *Travels*, V:67; Miranda, *Miranda i Danmark*, 163. See also Coxe, *Travels*, V:127–29; Otter, *Life and Remains*, 347.

19. Coxe, *Travels*, IV:9–13; Miranda, *Miranda i Danmark*, 186; La Tocnaye, *Promenade*, II:273–74; Clarke, *Travels*, V:626, 663, VI:407; Thomson, *Travels*, 275–76.

20. See, for example, Wraxall, *Cursory Remarks*, 27–33, 58–62, 119–21; Miranda, *Miranda i Danmark*, 76–80, 83, 127, 146, 148, 171–72, 210; Boisgelin, *Travels*, I, pt. 2, 22–35, II:56–96; Brougham, *Life and Times*, I:112–13; Clarke, *Travels*, VI:23–24.

21. See Torben Holck Colding, Jan Danielsen, Erik Lassen, and Vagn Poulsen, *Akademiet og Guldalderen 1750–1850* (Copenhagen, 1972); Andreas Lindblom, *Sveriges konsthistoria* (Stockholm, 1947); Carl Laurin, Emil Hannover, and Jens Thiis, *Scandinavian Art* (New York, 1922).

22. Küttner, *Travels*, 89–90; Boisgelin, *Travels*, II:107–16, esp. 110; Miranda, *Miranda i Sverige och Norge*, 140, 267; Brougham, *Life and Times*, I:120–22. See also Gunnar Jungmarker, ed., *Svenska mästartecknare. Sergel, Martin, Ehrensvärd* (Stockholm, 1955).

23. Miranda, *Miranda i Sverige och Norge*, 40, *Miranda i Danmark*, 157, compare 61, 118; Boisgelin, *Travels*, II:65, 68; Brougham, *Life and Times*, I:115–16; Clarke, *Travels*, VI:224; La Tocnaye, *Promenade*, I:72–75; Burr, *Private Journal*, I:223; Porter, *Travelling Sketches*, II:121; James, *Journal*, 115, 158–59.

24. La Tocnaye, *Promenade*, I:257, II:200–201; Wollstonecraft, *Letters*, 32, 78; Clarke, *Travels*, V:67, 70, 72, VI:39–41; Acerbi, *Travels*, I:94–95; Malthus, *Travel Diaries*, 60; Boisgelin, *Travels*, I, pt. 2, 201–3.

25. For example, Miranda, *Miranda i Danmark*, 83, 126–27, 146, 172, 210; Brougham, *Life and Times*, I:92; Clarke, *Travels*, V:70, VI:41. Regarding Swedish collections, see Davidsson, *Utländska resenärer*.

26. Boisgelin, *Travels*, I, pt. 2, 203; Clarke, *Travels*, V:70, 518, VI:37, 231, 442–43.

27. Acerbi, *Travels*, I:117, 134. See also Boisgelin, *Travels*, II:71–76; Clarke, *Travels*, VI:244–51.

28. James, *Journal*, 125; Wraxall, *Cursory Remarks*, 58, 111, 117; Clarke, *Travels*, V:479–80.

29. [Fredrick Calvert, Lord Baltimore,] *Gaudia poetica, composed in Latin, English and French in the Year 1769* (n.p., n.d. [1769]), xxv, xxvii; Beckmann, *Schwedische Reise*; Coxe, *Travels*, IV:195–203; Clarke, *Travels*, V:171, 479–80. Clarke refers here, besides Linnæus, evidently to the astronomer and physicist Anders Celsius (1701–44), remembered for his thermometer; the chemist and mineralogist Johan Gottschalk Wallerius (1709–85); Axel Fredrik Cronstedt (1722–65), also a chemist and mineralogist; Torbern Bergman (1735–84), a zoologist, physicist, mineralogist, and chemist; Fredrik Hasselquist (1722–52), a naturalist who died in Smyrna; Johann Christian Fabricius (1745–1808), a Danish disciple of Linnæus; and the Danish classical philologist and archaeologist Georg Zoëga (1755–1809), who spent most of his career in Rome. Regarding the international reputation of Linnæus, his widely traveled "disciples," and Swedish natural science generally, see Sörlin, "Scientific Travel," 96–123.

30. Beckmann, *Schwedische Reise*, 123; Wraxall, *Cursory Remarks*, 167–71; Boisgelin, *Travels*, II:253; Acerbi, *Travels*, I:153; James, *Journal*, 182; Consett, *Tour*, 41; Clarke, *Travels*, VI:203.

31. Clarke, *Travels*, VI:173–80, 188, 200–6. See also Sven G. Svensson, "Studentens klang- och jubeltid. Från Juntan till skandinavism," in *Uppsalastudenten genom tiderna* (Uppsala, 1950), 73–194; Barton, *Count Hans Axel von Fersen*, 274–82.

32. Brougham, *Life and Times*, I:140–42; Acerbi, *Travels*, I:149–56.

33. Miranda, *Miranda i Sverige och Norge*, 274–75; Clarke, *Travels*, VI:420–21, 430–32, 453; Otter, *Life and Remains*, 382–83.

34. Miranda, *Miranda i Danmark*, 153, 210; Brougham, *Life and Times*, I:94; Buch, *Travels*, 6; Küttner, *Travels*, 62; Coxe, *Travels*, V:35.

35. See H. Arnold Barton, "Gustav III of Sweden and the Enlightenment," *Eighteenth-Century Studies* 6 (1972): 1–34, esp. 8–9; Barton, *Scandinavia*. See also Charles Francis Sheridan, *History of the Late Revolution in Sweden* (Dublin, 1778). Note Coxe's commentary on the Swedish constitution of 1772 and his appendix giving the document in English translation, *Travels*, IV:108–31, 395–421.

36. Boisgelin, *Travels*, I, pt. 1, 201, II:171–72; Miranda, *Miranda i Sverige och Norge*, 267; Clarke, *Travels*, V:87–88; Acerbi, *Travels*, I:87–88, 94–95, 101–2, 167, 172; La Tocnaye, *Promenade*, I:75, 106.

37. Alfieri, *Memoirs*, 97–98; Miranda, *Miranda i Danmark*, 60, 63, 163; Boisgelin, *Travels*, II:338–39n.; Wollstonecraft, *Letters*, 74, 74–77, 79, 81, 83–84. See also Barton, *Scandinavia*, 110–11; Malthus, *Travel Diaries*, 60, 173–74; La Tocnaye, *Promenade*, II:259–60; Carr, *Northern Summer*, 61.

38. Miranda, *Miranda i Danmark*, 57, 63; Wollstonecraft, *Letters*, 225–27; Louis Bobé, ed., *Johann Caspar Lavaters Rejse til Danmark i Sommaren 1793* (Copenhagen, 1898), passim (text in the original German).

39. See Georg Landberg, *Gustav III i eftervärldens dom* (Stockholm, 1945).

40. Wraxall, *Cursory Remarks*, 111, 117–18, 126–33.

41. Boisgelin, *Travels*, II:350–97, esp. 350, 352–53, 355, 367, 370; La Tocnaye, *Promenade*, I:147–51, 222; Carr, *Northern Summer*, 123. See H. Arnold Barton, "Gustav III of Sweden and the French Revolution," *Personhistorisk tidskrift* 89 (1993): 81–101, *Scandinavia*, ch. 8.

42. Brougham, *Life and Times*, I:122–25, 125.

43. Clarke, *Travels*, V:245, VI:198–99, 220. See Barton, *Scandinavia*, 43.

44. Acerbi, *Travels*, I:82–88, 94, 101–2.

45. Ibid., 88–91.

46. Clarke, *Travels*, VI:217–18, 220–21, 239; La Tocnaye, *Promenade*, I:109–10, 218; Küttner, *Travels*, 84–85; Acerbi, *Travels*, I:92–95.

47. Malthus, *Travel Diaries*, 63; Miranda, *Miranda i Danmark*, 161–62, *Miranda i Sverige och Norge*, 108, 113, 135, 140; Fortia, *Travels in Sweden*, 393; Boisgelin, *Travels*, II:50–51; Clarke, *Travels*, VI:221–23; Porter, *Travelling Sketches*, II:132–35. See also Bobé, ed., *Lavaters Rejse til Danmark*, 37–38.

48. Burr, *Private Journal*, I:229, 231; James, *Journal*, 47, 114; Thomson, *Travels*, 438–39. On Bernadotte's role in the defeat of Napoleon, see Barton, *Scandinavia*, 357.

49. Wraxall, *Cursory Remarks*, 7–9, 23, 39–55. Compare Coxe, *Travels*, V:112–15,

138–40; Miranda, *Miranda i Danmark*, 48, 52, 59, 61–62, 119; John F. West, ed., *The Journals of the Stanley Expedition to the Faroe Islands and Iceland in 1789*, 3 vols. (Tórshavn, 1970), I:213n.; Clarke, *Travels*, V:85; Carr, *Northern Summer*, 58, 86, 88; See also Barton, *Scandinavia*, 67–76, 90–91, 107–8; Edvard Holm, *Danmark-Norges Historie fra den Store nordiske Krigs Slutning til Rigernes Skilelse 1720–1814*, 7 vols. (Copenhagen, 1891–1912), V:235–45.

50. Wollstonecraft, *Letters*, 64, 79, 106, 116, 138; La Tocnaye, *Promenade*, I:276–77, II:110; Malthus, *Travel Diaries*, 85, 92, 119, 152, 173–75, 195–96; Clarke, *Travels*, V:666–67, VI:260, 431–32; Brougham, *Life and Times*, I:99, 120, 128, 140, 142. Note Clarke's comments on Acerbi's enthusiasm for French democratic ideals (*Travels*, V:499).

51. Burr, *Private Journal*, I:233; Clarke, *Travels*, VI:293–94, 426; James, *Journal*, 214, 217–18; Porter, *Travelling Sketches*, II:150.

52. La Tocnaye, *Promenade*, II:133–34; Clarke, *Travels*, V:627–28, 666–68, VI:27; James, *Journal*, 142–45, 196; Malthus, *Travel Diaries*, 106.

53. Brougham, *Life and Times*, I:96; Wollstonecraft, *Letters*, 159; Buch, *Travels*, 104. See also Barton, *Scandinavia*, 346–47.

54. Brougham, *Life and Times*, I:136; Boisgelin, *Travels*, II:169; Wollstonecraft, *Letters*, 193; Burr, *Private Journal*, I:246; La Tocnaye, *Promenade*, I:107.

55. Clarke, *Travels*, V:270; Coxe, *Prisons and Hospitals*, esp. 32–33; Boisgelin, *Travels*, II:124–27.

56. Coxe, *Prisons and Hospitals*, 46; Miranda, *Miranda i Danmark*, 98–112, 145, 186.

57. Miranda, *Miranda i Sverige och Norge*, 105–7, 124, 132–33, 225, *Miranda i Danmark*, 68–69, 129–31; Boisgelin, *Travels*, II:127–31; Clarke, *Travels*, V:636. See also Coxe, *Prisons and Hospitals*.

58. Swinton, *Travels*, 29–30, 112–14, 163–72, 182–84, 191–92; Consett, *Tour*, 11; Porter, *Travelling Sketches*, II:138–41; Boisgelin, *Travels*, II:181; Acerbi, *Travels*, I:57n.; Lenz, *Bemerkungen*, I:147.

59. Miranda, *Miranda i Danmark*, 139; Boisgelin, *Travels*, II:168–69; Acerbi, *Travels*, I:92–93; Clarke, *Travels*, VI:79.

60. Boisgelin, *Travels*, II:48–49.

61. Coxe, *Travels*, IV:37; Acerbi, *Travels*, I:70–74; Clarke, *Travels*, VI:220–23. See also Boisgelin, *Travels*, II:50–51, 53–55.

62. Boisgelin, *Travels*, II:164–65, 165n.

63. Lenz, *Bemerkungen*, I:49–50; Wollstonecraft, *Letters*, 108–10; Clarke, *Travels*, V:132; Coxe, *Travels*, IV:351; Thomson, *Travels*, 70–74.

64. Acerbi, *Travels*, I:276.

65. Wraxall, *Cursory Remarks*, 137, 177; Clarke, *Travels*, V:129–32, 505, 539, 541, 627, VI:2, 207–8; Macdonald, *Travels*, 24, 35–36; La Tocnaye, *Promenade*, II:63–64.

66. Boisgelin, *Travels*, II:49; Brougham, *Life and Times*, I:117–18; Porter, *Travelling Sketches*, II:120; Burr, *Private Journal*, I:237; Clarke, *Travels*, V:628–30. See also La Tocnaye, *Promenade*, I:87–88; Malthus, *Travel Diaries*, 163.

67. Boisgelin, *Travels*, II:5, 49; Acerbi, *Travels*, I:45; Clarke, *Travels*, V:505, 663–64; La Tocnaye, *Promenade*, II:193–95; Carr, *Northern Summer*, 138. See also Consett, *Tour*, 56–57; Thomson, *Travels*, 11–13.

68. Clarke, *Travels*, VI:13–24; La Tocnaye, *Promenade*, II:228, 231; Küttner, *Travels*, 61–62; Coxe, *Travels*, V:38–40. See also Miranda, *Miranda i Sverige och Norge*, 177, 181; Malthus, *Travel Diaries*, 91–92, 99, 104; Burr, *Private Journal*, I:299.

69. Wraxall, *Cursory Remarks*, 178; Boisgelin, *Travels*, II:70; Acerbi, *Travels*, I:66–67, 276; Clarke, *Travels*, V:518.

70. Wollstonecraft, *Letters*, 202.

71. Clarke, *Travels*, V:506–8, 627; Buch, *Travels*, 35, 286; Acerbi, *Travels*, I:268–69, 277–83, 364–66. Baron Carl Göran Silfverhielm (1754–1808) had aroused much excitement in Stockholm during the 1780s as a "magnetizer," especially in the occult circle around Duke Carl of Södermanland.

72. Miranda, *Miranda i Danmark*, 126, 207, *Miranda i Sverige och Norge*, 228; La Tocnaye, *Promenade*, I:77, II:58; Brougham, *Life and Times*, I:95, 118; Lyttelton, *Correspondence*, 149–54, 158–59, 165; Acerbi, *Travels*, I:67–69, 77; James, *Journal*, 140–41; Boisgelin, *Travels*, II:15, 46; Wollstonecraft, *Letters*, 21–24. See also Kerguélen-Trémarec, *Relation*, 765.

73. Miranda, *Miranda i Sverige och Norge*; Burr, *Private Journal*, for example, I:232–33. See Paul Britten Austin, *The Life and Songs of Carl Michael Bellman, Genius of the Swedish Rococo* (New York, 1967).

74. Miranda, *Miranda i Sverige och Norge*, passim; Acerbi, *Travels*, I:63–64; Porter, *Travelling Sketches*, II:136; Lyttelton, *Correspondence*, 149–50, 152, 153, 160, 165; Swinton, *Travels*, 79; Macdonald, *Travels*, 24–25; Burr, *Private Journal*, I:226, 231; Carr, *Northern Summer*, 148–49.

75. Kerguélen-Trémarec, *Relation*, 765; Brougham, *Life and Times*, I:122–23; Acerbi, *Travels*, 64–65; Consett, *Tour*, 24–25, 42–43; Miranda, *Miranda i Sverige och Norge*, 150.

76. La Tocnaye, *Promenade*, I:25–26, II:148, 194; Clarke, *Travels*, VI:30; Wollstonecraft, *Letters*, 39–40, 66, 100, 193–94, 202; Carr, *Northern Summer*, 44–45.

77. Wollstonecraft, *Letters*, 13; Clarke, *Travels*, VI:76. See also Barton, *Scandinavia*, 243–44.

3. Landscapes and the Material Base

1. See Sandblad, "Edward D. Clarke och Giuseppe Acerbi."

2. Küttner, *Travels*, 2–6, 8–10, 13; Boisgelin, *Travels*, I, pt. 2, 4; Wollstonecraft, *Letters*, 238–40; Coxe, *Travels*, V:294, 298; Malthus, *Travel Diaries*, 48–49.

3. Küttner, *Travels*, 7–8; Wollstonecraft, *Letters*, 237; Macdonald, *Travels*, 12, 18; Buch, *Travels*, 460; Carr, *Northern Summer*, 20–21. On conditions in Denmark proper, see esp. Thorkild Kjærgaard, *The Danish Revolution, 1500–1800: An Ecohistorical Interpretation* (Cambridge, 1994). The present Danish South Jutland (Sønderjylland) was at that time the northern part of the duchy of Schleswig.

4. Swinton, *Travels*, 28; Boisgelin, *Travels*, I, pt. 2, 5; Küttner, *Travels*, 10–18, 27–29, 36; Macdonald, *Travels*, 57; Wraxall, *Cursory Remarks*, 77–78. See also Ketton-Cremer, *Windham*, 123–24; Coxe, *Travels*, V:293; Malthus, *Travel Diaries*, 49–52; Carr, *Northern Summer*, 33–35.

5. Wollstonecraft, *Letters*, 57, 115–16, 118, 146, 175. See also Küttner, *Travels*, 63–65; Malthus, *Travel Diaries*, 84, 93, 139; Buch, *Travels*, 24–25.

6. Buch, *Travels*, 72–73, 79–80, 86–87, 104–5, 118, 154, 207–8. See also Ketton-Cremer, *Windham*, 120; Coxe, *Travels*, V:560; Malthus, *Travel Diaries*, 138–39, 156, 159; Clarke, *Travels*, V:620; La Tocnaye, *Promenade*, II:90–94, 144, 224–26.

7. Malthus, *Travel Diaries*, 112, 131, 184–85; Buch, *Travels*, 87, 88, 161–62, 169, 177–78, 199–200; La Tocnaye, *Promenade*, II:191–92.

8. Küttner, *Travels*, 44–45, 48, 51, 53, 57–58; Malthus, *Travel Diaries*, 70–72. See also Ketton-Cremer, *Windham*, 122; Wollstonecraft, *Letters*, 51; Thomson, *Travels*, 20.

9. Miranda, *Miranda i Sverige och Norge*, 273; Boisgelin, *Travels*, II:6; Küttner, *Travels*, 109; La Tocnaye, *Promenade*, II:271, 275; Carr, *Northern Summer*, 109; James, *Journal*, 16–17; Coxe, *Travels*, IV:346.

10. Küttner, *Travels*, 103–4; Boisgelin, *Travels*, II:14.

11. Acerbi, *Travels*, I:27; Wraxall, *Cursory Remarks*, 96; Consett, *Tour*, 131–32; La Tocnaye, *Promenade*, I:48–50, 53, II:302; Thomson, *Travels*, 269. See also Boisgelin, *Travels*, II:42; Malthus, *Travel Diaries*, 78; Clarke, *Travels*, V:114, 126–27; James, *Journal*, 108–19.

12. Clarke, *Travels*, VI:89, 91, 96, 112; Küttner, *Travels*, 67–70.

13. Küttner, *Travels*, 70, 94–95, 97–99, 101; Consett, *Tour*, 106–9, 130; Coxe, *Travels*, IV:282–83, V:93–98; Burr, *Private Journal*, I:261, 274; Clarke, *Travels*, VI:111–12, 120–22. See also Miranda, *Miranda i Sverige och Norge*, 57, 75, 89; Brougham, *Life and Times*, I:138; La Tocnaye, *Promenade*, I:241–42, 244, 250–51, 262; Thomson, *Travels*, 151.

14. Clarke, *Travels*, V:184–90, 193, 209–14, 222, 543–49; La Tocnaye, *Promenade*, II:44–45; Consett, *Tour*, 96.

15. Clarke, *Travels*, V:495, 512–13, 515, 519, 547–48, VI:389–90; Wraxall, *Cursory Remarks*, 196; Boisgelin, *Travels*, II:313, 321.

16. Küttner, *Travels*, 111.

17. Miranda, *Miranda i Danmark*, 193; Brougham, *Life and Times*, I:90; Clarke, *Travels*, V:56; Malthus, *Travel Diaries*, 59–61; Macdonald, *Travels*, 30, 43.

18. Malthus, *Travel Diaries*, 156, 159, 164, 172, 196, 202–6; Clarke, *Travels*, V:631, 636, 676, 737; Buch, *Travels*, 221; La Tocnaye, *Promenade*, II:93–94, 129, 144; Küttner, *Travels*, 63–64; Ketton-Cremer, *Windham*, 110; Coxe, *Travels*, V:12. Before Malthus, Consett had also spoken of how rapidly crops grew during the short summers in far northern Sweden (*Tour*, 121).

19. La Tocnaye, *Promenade*, I:220; Burr, *Private Journal*, I:261; James, *Journal*, 16–17, 110, 128–30; Malthus, *Travel Diaries*, 164.

20. Clarke, *Travels*, V:512–13, 515, 519; La Tocnaye, *Promenade*, II:26, 43, 60–61. Thomson noted considerable tobacco cultivation in Sweden in 1812 (*Travels*, 65–66).

21. Küttner, *Travels*, 11–12; Coxe, *Travels*, V:294; Malthus, *Travel Diaries*, 49–52; Wollstonecraft, *Letters*, 237; Buch, *Travels*, 459; Macdonald, *Travels*, 28–32, 43–44, 47, 54–55.

22. Brougham, *Life and Times*, I:100, 110; Clarke, *Travels*, V:126–27, 133–34; Macdonald, *Travels*, 83, 85; Consett, *Tour*, 119–20; Thomson, *Travels*, 26–27, 65–66, 83–88, 425–30.

23. Wraxall, *Cursory Remarks*, 153–59, 174–77; Coxe, *Travels*, V:102–6; Küttner, *Travels*, 95–96; Thomson, *Travels*, 187–92, 194–95; Boisgelin, *Travels*, II:42; Clarke, *Travels*, VI:163–64; La Tocnaye, *Promenade*, I:60–61; Carr, *Northern Summer*, 160–61; Buch, *Travels*, 382–83, 388.

24. Consett, *Tour*, 106; Clarke, *Travels*, VI:47–66, 126–54, 166–70; Küttner, *Travels*, 97–99; Malthus, *Travel Diaries*, 112; La Tocnaye, *Promenade*, I:239–40, 244–48, II:77, 235–36; Thomson, *Travels*, 217–22, 235–41, 304. The Falun mine remained in operation until 1994.

25. Buch, *Travels*, 25; Ketton-Cremer, *Windham*, 120; Swinton, *Travels*, 48; La Tocnaye, *Promenade*, II:240; Clarke, *Travels*, V:87–88, 519, VI:27.

26. Buch, *Travels*, 148, 154, 158–59, 161–62, 264–70. See also Malthus, *Travel Diaries*, 175.

27. Coxe, *Travels*, V:234–36; Miranda, *Miranda i Danmark*, 172–74; Boisgelin, *Travels*, I, pt. 2, 66, II:132–41; Canzler, *Mémoires*, 378–81; Clarke, *Travels*, VI:270–71; Küttner, *Travels*, 72, 75, 86. See also La Tocnaye, *Promenade*, I:83–84; Thomson, *Travels*, 40. Cf. Fortia, *Travels in Sweden*, 435, for his figures for the value of Swedish manufactures, which differ from his companion Boisgelin's.

28. Miranda, *Miranda i Sverige och Norge*, 198; Acerbi, *Travels*, I:21; James, *Journal*, 4–5, 111; Coxe, *Travels*, IV:76–85, 318–19, V:301–5; Küttner, *Travels*, 51–53.

29. Swinton, *Travels*, 29.

30. Wraxall, *Cursory Remarks*, 24–26; Boisgelin, *Travels*, I, pt. 2, 139 (page misnumbered "193"), 144; Malthus, *Travel Diaries*, 58; Wollstonecraft, *Letters*, 135; Thomson, *Travels*, 6, 9. For Scandinavian neutral maritime trade during the American and the French Revolutionary and Napoleonic Wars, see Barton, *Scandinavia*, 222, 226–27, 253, 265–66, 272–73, 276, 318–19.

31. Boisgelin, *Travels*, II:185; Brougham, *Life and Times*, I:145; James, *Journal*, 10, 95; Wollstonecraft, *Letters*, 19; Clarke, *Travels*, V:630, VI:450n.

32. Clarke, *Travels*, V:639, VI:449, 461; La Tocnaye, *Promenade*, I:18, II:94, 146, 230, 245; Buch, *Travels*, 262–70.

33. Küttner, *Travels*, 24–25; Lenz, *Bemerkungen*, I:195–96; La Tocnaye, *Promenade*, I:92; Thomson, *Travels*, 14, 19; James, *Journal*, 134. See also Carr, *Northern Summer*, 81, 116; Lyttelton, *Correspondence*, 146, 164.

34. Küttner, *Travels*, 11–12, 13; Macdonald, *Travels*, 47; Boisgelin, *Travels*, II:183–85; Canzler, *Mémoires*, 186–87; Clarke, *Travels*, V:667–68; Lenz, *Bemerkungen*, I:163–65. See also Barton, *Scandinavia*, 6, 367.

35. Consett, *Tour*, 120–21; Küttner, *Travels*, 13.

36. Boisgelin, *Travels*, II:132; Thomson, *Travels*, 296; Macdonald, *Travels*, 26; Lenz, *Bemerkungen*, I:164–65; Coxe, *Travels*, IV:336; Consett, *Tour*, 106, 117.

37. Boisgelin, *Travels*, II:183–84n.; La Tocnaye, *Promenade*, II:13, 288–89; Küttner, *Travels*, 101–3; Thomson, *Travels*, 431–32; Coxe, *Travels*, IV:358; Macdonald, *Travels*, 28, 83. See also Buch, *Travels*, 391–92; Clarke, *Travels*, V:271, VI:163; Wollstonecraft, *Letters*, 85.

38. Malthus, *Travel Diaries*, 153–54, 156–57; Wollstonecraft, *Letters*, 169; Buch, *Travels*, 158–59, 213–16; La Tocnaye, *Promenade*, II:189–90.

39. Canzler, *Mémoires*, 387; Lenz, *Bemerkungen*, I:194–95; La Tocnaye, *Promenade*, I:104, 111–12; Thomson, *Travels*, 94. See also Küttner, *Travels*, 86; Consett, *Tour*, 142.

40. Baltimore, *Gaudia poetica*, xvii; Acerbi, *Travels*, I:172–73, 285–87; James, *Journal*, III.

4. The Inhabitants of the North

1. Swinton, *Travels*, 78; James, *Journal*, 141–42. Compare Samuel Johnson's reflections in 1775 on this theme; see Pat Rogers, ed., *Johnson and Boswell in Scotland* (New Haven, 1993), 55.

2. La Tocnaye, *Promenade*, II:55–56, 85.

3. Küttner, *Travels*, 2–10.

4. Miranda, *Miranda i Danmark*, 196, 198; Wollstonecraft, *Letters*, 244–45, 246–47; Carr, *Northern Summer*, 26. See also Boisgelin, *Travels*, I, pt. 2, 4; Clarke, *Travels*, V:40–51; Malthus, *Travel Diaries*, 40–49, 59.

5. Malthus, *Travel Diaries*, 48–49, 59. See also Barton, *Scandinavia*, 22–23, 26, 235, 244–45, 208–9, 259–60.

6. Küttner, *Travels*, 6, 8, 13–16, 27; Macdonald, *Travels*, 12, 30, 54–55; Malthus, *Travel Diaries*, 49, 52; Ketton-Cremer, *Windham*, 124; Coxe, *Travels*, V:126.

7. Miranda, *Miranda i Danmark*, 194; Küttner, *Travels*, 36; Coxe, *Travels*, V:132–33; La Tocnaye, *Promenade*, II:266; Carr, *Northern Summer*, 80; Wollstonecraft, *Letters*, 75; Malthus, *Travel Diaries*, 49, 59–60, 62, 64–65.

8. Malthus, *Travel Diaries*, 52, 55–56, 57; Swinton, *Travels*, 78; Carr, *Northern Summer*, 33.

9. Coxe, *Travels*, V:11; Clarke, *Travels*, V:598–99, VI:8–9, 70; Malthus, *Travel Diaries*, passim; Swinton, *Travels*, 38.

10. Coxe, *Travels*, V:31; Wollstonecraft, *Letters*, 165; Malthus, *Travel Diaries*, 140, 161, 164, 202; Küttner, *Travels*, 63; Ketton-Cremer, *Windham*, 120.

11. Wollstonecraft, *Letters*, 128; Clarke, *Travels*, V:598, 678; Malthus, *Travel Diaries*, 199.

12. Clarke, *Travels*, V:701; Ketton-Cremer, *Windham*, 118, 120.

13. Clarke, *Travels*, V:616–17, 739, 742; Malthus, *Travel Diaries*, 112, 185, 217; La Tocnaye, *Promenade*, II:237; Buch, *Travels*, 87–88.

14. La Tocnaye, *Promenade*, II:144–45, 156–58, 160, 207, 191–92, 209–10, 220–21, 223; Malthus, *Travel Diaries*, 138.

15. Acerbi, *Travels*, I:181. See also La Tocnaye, *Promenade*, I:22; James, *Journal*, 140–41. For a useful survey of some of these travelers' views of peasant conditions in Sweden, see Utterström, *Jordbrukets arbetare*, I:81–96.

16. Küttner, *Travels*, 44; Clarke, *Travels*, V:96; Macdonald, *Travels*, 83. See also Wollstonecraft, *Letters*, 186; La Tocnaye, *Promenade*, I:22; Malthus, *Travel Diaries*, 72. It is worth noting that a fairly recent survey by the Stockholm newspaper *Dagens nyheter* showed Halland to be Sweden's most livable province. See the Swedish-American newspaper *Nordstjernan* (New York), 6 Feb. 1986.

17. Wollstonecraft, *Letters*, 26, 195–96; Brougham, *Life and Times*, I:150. See also Miranda, *Miranda i Sverige och Norge*, 196.

18. Clarke, *Travels*, V:109–10, 134, VI:89–90.

19. Lenz, *Bemerkungen*, I:211–12, 215–16; Brougham, *Life and Times*, I:102–3; Coxe, *Travels*, IV:330, 333–35.

20. Carr, *Northern Summer*, 110–11; Clarke, *Travels*, V:109–10; James, *Journal*, 107; Wollstonecraft, *Letters*, 37; Macdonald, *Travels*, 86; Malthus, *Travel Diaries*, 78.

21. Clarke, *Travels*, V:134–35; Küttner, *Travels*, 55–56.

22. Miranda, *Miranda i Sverige och Norge*, 269, 273; James, *Journal*, 16–17. See Barton, *Scandinavia*, 256–57.

23. Küttner, *Travels*, 71, 94–95; Thomson, *Travels*, 31–32; Clarke, *Travels*, V:170, VI:111–12, 298; Boisgelin, *Travels*, II:291, 295. See also Miranda, *Miranda i Sverige och Norge*, 57; James, *Journal*, 193–95.

24. La Tocnaye, *Promenade*, I:241–42, 256–57; Clarke, *Travels*, VI:120, 122.

25. James, *Journal*, 107–8. See also Buch, *Travels*, 393.

26. Clarke, *Travels*, V:169–70, 178–79, 184–85, 193, 200–201, 209–14, 543–45, 547–48. See also Consett, *Tour*, 44–46.

27. Clarke, *Travels*, V:109–10, 595, VI:209–10; Thomson, *Travels*, 29.

28. Clarke, *Travels*, V:464–72, 512–16; Acerbi, *Travels*, I:218–19. In 1809, following the Russian conquest, that part of Norrbotten lying east of the Torne and Kemi Rivers was allotted to the new grand duchy of Finland under Russian overlordship.

29. Acerbi, *Travels*, I:198–200; Clarke, *Travels*, VI:311, 318–19, 328–29, 334–38.

30. Clarke, *Travels*, VI:354–56, 375–77, 454, 466; Carr, *Northern Summer*, 192–95.

31. Clarke, *Travels*, VI:432–36, 451–52.

32. Ibid., 466–68, 471–74, 482–83; James, *Journal*, 223–28; Carr, *Northern Summer*, 208–9, 218.

33. Clarke, *Travels*, V:139–40, 549–53; La Tocnaye, *Promenade*, II:3–4; Brougham, *Life and Times*, I:103; Burr, *Private Journal*, I:235–36.

34. Clarke, *Travels*, V:94–95; La Tocnaye, *Promenade*, I:94–98.

35. Küttner, *Travels*, 29–30; Clarke, *Travels*, VI:432–36; Buch, *Travels*, 30–31.

36. La Tocnaye, *Promenade*, I:96; Brougham, *Life and Times*, I:90; Macdonald, *Travels*, 25–26; Clarke, *Travels*, V:194, 470, 512.

37. La Tocnaye, *Promenade*, I:96–97.

38. Acerbi, *Travels*, I:219, 283–84; Clarke, *Travels*, V:255–56, 439–41, 503; Otter, *Life and Remains*, 53. See also Consett, *Tour*, 101.

39. La Tocnaye, *Promenade*, I:97, II:131; Clarke, *Travels*, V:144–45; Acerbi, *Travels*, I:329–30; Swinton, *Travels*, 51–52, 77–78.

40. Alfieri, *Memoirs*, 99; Macdonald, *Travels*, 79; Küttner, *Travels*, 35.

41. Lenz, *Bemerkungen*, I:101–8; Carr, *Northern Summer*, 192; Clarke, *Travels*, V:473–75, VI:443–46, 449; Otter, *Life and Remains*, 368. See also La Tocnaye, *Promenade*, II:126–28.

42. Clarke, *Travels*, V:521; La Tocnaye, *Promenade*, I:241–32, 252–53, 255, 256, 260; Thomson, *Travels*, 202.

43. Acerbi, *Travels*, I:283–84, 300–323. See also Clarke, *Travels*, VI:447–49.

44. Acerbi, *Travels*, I:293–99, 337–39.

45. Burr, *Private Journal*, I:267–68. See also Clarke, *Travels*, VI:377.

46. Boisgelin, *Travels*, II:166–67; Burr, *Private Journal*, I:246, 312–13, 316; Lenz, *Bemerkungen*, I:124–25, 152. See also Wraxall, *Cursory Remarks*, 92; Clarke, *Travels*, VI:207–8; La Tocnaye, *Promenade*, II:54–55.

47. Carr, *Northern Summer*, 116–17; Thomson, *Travels*, 31, 33; Boisgelin, *Travels*, II:v, 166–67, 240; La Tocnaye, *Promenade*, I:62, 123, II:160, 162–63, 195–97; Consett, *Tour*, 53–54; Clarke, *Travels*, V:169–70, 223, 266, VI:205–6. See also Brougham, *Life and Times*, I:110, 129; Miranda, *Miranda i Danmark*, 191–92; James, *Journal*, 107–8.

48. Boisgelin, *Travels*, II:236–37. See also Carr, *Northern Summer*, 139–42; Clarke, *Travels*, VI:121.

49. Clarke, *Travels*, VI:209; James, *Journal*, 105–6.

50. Clarke, *Travels*, V:247. See also Lenz, *Bemerkungen*, I:155.

51. Consett, *Tour*, 26–27; Boisgelin, *Travels*, II:169; Acerbi, *Travels*, I:136, 138; James, *Journal*, 105; La Tocnaye, *Promenade*, I:271; Macdonald, *Travels*, 87–88; Clarke, *Travels*, V:644–45, 656; Swinton, *Travels*, 55.

52. Lenz, *Bemerkungen*, I:157; Malthus, *Travel Diaries*, 167. See also Barton, *Scandinavia*, esp. 38–39, 330–32; H. Arnold Barton, "Popular Education in Eighteenth-Century Sweden: Theory and Practice," in *Aspects of Education in the Eighteenth Century*, ed. James Leith, Studies in Voltaire and the Eighteenth Century 167 (Oxford, 1977), 523–41; and Carol Gold, "Educational Reform in Denmark, 1784–1814," in Leith, ed., *Aspects of Education*, 49–64; Mauno Jokipii and Ilka Nummela, eds., *Ur nordisk kulturhistoria. Läskunnighet och folkbildning före folkskoleväsendet* (Jyväskylä, 1981).

53. Wollstonecraft, *Letters*, 31; Malthus, *Travel Diaries*, 152; Boisgelin, *Travels*, II:169. See also Clarke, *Travels*, V:656.

54. Boisgelin, *Travels*, II:v, 132; Baltimore, *Gaudia poetica*, xvii.

55. See Barton, *Scandinavia*, 20–21, 22, 26, 90, 144–47, 184, 187.

56. Coxe, *Travels*, V:135; Consett, *Tour*, 144; Lenz, *Bemerkungen*, I:49–50, 104–5; Malthus, *Travel Diaries*, 49, 59–60, 64–65.

57. Lenz, *Bemerkungen*, I:49–50, 103, 147, 157, 179–80, 215–17; Brougham, *Life and Times*, I:129, 134; Malthus, *Travel Diaries*, 59.

58. Boisgelin, *Travels*, II:132, 166–67; Küttner, *Travels*, 56; Wollstonecraft, *Letters*, 26; La Tocnaye, *Promenade*, I:126, II:250–51; Lenz, *Bemerkungen*, I:163–65; Clarke, *Travels*, VI:206, 437. See also Swinton, *Travels*, 77; Malthus, *Travel Diaries*, 72.

59. Carr, *Northern Summer*, 139.

60. Küttner, *Travels*, 71; Macdonald, *Travels*, 35, 87; Miranda, *Miranda i Sverige och Norge*, 80, *Miranda i Danmark*, 210; Malthus, *Travel Diaries*, 78, 137; Clarke, *Travels*, V:269, 706, VI:68; Ketton-Cremer, *Windham*, 122–23.

61. Consett, *Tour*, 108–9; Wollstonecraft, *Letters*, 27, 66.

62. Baltimore, *Gaudia poetica*, xix; Miranda, *Miranda i Danmark*, 145; Malthus, *Travel Diaries*, 153, 172; Wollstonecraft, *Letters*, 215; La Tocnaye, *Promenade*, II:51–53, 195.

63. Acerbi, *Travels*, I:392–93; Miranda, *Miranda i Danmark*, 184, 188, 190.

64. La Tocnaye, *Promenade*, II:52; Acerbi, *Travels*, I:64–65; Wollstonecraft, *Letters*, 38.

65. Clarke, *Travels*, VI:258; Miranda, *Miranda i Sverige och Norge*, 122; Boisgelin, *Travels*, II:167; Wollstonecraft, *Letters*, 213.

66. Carr, *Northern Summer*, 16–17.

67. Burr, *Private Journal*, I:301; Miranda, *Miranda i Sverige och Norge*, 183, *Miranda i Danmark*, for example, 58, 154, 161, 165. See also Milton Lomask, *Aaron Burr: The Conspiracy and Years of Exile, 1805–1836* (New York, 1982), esp. 299–301, 316–21.

68. Wollstonecraft, *Letters*, 238–40; Carr, *Northern Summer*, 9–11.

69. Malthus, *Travel Diaries*, 49, 52. See also Consett, *Tour*, 139; the contemporary Norwegian-born Danish writer Henrik Steffens's strictures in the same vein against his countrymen, in *Was ich erlebte*, 10 vols. (Breslau, 1840–44), II:71–72.

70. Macdonald, *Travels*, 78–79; Malthus, *Travel Diaries*, 77; Clarke, *Travels*, V:106; Burr, *Private Journal*, I:317; Thomson, *Travels*, 31; Lenz, *Bemerkungen*, I:101–3.

71. Clarke, *Travels*, V:599, 616–17, VI:89; Wollstonecraft, *Letters*, 192; La Tocnaye, *Promenade*, II:92, 133–34, 145, 160; Swinton, *Travels*, 46–47.

72. Clarke, *Travels*, V:270, 483–84, 492, VI:434–36.

73. Clarke, *Travels*, VI:456–57, 466–75; Swinton, *Travels*, 455–65.

5. Ultima Thule

1. Clarke, *Travels*, V:451; Acerbi, *Travels*, II:29, 131.

2. Maupertuis, *Rélation d'un Voyage*; Jean-François Regnard, *Voyage en Lapponie* (Paris, 1731), English trans. in Pinkerton, ed., *General Collection*, I; Carl Linnæus, *Iter Lapponica Dei gratia institutum 1732*, ed. T. M. Fries (Uppsala, 1913), and *Lachesis Lapponica; or, a Tour in Lapland, now first published from the original Manuscript of the celebrated Linnaeus; by James Edward Smith*, 2 vols. (London, 1811); Eggert Ólafsson, *Ennarrationes Historicæ de Natura et Constitutione Islandiæ* (Copenhagen, 1749), in English, *Travels in Iceland* (London, 1772); Knud Leem, *Beskrivelse over Finnmarkens Lapper* (Copenhagen, 1767), with parallel Latin text, English trans. in Pinkerton, ed., *General Collection*, I:376–490.

3. Küttner, *Travels*, 83; Acerbi, *Travels*, I:347–48; Clarke, *Travels*, V:348. See also Johann Gerhard Scheller, *Reise-Beschreibung von Lappland und Bothnien* (Jena, 1727); Acerbi mistakenly dated his account 1792. The duke of Orleans kept detailed diaries from his years of exile, some of which have since been published, but none has been preserved for his travels in Scandinavia during 1796. Swedish descendants of his ille-

gitimate son presently maintain amicable relations with the count of Paris, the current pretender to the French throne. "Stuart" was in fact the British adventurer John Stewart (1749–1822), who had been in India, Persia, and Abyssinia, before traveling through Europe in 1789 and residing in the United States during the 1790s; see Stewart, *Travels over the Most Interesting Parts of the Globe, to Discover the Source of Moral Motion* (London [1810]), which briefly touches on Sweden and Lapland (172–74).

4. Clarke, *Travels*, V:286–87, 420, 422; Acerbi, *Travels*, I:395; Consett, *Tour*. Thomson's extensive "Account of Lapland," in his *Travels*, 311–67, is not based upon personal observation. Other travelers, too, offer some secondhand information on the Far North. The Italian Francesco Negri had, of course, visited the North Cape in the 1660s.

5. Clarke, *Travels*, V:286, 308, 310–11, 312–13, 338, 356, 361, 452; Consett, *Tour*, 49; Acerbi, *Travels*, I:356, 373–74, II:5, 47, 50–51.

6. Acerbi, *Travels*, I:372; Clarke, *Travels*, 323–24.

7. Clarke, *Travels*, V:379. Malthus, *Travel Diaries*, 189. See also Buch, *Travels*, 247–48, 346.

8. Consett, *Tour*, 82–84, 85; Olaus Magnus, *Historia de gentibus septentrionalibus* (1555), bk. 4, ch. 5, bk. 20, ch. 1, in English trans., *A Compendious History of the Goths, Svvedes, & Vandals, and Other Northern Nations* (London, 1658); Linnæus, *Linné i Lappland*, 112–13; Hoxie Neale Fairchild, *The Noble Savage: A Study in Romantic Naturalism* (New York, 1928), 58; Alan Dugald McKillop, *The Background of Thomson's Seasons* (Minneapolis, 1942), 111–22.

9. Consett, *Tour*, 62–63, 148–57; La Tocnaye, *Promenade*, II:36–43, 74, 79–81.

10. Clarke, *Travels*, V:350, 352, 389, 415–16, 434–35; Otter, *Life and Remains*, 352. See also Acerbi, *Travels*, II:151–56; Buch, *Travels*, 354–55.

11. Acerbi, *Travels*, II:29, 47, 52–53, 59, 62, 64; Buch, *Travels*, 300–301, 314; Consett, *Tour*, 62.

12. Clarke, *Travels*, V:353, 400, 404; Buch, *Travels*, 295, 296–99. See also Acerbi, *Travels*, II:47, 55; La Tocnaye, *Promenade*, II:42.

13. Clarke, *Travels*, V:390.

14. Acerbi, *Travels*, II:18, 67, 325–36; Clarke, *Travels*, V:351.

15. Consett, *Tour*, 64–66; Clarke, *Travels*, V:404–5, 418; Acerbi, *Travels*, II:56, 125, 299–300.

16. Clarke, *Travels*, V:395–97; Otter, *Life and Remains*, 54–55, 352, 355; Malthus, *Travel Diaries*, 14.

17. Acerbi, *Travels*, II:54–56, 299–300.

18. Buch, *Travels*, 295, 320, 325, 328.

19. Clarke, *Travels*, V:362–63, 428–29, 453; Acerbi, *Travels*, II:104–6. See also La Tocnaye, *Promenade*, II:35; Buch, *Travels*, 291–91, 323.

20. Acerbi, *Travels*, II:137–380. See also Leem, *Beskrivelse over Finnmarkens Lapper*.

21. Clarke, *Travels*, V:294–95, 379, 383; Buch, *Travels*, 222, 229, 245, 329, 370–74, 378, 381.

22. Clarke, *Travels*, V:435. See also Buch, *Travels*, 354–55; Consett, *Tour*, 87–88.

23. Acerbi, *Travels*, II:47, 62; Buch, *Travels*, 221, 229, 245–46, 329, 356–59, 365–68; Clarke, *Travels*, V:448, 464–69.

24. Buch, *Travels*, 300–301, 354–55, 366; Clarke, *Travels*, V:294–95, 309, 315, 330, 334, 340–41; Acerbi, *Travels*, II:21.

25. Buch, *Travels*, 262–70, 300. See also chapter 3, above.

26. Acerbi, *Travels*, II:15–17, 124; Clarke, *Travels*, V:368–70, 377–79; Buch, *Travels*, 286, 360, 381. See also Eric Grape, "Utkast till beskrifning öfver Enontekis sokn i Torneå Lappmark," *Kungl. Vetenskapsakademiens nya handlingar*, 24 (Stockholm, 1803): 197–226. Clarke states that Grape made him a transcription of "the whole of his statistical account" of his district, which Clarke deposited in the Cambridge University Library (*Travels*, V:ix–x). On Pastor Matthias Kolström at Muonioniska, see Sandblad, "Edward D. Clarke och Giuseppe Acerbi," 173–75.

27. Clarke, *Travels*, V:393, 448; Buch, *Travels*, 246, 295–96, 301, 332, 371.

28. Acerbi, *Travels*, II:132; Clarke, *Travels*, V:450.

29. Kerguélen-Trémarec, *Relation*, esp. 736–68.

30. Halldór Hermannsson, *Sir Joseph Banks and Iceland* (Ithaca, N.Y., 1928), on Johnson, see p. 1; Roy A. Rauschenberg, ed., "The Journals of Sir Joseph Banks's Voyage up Great Britain's West Coast to Iceland and to the Orkney Islands, July to October, 1772," *Proceedings of the American Philosophical Society* 117 (1973): 186–226. See also Uno von Troil, *Bref rörande en resa till Island* (Uppsala, 1777), or English trans., *Letters on Iceland* (London, 1780), or rev. ed., in Pinkerton, ed., *General Collection*, I:671–734.

31. Andrew Wawn, "John Thomas Stanley and Iceland: The Sense and Sensibility of an Eighteenth-Century Explorer," *Scandinavian Studies* 53 (1981): 52–76; West, ed., *Journals*, I:viii–xi. Vol. I comprises Wright's diary; vol. II, Benners's; vol. III, Baine's. I have not found any of their birth and death dates.

32. William Jackson Hooker, *Journal of a Tour in Iceland in the Summer of 1809*, 2 vols. (2d ed., London, 1813; first ed. privately printed, Yarmouth, 1811). See also Hermannsson, *Joseph Banks*, 58–59, 87.

33. George S. Mackenzie, *Travels in the Island of Iceland during the Summer of the Year 1810* (Edinburgh, 1811); my references are to the 2d ed. (Edinburgh, 1812). Also Holland, *Icelandic Journal*.

34. Ebenezer Henderson, *Iceland; or, the Journal of a Residence on that Island during the Years 1814 and 1815*, 2 vols. (Edinburgh, 1818). On Henderson, see *Dictionary of National Biography*, 9 (1917):397–98.

35. The fullest account of the Færøes in this period is "Indberetninger indhendtede paa en Reise i Færøe i Aarene 1781 og 1782" (manuscript in 7 octavo volumes) by the Færøese-born Jens Christian Svabo, from which excerpts have been published in M. A. Jacobsen, ed., *Føroyaferðin 1781–82* (Tórshavn, 1924).

36. West, ed., *Journals*, I:29.

37. Ibid., 47.

38. Ibid., 175–76n., 189n. On the smuggling trade via Tórshavn, see John F. West, *Faroe: The Emergence of a Nation* (London, 1972), 45–48; Barton, *Scandinavia*, 116.

39. West, ed., *Journals*, I:26–28, 33, 45, 47–50, 183n.

40. Ibid., 28, 36, III:38–39.

41. West, ed., *Journals*, I:43, III:58–59.

42. Holland, *Icelandic Journal*, 32; West, ed., *Journals*, III:95; Mackenzie, *Travels*, 242.

43. West, ed., *Journals*, III:209n.; Hooker, *Journal*, I:xcvi–vii; Henderson, *Iceland*, II:238–39. On the natural disasters, see Barton, *Scandinavia*, 126.

44. West, ed., *Journals*, I:196–97; Henderson, *Iceland*, I:359–60.

45. Holland, *Icelandic Journal*, 150, 210–11; Henderson, *Iceland*, I:29–30; West, ed., *Journals*, I:70–71, 128, III:89, 170. Mackenzie describes these tents in *Travels*, 163.

46. Holland, *Icelandic Journal*, 137; Henderson, *Iceland*, I:xxxiii–iv; West, ed., *Journals*, III:81, 209n.; Hooker, *Journal*, I:10–11, 15, 18, 176; Wawn, "Stanley and Iceland," 63, 65, 70.

47. Mackenzie, *Travels*, 168–69.

48. West, ed., *Journals*, I:59–60, 67, 73, 107, 199n.; Hooker, *Journal*, I:cv–cvi; Henderson, *Iceland*, II:130.

49. Henderson, *Iceland*, I:308–9.

50. Ibid., 363–66, II:157–58.

51. West, ed., *Journals*, I:59–60, III:116–17, 175, 178; Henderson, *Iceland*, I:136, 138–39, 348; Mackenzie, *Travels*, 188, 197, 270–281.

52. West, ed., *Journals*, III:183, 212n.; Henderson, *Iceland*, I:162–63; Hooker, *Journal*, I:lxxxv–vi, 119; Mackenzie, *Travels*, 282–87.

53. Hooker, *Journal*, I:53–56, 78, 88–89, 222–23, 324–25, 334–35, 357–58, 363, II:7–57. Mackenzie's account of the revolution, in *Travels*, 474–81, obviously builds upon Hooker's, although Mackenzie dismissed Jørgensen as an impostor. See also Hermannsson, *Joseph Banks*, 53–72; Barton, *Scandinavia*, 298–99.

54. Hooker, *Journal*, I:280–81, II:58–63; Henderson, *Iceland*, II:163–64. See also Hermannsson, *Joseph Banks*, 19–20, 24–86, passim.

55. West, ed., *Journals*, I:87; Holland, *Icelandic Journal*, 85, 139; Henderson, *Iceland*, I:10–12; Hooker, *Journal*, I:25–26, 32–33.

56. Henderson, *Iceland*, I:75–76; Holland, *Icelandic Journal*, 86, 126–27, 150; West, ed., *Journals*, I:201n.; Hooker, *Journal*, I:109–12.

57. Henderson, *Iceland*, I:xxxiii–iv, 291–97; Hooker, *Journal*, I:xcviii–ix; West, ed., *Journals*, I:62, 84–85, III:101; Holland, *Icelandic Journal*, 86, 210, and his chapter in Mackenzie, *Travels*, entitled "On the Diseases of the Icelanders," 280–81.

58. Henderson, *Iceland*, I:77, II:76–77, 88, 96, 211; Holland, *Icelandic Journal*, 150, 170–71; Mackenzie, *Travels*, 156.

59. West, ed., *Journals*, I:137, III:101, 146, 170; Mackenzie, *Travels*, 202; Holland, *Icelandic Journal*, 32; Henderson, *Iceland*, I:lix, 77, 88, 96, 374, 377, II:167–69. See also Hooker, *Journal*, I:135n.

60. Henderson, *Iceland*, I:114–15, 254. See also Hooker, *Journal*, I:257, 274–75.

61. Holland, *Icelandic Journal*, 32, 299–301; Mackenzie, *Travels*, 310; Henderson, *Iceland*, I:xli–ii.

62. West, ed., *Journals*, I:115, III:148–50; Henderson, *Iceland*, I:109–11, 370.

63. West, ed., *Journals*, I:93–94, III:105; Holland, *Icelandic Journal*, 116–19; Henderson, *Iceland*, I:370–74; Mackenzie, *Travels*, 310–13; Hooker, *Journal*, I:351–55.

64. Wawn, "Stanley and Iceland," 70; Mackenzie, *Travels*, 18; Henderson, *Iceland*, I:xxxv, xxxviii–xli, 77, 366–67, II:104; Hooker, *Journal*, I:lxxxix–xc; Holland, *Icelandic Journal*, 154.

65. West, ed., *Journals*, I:74; Hooker, *Journal*, I:xci–iin.; Miranda, *Miranda i Danmark*, 107; Swinton, *Travels*, 6–7.

66. West, ed., *Journals*, III:150; Mackenzie, *Travels*, 151, 322–35; Hooker, *Journal*, I:294; Holland, in Mackenzie, *Travels*, 322–24. For a contemporary Icelandic account of literary life, see Magnus Stephensen, *Island i det 18. Aarhundrede, historisk-politisk skildret* (Copenhagen, 1808), 154–65.

67. Henderson, *Iceland*, I:xli–xlii; Holland, "Disease," in Mackenzie, *Travels*, 319.

68. Henderson, *Iceland*, I:93–100, 336, II:103, 153–54. Henderson provides selections from Jon Thorlakson's Icelandic translation of Milton's *Paradise Lost*, with parallel English text (II:386–400).

69. West, ed., *Journals*, I:136, 204n.

70. Ibid., 207–8n., III:100–101; Mackenzie, *Travels*, 266–68; Hooker, *Journal*, I:xc–xci; Henderson, *Iceland*, II:245. During the late nineteenth century, a sizable part of Iceland's small population did in fact emigrate to Canada, in particular to Manitoba.

6. The Rise and Fall of a New Arcadia

1. See Batten, *Pleasurable Instruction*, esp. 92, 96–99, 114–5.

2. Ibid., esp. 25–28, 119; Swinton, *Travels*, vi–vii.

3. Batten, *Pleasurable Instruction*, 29–30, 39, 46, 72, 74–75, 77–84, 99–110. See also Laurence Sterne, *Sentimental Journey through France and Italy* (London, 1768); William Gilpin's series of travel accounts from Britain, commencing with *Observations on the River Wye, and Several Parts of South Wales, &c. Relative Chiefly to Picturesque Beauty; Made in the Summer of the Year 1770* (London, 1782), esp. 1–2.

4. Wraxall, *Cursory Remarks*, 3–5; Wollstonecraft, *Letters*, "Advertisement" (n.p.); La Tocnaye, *Promenade*, I:67, II:138–39.

5. I must disagree in part with Batten, who stresses the search for novelty and is skeptical of the preromantic influence (*Pleasurable Instruction*, 115). See also George P. Parks, "The Turn to the Romantic in the Travel Literature of the Eighteenth Century," *Modern Language Quarterly* 25 (1964): 22–33. The literature on romanticism is, of course, immense; specifically on eighteenth-century preromanticism, considerably sparser. However, see, for example, Henry A. Beers, *A History of English Romanticism in the Eighteenth Century* (New York, 1898); Martin Lamm, *Upplysningstidens romantik*, 2 vols. (Stockholm, 1918–20); Daniel Mornet, *Le Romantisme en France au*

XVIIIe siècle, 2d ed. (Paris, 1925); Pierre van Tieghem, *Le Préromantisme*, 3 vols. (Paris, 1929–48); Walter Jackson Bate, *From Classic to Romantic: Premises of Taste in Eighteenth-Century England* (Cambridge, Mass., 1946); Gerhard Kaiser, *Von der Aufklärung bis zum Sturm und Drang 1730–1785* (Gütersloh, 1966).

6. Batten, *Pleasurable Instruction*, 97, 104–7.

7. Edmund Burke, *Philosophic Enquiry into the Origin of Our Ideas of the Sublime and Beautiful* (London, 1757), 39–40. See also Margaret Omberg, *Scandinavian Themes in English Poetry, 1760–1800* (Uppsala, 1976), 62–64.

8. Wraxall, *Cursory Remarks*, 110–11, 160–65.

9. Alfieri, *Memoirs*, 99–100; Küttner, *Travels*, 67, 103–4; Coxe, *Travels*, V:278, 99–100; Malthus, *Travel Diaries*, for example, 127–28; Boisgelin, *Travels*, II:27–29, 38; Wollstonecraft, *Letters*, 189–92; James, *Journal*, 3; Ketton-Cremer, *Windham*, 105–6, 109–10, 116; La Tocnaye, *Promenade*, esp. II:145, 155–56; Acerbi, *Travels*, II:110–11; West, ed., *Journals*, I:82; Clarke, *Travels*, V:721.

10. The classic study of this concept remains Fairchild, *Noble Savage*.

11. Beers, *History of English Romanticism*, 223; Paul Henri Mallet, *Northern Antiquities; or, An Historical Account of the Manners, Customs, Religion, and Laws, Maritime Expeditions and Discoveries, and Language of the Ancient Scandinavians. Translated from the French of M. Mallet by Bishop Percy*, new edition, ed. I. A. Blackwell (London, 1847; rpt. New York, 1968), 55.

12. Johann Wolfgang von Goethe, *Die Leiden des jungen Werthers* (Leipzig, 1774), epistle of 12 Oct. 1771. Mallet, *Northern Antiquities*. There exists an extensive and fascinating literature on the Nordic vogue of the period. See esp. Frank E. Farley, *The Scandinavian Influence in the English Romantic Movement* (Cambridge, Mass., 1903); Anton Blanck, *Den nordiska renässansen i sjuttonhundratalets litteratur* (Stockholm, 1911); Lamm, *Upplysningstidens romantik*; van Tieghem, *Préromantisme*, I; Thor J. Beck, *Nordic Antiquities in French Learning and Literature (1755–1855): A Study in Pre-Romantic Ideas*, 2 vols. (New York, 1934); E. V. Gordon, *An Introduction to Old Norse*, rev. A. R. Taylor (Oxford, 1957), lxviii–lxxvii; Omberg, *Scandinavian Themes*; Holland, *Icelandic Journal*, Andrew Wawn's introduction, 1–67. Hayley's verse quoted in Omberg, *Scandinavian Themes*, 46. For examples of the "runic odes" of the period, see *Poems by Mr. Gray* (London, 1768); and, for example, T. J. Mathias, *Runic Odes from the Norse Tongue in the Manner of Mr. Gray* (London, 1781), and Joseph Sterling, *Poems* (Dublin, 1782).

13. Mallet, *Northern Antiquities*, 2–21; Beck, *Nordic Antiquities*, I:10–11; Omberg, *Scandinavian Themes*, 49–50; Malthus, *Travel Diaries*, 138; Clarke, *Travels*, V:121–22, 708, VI:129–30; Wawn, "Stanley and Iceland," 62.

14. Beck, *Nordic Antiquities*, esp. I:68, 113, 121–23; Olof Rudbeck, *Atland eller Manhem* (Uppsala, 1679). See also, for example, Viggo Starcke, *Denmark in World History* (Philadelphia, 1963). Regarding more recent debate on the Swedish origins of the Goths, see Franklin D. Scott, *Sweden: The Nation's History*, enlarged ed. (Carbondale, Ill., 1988), 11.

15. Mallet, *Northern Antiquities*, 79–82; Swinton, *Travels*, 64–67; La Tocnaye, *Promenade*, I:170–84; McKillop, *Background of Thomson's Seasons*, 109–10. See also Snorri

Sturluson, *Heimskringla*, Lee Hollander, trans. and ed. (Austin, Tex., 1964), 6–13; also Snorri Sturluson, *The Prose Edda*, trans. and ed., A. C. Brodeur (New York, 1929), 6–9.

16. On the theme of "Gothic" liberty, see esp. Samuel M. Kliger, *The Goths in England: A Study in Seventeenth- and Eighteenth-Century Thought* (Cambridge, Mass., 1952); also Beck, *Nordic Antiquities*, I, esp. 22–23, 63–64; Omberg, *Scandinavian Themes*, 53–54, 87, 91, 97, Hayley quoted p. 97. See also Baron de La Brède et de Montesquieu [Charles-Louis de Secondat], *L'Esprit des lois* (Paris, 1748), bk. 17, ch. 2; Mallet, *Northern Antiquities*, 57–58, 82–84, 122–34.

17. Swinton, *Travels*, 40–41, 64–67, 74–75; La Tocnaye, *Promenade*, II:276; Clarke, *Travels*, V:iv–vii, VI:129–30.

18. Coxe, *Travels*, V:293; Swinton, *Travels*, 62; James Thomson, *Complete Works* (London, 1908), 368, 479–80; Miranda, *Miranda i Danmark*, 146. See also Beck, *Nordic Antiquities*, I:68, 85; McKillop, *Background of Thomson's Seasons*, 111; Omberg, *Scandinavian Themes*, 108–16.

19. Clarke, *Travels*, V:598, 620, 712–13; La Tocnaye, *Promenade*, I:2.

20. Swinton, *Travels*, 6–7, 66–67, 76, 254, 262–64, 304–5, 382; La Tocnaye, *Promenade*, I:163, 170–71, 195–96; Hooker, *Journal*, I:lxvii; Clarke, *Travels*, VI:446–47; Buch, *Travels*, 358; James, *Journal*, 216. See also *Dissertation on the Origin and Progress of the Scythians or Goths* (London, 1797) by the Scottish antiquarian and Scandophile John Pinkerton, who later published a number of accounts of travel in Scandinavia in his *General Collection*. See also Beck, *Nordic Antiquities*, I:121–23 (on Pinkerton), and vol. II, subtitled *The Odin Legend and the Oriental Fascination*, esp. 1–18. The Ostyaks and Cheremis, who speak Fenno-Ugric tongues, are today generally called the *Mari* and *Khanty*, respectively.

21. Omberg, *Scandinavian Themes*, 87, 98–100, 102, 119–23; Henderson, *Iceland*, II:325–26. See also Mallet, *Northern Antiquities*, 199–205, 233–40.

22. Swinton, *Travels*, 53–54, 60; Holland, *Icelandic Journal*, 10, 301; Mackenzie, *Travels*, 18; Henderson, *Iceland*, I:xxxv–xxxvii.

23. Fairchild, *Noble Savage*, 173; Barton, *Count Hans Axel von Fersen*, 15.

24. Quoted in Walter Schmid, *Romantic Switzerland Mirrored in the Literature and Graphic Art of the 18th and 19th Centuries* (Berne, 1965), 7.

25. Macdonald, *Travels*, 40; Küttner, *Travels*, 60–61, 65; Clarke, *Travels*, V:179, 543, 665, 686–87; Otter, *Life and Remains*, 352, 361, 364, 365–66; Acerbi, *Travels*, II:102. See also Wollstonecraft, *Letters*, 56; Buch, *Travels*, 26; Wawn, "Stanley and Iceland," 53–54; McKillop, *Background of Thomsons's Seasons*, 123–24.

26. Carr, *Northern Summer*, 114–15; Wollstonecraft, *Letters*, 11.

27. Acerbi, *Travels*, I:33, 76, 172–73, 181, 218, 226, 235–36, 327, 336, II:14, 17, 29, 104–6, 122–23; Baltimore, *Gaudia poetica*, xxix; Clarke, *Travels*, V:525–26, VI:328–29. See also Consett, *Tour*, 69; Miranda, *Miranda i Danmark*, 98; Henderson, *Iceland*, I:188. Consett quotes at length from James Thomson's poetic idealization of the Lapps' simple way of life in his "Winter," from 1726 (Consett, *Tour*, 82–84).

28. Miranda, *Miranda i Danmark*, 172, 178, 181, 183–84, 189–90; Clarke, *Travels*, V:121–22; La Tocnaye, *Promenade*, II:283–85; Porter, *Travelling Sketches*, II:167–74; Macdonald, *Travels*, 39–40; Acerbi, *Travels*, I:219–20; Henderson, *Iceland*, I:366–67.

29. Clarke, *Travels*, V:94–95, 255, VI:123.
30. Wollstonecraft, *Letters*, 8–9, 21–24, 30, 32, 40, 119, 128, 135.
31. La Tocnaye, *Promenade*, I:252–53, 273–75, II:20; Lyttelton, *Correspondence*, 158; Clarke, *Travels*, II:75–76; James, *Journal*, 141–42.
32. Buch, *Travels*, 30–33, 80–81, 299, 371.
33. Ibid., 104–5.
34. Wollstonecraft, *Letters*, 115–18, 132, 136–37, 167–68, 170, 182, 218, 245.
35. Clarke, *Travels*, V:680–82; La Tocnaye, *Promenade*, I:25–29, 46–47, 59–60, 67, 133–36, 138–39, II:136–40, 207.
36. See Barton, *Scandinavia*, chs. 12–14.
37. Macdonald, *Travels*, esp. 18–20, 35–36, 42–43, 63–76, 78.
38. Omberg, *Scandinavian Themes*, 139.
39. Porter, *Travelling Sketches*, II:126; Clarke, *Travels*, VI:241–42, 293–94, 450n. That Clarke's apprehensions were not simply the wisdom of afterthought is shown by his letter of 15 Dec. 1799 to a friend in Cambridge (Otter, *Life and Remains*, 373). On unrest in Sweden during 1799–1801, see Barton, *Scandinavia*, 235–41, and *Count Hans Axel von Fersen*, 273–96.

Conclusion: "The Eye of the Beholder"

1. La Tocnaye, *Promenade*, II:232. See also Mungo Park, *Travels in the Interior Districts of Africa Performed in the Years 1795, 1796, & 1797* (London, n.d. [1799]).
2. Lyttelton, *Correspondence*, 152; Baroness de Staël-Holstein, *Ten Years' Exile* (Fontwell, Sussex, 1968, facsimile of 1812 original), 425–33; E. Beau de Loménie, ed., *Lettres de Madame de Staël à Madame Récamier* (Paris, 1952), 238–43. See also Anne-Louise-Germaine de Staël, *Corréspondance générale*, ed. Béatrice Jasinski (Paris, 1962–); J. Christopher Herold, *Mistress to an Age: A Life of Madame de Staël* (New York, 1958), 430–34.
3. James, *Journal*, 143–45. See also Küttner, *Travels*, 75–76.
4. Clarke, *Travels*, V:87–88, VI:433; Acerbi, *Travels*, II:132; West, ed., *Journals*, III:183–84; Buch, *Travels*, 295–96, 332; Wollstonecraft, *Letters*, 127. Nootka Sound was a familiar name due to a confrontation there between a British and a Spanish war vessel, which nearly precipitated a war in 1790.
5. Robert Burns, "To a Louse," *Poems of Robert Burns*, ed. Henry W. Meikle and William Beattie (Harmondsworth, 1946), 82.
6. See Barton, *Scandinavia*.
7. See Skjöldebrand, *Premier supplément*; his criticisms are summarized by Boisgelin (*Travels*, II:xii–xx); Henrik Steffens, *Was ich erlebte*, I:319–21.
8. Wollstonecraft, *Letters*, 225.
9. James, *Journal*, 140.
10. Note Batten's observations on the approved requisites for "reflections" in eighteenth-century travel literature (*Pleasurable Instruction*, 110).

11. Clarke, *Travels*, VI:377.

12. See chapter 2, above.

13. Molesworth, *Account of Denmark*; Beck, *Nordic Antiquities*, I:12–16, 71, 124, 189; Swinton, *Travels*, 69; Miranda, *Miranda i Danmark*, 89.

14. Swinton, *Travels*, 31, 73–76. See also Coxe, *Travels*, V:144–69, esp. 169; Miranda, *Miranda i Danmark*, 157; Stanley, in West, ed., *Journals*, III:101n., 183–84n.; Wollstonecraft, *Letters*, 212. Regarding appreciation for the benevolent aspects of Danish absolutism, see chapter 2, above.

15. The exception was, of course, Macdonald, who unintentionally visited Denmark around the turn of the year 1808–9 thanks to his being shipwrecked at Skagen.

16. Matti Klinge, *Let Us Be Finns: Essays on History* (Helsinki, 1990), 79–80; Charles Loring Brace, *The Norse Folk; or, a Visit to the Homes of Norway and Sweden* (New York, 1857), iii, also 133.

17. See Barton, *Scandinavia*, 321, 339, 348–51; Herold, *Mistress to an Age*, 430–33; Franklin D. Scott, *Bernadotte and the Fall of Napoleon* (Cambridge, Mass., 1935); Terje I. Leiren, "1814 and British Opinion," *Scandinavian Studies* 47 (1975):364–82.

18. Franzén quoted in Hirn, "Finland," 149; Küttner, *Travels*, 21–22; Davidsson, *Utländska resenärer*, 8. See also J. W. Eaton, *German Influence on Danish Literature in the Eighteenth Century* (Cambridge, Mass., 1929); Swinton, *Travels*, 84–85. On the growth of "Scandinavianist" sentiment, see Barton, *Scandinavia*, 44, 155, 160, 200, 227–28, 281, 310, 312; Julius Clausen, *Skandinavismen historisk fremstillet* (Copenhagen, 1900), 1–20.

19. Otter, *Life and Remains*, 537; La Tocnaye, *Promenade*, II:139, 310.

20. Consett, *Tour*, 147.

Select Bibliography

Acerbi, Giuseppe [Joseph]. *Travels through Sweden, Finland, and Lapland to the North Cape in the Years 1798 and 1799.* 2 vols. London, 1802.

Alfieri, Vittorio. *Memoirs.* Anonymous translation of 1810, revised and ed. by E. R. Vincent. London, 1961.

Austin, Paul Britten. *The Life and Songs of Carl Michael Bellman, Genius of the Swedish Rococo.* New York, 1967.

[Baltimore, Frederick Calvert, Lord.] *Gaudia poetica, composed in Latin, English and French in the Year 1769.* N.p., n.d. [1769].

Barton, H. Arnold. *Count Hans Axel von Fersen: Aristocrat in an Age of Revolution.* Boston, 1975.

——. "Gustav III of Sweden and the Enlightenment." *Eighteenth-Century Studies* 6 (1972): 1–34.

——. "Gustav III of Sweden and the French Revolution." *Personhistorisk tidskrift* 89 (1993): 81–101.

——. "*Iter Scandinavicum:* Foreign Travelers' Views of the Late Eighteenth-Century North." *Scandinavian Studies* 68 (1996): 1–18.

——. *Scandinavia in the Revolutionary Era, 1760–1815.* Minneapolis, 1986.

Bate, Walter Jackson. *From Classic to Romantic: Premises of Taste in the Eighteenth-Century.* Cambridge, Mass., 1946.

Batten, Charles L., Jr. *Pleasurable Instruction: Form and Convention in Eighteenth-Century Travel Literature.* Berkeley, 1978.

Bech, Svend Cedergreen. *Københavns historie gennem 800 år.* Copenhagen, 1967.

Beck, Thor J. *Nordic Antiquities in French Learning and Literature (1755–1855): A Study in Pre-Romantic Ideas.* 2 vols. New York, 1934.

Beckmann, Johann. *Schwedische Reise in den Jahren 1765–1766. Tagebuch.* Ed. Th. Fries. Uppsala, 1911.

Beers, Henry A. *A History of English Romanticism in the Eighteenth Century.* New York, 1898.

Blanck, Anton. *Den nordiska renässansen i sjuttonhundratalets litteratur.* Stockholm, 1911.

Bobé, Louis, ed. *Johann Caspar Lavaters Rejse til Danmark i Sommeren 1793.* Copenhagen, 1898.

Boisgelin [de Kerdu, Pierre Marie] Louis [de]. *Travels through Denmark and Sweden.* 2 vols. London, 1810.

Bring, Samuel E. *Itineraria Svecana. Bibliografisk förteckning över resor i Sverige fram till 1950*. Stockholm, 1954.

[Brougham, Henry Peter.] *The Life and Times of Henry, Lord Brougham. Written by Himself*. 3 vols. London, 1871. I.

Buch, Leopold von. *Travels through Norway and Lapland during the Years 1806, 1807 and 1808*. Trans. John Black. London, 1813.

Burr, Aaron. *The Private Journal during His Residence of Four Years in Europe*. Ed. M. L. Davis. 2 vols. New York, 1836.

Canzler, Johann Georg. *Mémoires pour servir à la connoissance des affaires politiques et économiques du Royaume de Suède jusqu'à la fin de la 1775me année*. 2 vols. in 1. London, 1776.

Carr, John. *A Northern Summer; or, Travels round the Baltic through Denmark, Sweden, Russia, Prussia, and Part of Germany in the Year 1804*. London, 1805.

Clarke, Edward Daniel. *Travels in Various Countries of Europe, Asia, and Africa*. 6 vols. London, 1810–23. V, VI.

Colding, Torben Holck, Jan Danielsen, Erik Lassen, and Vagn Poulsen. *Akademiet og Guldalderen, 1750–1850*. Copenhagen, 1972.

Consett, Matthew. *A Tour through Sweden, Swedish-Lapland, Finland and Denmark*. Stockton, 1789.

Cox, Edward Godfrey. *A Reference Guide to the Literature of Travel*. 3 vols. Seattle, 1935–46. I.

Coxe, William. *Account of the Prisons and Hospitals in Russia, Sweden and Denmark*. London, 1781.

———. *Travels into Poland, Russia, Sweden and Denmark*. 4th ed. 5 vols. London, 1792. IV, V.

Davidsson, Åke. *Med utländska resenärer i svenska bibliotek*. Stockholm, 1975.

Eaton, J. W. *German Influence on Danish Literature in the Eighteenth Century*. Cambridge, Mass., 1929.

Fairchild, Hoxie Neale. *The Noble Savage: A Study in Romantic Naturalism*. New York, 1928.

Farley, Frank E. *The Scandinavian Influence in the English Romantic Movement*. Cambridge, Mass., 1903.

Fortia [de Piles, Alphonse.] *Travels in Sweden*. In Pinkerton, ed., *General Collection*, VI. London, 1809. Pp. 375–569.

Grimberg, Carl. *Svenska folkets underbara öden*. Rev. ed. Ed. A. Åberg. 10 vols. Stockholm, 1959–63.

Henderson, Ebenezer. *Iceland; or, the Journal of a Residence on That Island during the Years 1814 and 1815*. 2 vols. Edinburgh, 1818.

Hermannsson, Halldór. *Sir Joseph Banks and Iceland*. Ithaca, N.Y., 1928.

Herold, J. Christopher. *Mistress to an Age: A Life of Madame de Staël*. New York, 1958.

Hibbert, Christopher. *The Grand Tour*. London, 1987.

Hirn, Yrjö. "Finland i den utländska reselitteraturen under slutet av sjuttonhundratalet." *Skrifter utgivna av Svenska litteratursällskapet i Finland* 36: *Förhandlingar och uppsatser* 11 (1898): 149–74.

[Holland, Henry.] *The Icelandic Journal of Henry Holland.* Ed. Andrew Wawn. Issued by the Hakluyt Society. 2d ser., 168. London, 1987.

———. "On the Diseases of the Icelanders." In Mackenzie, *Travels.* Edinburgh, 1812. Pp. 397–408.

Holm, Edvard. *Danmark-Norges Historie fra den Store nordiske Krigs Slutning til Rigernes Adskillelse 1720–1814.* 7 vols. Copenhagen, 1891–1912. V.

Hooker, William Jackson. *Journal of a Tour in Iceland in the Summer of 1809.* 2d ed. 2 vols. London, 1813 (first ed., 1811).

Huitfeldt, Carl. *Norge i andres øine. Utdrag av utenlandske reisebeskrivelser gjennem 2000 år.* Oslo, 1932.

James, John Thomas. *Journal of a Tour in Germany, Sweden, Russia, and Poland during the Years 1813 and 1814.* London, 1816.

———. *Views in Russia, Sweden, Poland, and Germany.* London, 1826.

Julius, Arvid. *Sverige med främlingsögon. Utdrag ur utländska resenärers skildringar före 1800.* Stockholm, 1930.

Kaiser, Gerhard. *Von der Aufklärung bis zum Sturm und Drang 1730–1785.* Gütersloh, 1966.

Kerguélen-Trémarec, [Yves-Joseph] de. *Relation of a Voyage in the North Sea.* In Pinkerton, ed., *General Collection*, I. London, 1808. Pp. 735–803.

Ketton-Cremer, Robert Wyndham. *The Early Life and Letters of William Windham.* London, 1930.

Kirby, David. *The Baltic World, 1772–1993: Europe's Northern Periphery in an Age of Change.* London, 1995.

Kjærgaard, Thorkild. *The Danish Revolution, 1500–1800: An Ecohistorical Interpretation.* Cambridge, 1994.

Kliger, Samuel M. *The Goths in England: A Study in Seventeenth- and Eighteenth-Century Thought.* Cambridge, Mass., 1952.

Küttner, Carl [Charles] Gottlob. *Travels through Denmark, Sweden, Austria and Part of Italy in 1798 & 1799.* Trans. from the German. London, 1805.

Lamm, Martin. *Upplysningstidens romantik.* 2 vols. Stockholm, 1918–20.

La Tocnaye, Jacques-Louis de Bourgrenet de. *En franskmann i Norge i 1799.* Oversatt av Axel Amlie. Oslo, 1980. Norwegian trans. of part of vol. II of *Promenade d'un français en Suède et en Norvège.*

———. *Promenade d'un français en Suède et en Norvège.* 2 vols. Brunswick, 1801.

Laurin, Carl, Emil Hannover, and Jens Thiis. *Scandinavian Art.* New York, 1922.

Leem, Knud. *Beskrivelse over Finnmarkens Lapper.* English trans. in Pinkerton, ed., *General Collection*, I. London, 1808. Pp. 376–490.

Lenz, Christian Ludwig. *Bemerkungen auf Reisen in Dänemark, Schweden und Frankreich.* 2 vols. Gotha, 1800–1801.

Lindblom, Andreas. *Sveriges konsthistoria*. Stockholm, 1947.

[Linnæus, Carl.] *Iter Lapponicum*. 1732.

——. *Linné i Lappland*. Ed. Bertil Gullander. Stockholm, 1969.

[Lyttelton, Sarah.] *The Correspondence of Sarah Spencer, Lady Lyttelton, 1787–1870*. Ed. Mrs. Hugh Wyndham. London, 1912.

Macdonald, James. *Travels through Denmark and Part of Sweden, during the Winter and Spring of the Year 1809*. 2d ed. London, 1810.

Mackenzie, George S. *Travels in the Island of Iceland during the Summer of the Year 1810*. 2d ed. Edinburgh, 1812.

Mallet, Paul Henri. *Introduction à l'histoire de Dannemarc*. Copenhagen, 1755.

——. *Monumens de la mythologie et de la poésie des Celtes, et particulièrement des anciens Scandinaves: pour servir de supplement et des preuves à l'histoire de Dannemarc*. Copenhagen, 1756.

——. *Northern Antiquities; or, An Historical Account of the Manners, Customs, Religion, and Laws, Maritime Expeditions and Discoveries, and Language of the Ancient Scandinavians. Translated from the French of M. Mallet by Bishop Percy*. New ed. Ed. I. A. Blackwell. London, 1847. Rpt. New York, 1968. Orig. ed. 1779.

[Malthus, Thomas.] *The Travel Diaries of Thomas Robert Malthus*. Ed. Patricia James. Cambridge, 1966.

Maupertuis, Pierre Louis Moreau de. *Rélation d'un Voyage fait dans la Lapponie septentrionale*. Berlin, 1747.

McKillop, Alan Dugald. *The Background of Thomson's Seasons*. Minneapolis, 1942.

[Miranda, Francisco de.] *Miranda i Danmark. Francisco de Miranda's danske rejsedagbog 1787–1788*. Trans. and ed. Haarvard Rostrup. Copenhagen, 1987.

[——.] *Miranda i Sverige och Norge 1787. General Francisco de Mirandas dagbok från hans resa september–december 1787*. Trans. and ed. Stig Rydén. Stockholm, 1950.

Molesworth, Robert. *An Account of Denmark as It Was in the Year 1692*. London, 1694.

Montesquieu, Baron de La Bräde et de Montesquieu [Charles-Louis de Secondat]. *L'Esprit des lois*. Paris, 1748.

Mornet, Daniel. *Le Romantisme en France au XVIIIe siècle*. 2d ed. Paris, 1925. Orig. ed. 1912.

Omberg, Margaret. *Scandinavian Themes in English Poetry, 1760–1800*. Uppsala, 1976.

Otter, William. *The Life and Remains of the Rev. Edward Daniel Clarke, LL.D.* London, 1824.

Parks, George P. "The Turn to the Romantic in the Travel Literature of the Eighteenth Century," *Modern Language Quarterly* 25 (1964): 22–33.

Pettersen, Hjalmar. *Utlændingers Reiser i Norge*. Universitets-Bibliothekets Aarbog for 1895. Christiania, 1897.

Pinkerton, John. *Dissertation on the Origin and Progress of the Scythians or Goths*. London, 1787.

——, ed. *A General Collection of the Best and Most Interesting Voyages in All Parts of the World*. 17 vols. London, 1808–14.

Pontoppidan, Erik. *The Natural History of Norway*. 2 vols. London, 1755.

Porter, Robert Ker. *Travelling Sketches in Russia and Sweden during the Years 1805, 1806, 1807, 1808*. 2 vols. London, 1809. II.

Rauschenberg, Roy A. "The Journals of Sir Joseph Banks's Voyage up Great Britain's West Coast to Iceland and to the Orkney Islands, July to October, 1772." *Proceedings of the American Philosophical Society* 117 (1973): 186–226.

Rühs, Friedrich. *Finnland und seine Bewohner*. Leipzig, 1809.

Sandblad, Henrik. "Edward D. Clarke och Giuseppe Acerbi, upptäcktsresande i Norden 1798–1800." *Lychnos* (1979–80): 155–205. English summary, 202–5.

Schiøtz, Eiler H. *Utenlendingers reiser i Norge. En bibliografi*. 2 vols. Oslo, 1970, 1986.

Skjöldebrand, Anders Fredrik. *Picturesque Journey to the North Cape*. London, 1813.

——. *Premier supplément du voyage pittoresque à Cap Nord, contenant des remarques sur le premier cahier de cet ouvrage et sur le voyage de Mr. Joseph Acerbi*. Stockholm, 1802.

Sörlin, Sverker. "Scientific Travel—the Linnean Tradition." In Tore Frängsmyr, ed., *Science in Sweden: The Royal Swedish Academy of Sciences, 1739–1989*. Canton, Mass., 1989. Pp. 96–123.

Stafford, Barbara M. *Voyage into Substance: Art, Science, and the Illustrated Travel Account, 1760–1840*. Cambridge, Mass., 1984.

Steffens, Henrik. *Was ich erlebte*. 10 vols. Breslau, 1840–44. I, II.

Stephensen, Magnus. *Island i det 18. Aarhundrede, historisk-politisk skildret*. Copenhagen, 1808.

Swinton, Andrew. *Travels into Norway, Denmark and Russia in the Years 1788, 1789, 1790 and 1791*. London, 1792.

Tacitus, *Germania*. In Tacitus, *On Britain and Germany*. Trans. H. Mattingly. Harmondsworth, 1948.

Thomson, Thomas. *Travels in Sweden during the Autumn of 1812*. London, 1813.

Treese, Geoffrey, *The Grand Tour*. London, 1967.

Tucker, Susie I. "Scandinavica for the Eighteenth-Century Reader." *Saga-Book of the Viking Society for Northern Research* 16 (1962–65): 233–47.

Utterström, Gustaf. *Jordbrukets arbetare. Levnadsvillkor och arbetsliv på landsbygden från frihetstiden till mitten av 1800–talet*. 2 vols. Stockholm, 1957.

Van Tieghem, Pierre. *Le Préromantisme*. 3 vols. Paris, 1929–48. I.

Wawn, Andrew. "John Thomas Stanley and Iceland: The Sense and Sensibility of an Eighteenth-Century Explorer." *Scandinavian Studies* 53 (1981): 52–76.

West, John F. *Faroe: The Emergence of a Nation*. London, 1972.

——, ed. *The Journals of the Stanley Expedition to the Faroe Islands and Iceland in 1789*. 3 vols. Tórshavn, 1970–76.

Williams, John. *The Rise, Progress and Present State of the Northern Governments; vis. the United Provinces, Denmark, Sweden, Russia and Poland*. 2 vols. London, 1777. I.

Wollstonecraft, Mary. *Letters Written during a Short Residence in Sweden, Norway, and Denmark*. Facsimile of original, with introduction by Sylvia Norman. Fontwell, 1970.

[Wraxall, Sir Nathanael William.] *Cursory Remarks Made on a Tour through Some of the Northern Parts of Europe, Particularly Copenhagen, Stockholm, and Petersburgh*. London, 1775.

——. *The Historical and Posthumous Memoirs of Sir Nathanael William Wraxall, 1772–1784*. Ed. Henry B. Wheatley. 5 vols. London, 1884. IV.

Index

Aabenraa (Apenrade), northern
Schleswig, 82
Aalborg, Denmark, 51, 56, 62, 69, 83, 97, 166
Åbo (Turku), Finland, 17, 20, 27, 29, 31, 34, 59, 60, 66, 93, 94, 96, 100, 155, 169; University of, 37–38, 45
academies and learned societies, 34
Acerbi, Giuseppe (Joseph), 1, 4, 10, 13, 16–17, 19, 20, 22, 23, 27, 36, 37, 39, 42, 43, 45, 48–51, 53, 54, 55–57, 60, 64, 74, 80, 98, 100, 101, 104, 110, 115–18, 120–22, 123–26, 149, 157, 158, 159, 164, 170, 171, 178, 190n50
Addison, Joseph, 150
Adolf Fredrik (king of Sweden, 1751–71), 40
Agre, Norway, 85
agriculture: Denmark, 50, 62, 66, 68–69, 83, 105–6; Færø Islands, 129–30; Finland, 65–66, 67, 68, 70, 93, 95, 115; Iceland, 133–34; Norway, 63, 67, 72, 79, 124; Scandinavia, 23, 66–70; Schleswig-Holstein, 82; Sweden, 62–65, 67–68, 69–70, 77, 78, 87–88, 90, 109, 124, 170, 192nn18, 20
Akureyri, Iceland, 143
Åland Islands (Finland), 17, 20, 59, 93
alcohol. See morality: sobriety
Alexander I (emperor of Russia, 1801–25), 46, 169
Alfieri, Vittorio, 8, 13, 14, 15, 19, 39, 99, 148, 177
Alta Fjord (Norway), 22, 123
Älvkarleby, Sweden, 148
Amager (island of Denmark), 84, 105
Amalienborg Palace (Copenhagen), 24

America and the Americans (North and South), 1, 6, 9, 12, 13, 19, 21, 27, 36, 55, 64, 74, 75, 105, 109, 120, 126, 141, 144, 155, 162, 170, 178, 198n3, 201n70, 204n4
Anckarström, Johan Jakob, 47
Ångermanland (province in Sweden), 60, 65, 68, 92, 157
Anker, Berndt, 52, 72
Anker, Peder, 31, 52
antiquity: classic, 3, 159–60, 163; Nordic, 3, 9, 33, 35, 129, 132, 135, 140–44, 150–56, 159, 167, 174, 175, 176
Arkhangelsk (Archangel), Russia, 76, 117
Arndt, Ernst Moritz, 182n11
art: collections in Scandinavia, 31; European, 23; Scandinavian, 29, 31–32, 43, 73, 171–72
Åsele, Swedish Lapland, 60
Avesta, Sweden, 65, 71

Baggesen, Jens, 1
Baine, John, 128, 130, 131, 132, 134, 137, 138, 140, 141, 143
Baltic Sea, 17–18
Baltimore, Lord (Frederick Calvert), 35, 80, 109, 158
Banks, Sir Joseph, 127, 128, 135, 144
Batten, Charles L., Jr., 145–46, 201n5
Beck, Thor J., 173–74
Beckmann, Johann, 7, 13, 14, 31, 35, 36, 177
Beers, Henry A., 150
Bellman, Carl Michael, 55
Benners, Isaac, 128
Bergen, Norway, 8, 19, 26, 28, 52, 57, 60, 61, 63, 72, 79, 87, 108

H. Arnold Barton is a professor emeritus of history at Southern Illinois University at Carbondale. He graduated from Pomona College and received his Ph.D. at Princeton University. Previously he has taught at the University of Alberta and the University of California at Santa Barbara. His earlier publications include *Count Hans Axel von Fersen: Aristocrat in an Age of Revolution* (1975) and *Scandinavia in the Revolutionary Era, 1760–1815* (1986). He has also published extensively in the area of Swedish-American history and served as the editor of the *Swedish-American Historical Quarterly* from 1974 to 1990. In 1989 he received an honorary doctorate from Uppsala University in Sweden.